The Maui Millionaires for Business

The Five Secrets to Get on the Millionaire Fast-Track™

DAVID FINKEL
DIANE KENNEDY, CPA

John Wiley & Sons, Inc.

Published by John Wiley & Sons, Inc., Hoboken, New Jersey.
Published simultaneously in Canada.

Wiley Bicentennial Logo: Richard J. Pacifico

For general information on our other products and services or for technical support, please
contact our Customer Care Department within the United States at (800) 762-2974, outside the
United States at (317) 572-3993 or fax (317) 572-4002.

Wiley also publishes its books in a variety of electronic formats. Some content that appears in print
may not be available in electronic books. For more information about Wiley products, visit our web
site at www.wiley.com.

The following trademarks are the exclusive property of Maui Millionaires, LLC and are used with
permission: Maui Millionaire™, Maui Millionaires™, Self Employment Trap™, Money Plus™,
Gateway Offer™, Core Value Process™, Millionaire Fast-Track™, The Five Languages of
Financial Fluency™, Wealth Matrix™ (and the Wealth Matrix Diagram shown in Chapter 10),
The Inside/Outside Asset Protection Plan™, Tax Efficiency Rate™, Tax Power Percentage™,
Wealth Frame™, Wealth Map™, Wealth Curve™, The Great Risk Hoax™, Cash Flow
Maximizer™, Preemptive Tax Strategy™, The Five Wealth Factors™, Z-Cost™,
Unique Advantages™, E-Ratio™.

The following trademarks are the exclusive property of Maui Mastermind (NV), LLC and are used
with permission: Maui Mastermind™, the most exclusive wealth retreat in the world™, the world's
most exclusive wealth retreat™.

The following trademarks are the exclusive property of New Edge Financial, LLC and are used with
permission: Wealth Operating System™, Wealth Factor Test™, S-Factor™, R-Score™.

Library of Congress Cataloging-in-Publication Data:
Finkel, David.
    The Maui millionaires for business : the five secrets to get on the millionaire fast-track™ /
David Finkel, Diane Kennedy.
        p.   cm.
    ISBN 978-0-470-16495-2 (cloth)
        1. Entrepreneurship—United States.   2. Success in business—United States.   3. Wealth—
United States.   4. Millionaires—United States.   I. Kennedy, Diane, 1956–.   II. Title.
    HB615.F56   2008
    332.024'01—dc22
                                                                                    2007020650

Printed in the United States of America.

10 9 8 7 6 5 4 3 2 1

This book is dedicated to the extraordinary members of the Maui Millionaire community. Your commitment to build, enjoy, and share great wealth is an inspiration. You have changed our world. Thank you.

CONTENTS

PART TWO
Invest in Yourself

SECRET #3: Become Financially Fluent and Guarantee Your Future!

SECRET #4: Create Your Wealth Map and Build Your Passive Residual Income

PART THREE
Invest in the Greater Good

SECRET #5: Invest in the Greater Good and Reap Enduring Rewards!

After we wrote *The Maui Millionaires* we realized there was more we wanted to say. This time, we wanted to write about one of the things we are most passionate about—building businesses that help create freedom. *The Maui Millionaires for Business* is about how to, step-by-step, create a Maui Millionaire lifestyle with a new or existing business. The best leverage comes with a highly functional team. There are a lot of people that we want to thank on our team.

This book series wouldn't have existed without the vision of Laurie Harting and her team at John Wiley & Sons, the determination of Larry Jellen, and the in-the-trenches work of Megan Hughes and Eva Brunnette (Apex Designs). We also want to give a huge thank-you to Diana Arsenenian (www.darsenian.com), the talented artist at Maui Mastermind who created the iconography you see spaced throughout this book.

We also want to thank the Maui faculty, including Elizabeth Kanna, Steve Maxwell, Blake Mitchell, Beverly Sallee, Michael Schinner, Bill Shopoff, David Bolls, Stephen and Susan Wilklow, and Morgan Smith. You are all inspirations and friends.

Next we want to thank all of the participants over the past several years at Maui Mastermind and in the Maui Millionaires community. Your commitment to building wealth and doing good in the world has inspired us to write this book and keep sharing these ideas. We savor our connection with you and are humbled by your energy and ambition.

Our deepest gratitude to the team that makes all of this possible: To Amy, Larry, Gabe, Bill, Joel, Christina, Carolyn, and Megan—your commitment to making a difference in the world through Maui Millionaires and your willingness to do whatever it takes to give our clients a world-class experience are changing the world.

In addition, David would like to acknowledge:

First, my wife Heather. I want to thank you for always being there to listen, to share, and to love me. I feel so grateful to be living our lives together. I love you with all my heart. Next, I want to thank my friends and family for your love and friendship. Finally, I want to dedicate this book to my grandfather, Morey Spivak. You have touched and shaped much of who I am, and I will miss you dearly.

In addition, Diane would like to acknowledge:

As always, my husband Richard and son David. Richard, you have the strength when I am tired, the insight when I have lost my vision, and the balance to hold me fast. David, this is all for you and the generation you represent. My heartfelt wish is that you inherit the best world when it is your time to lead.

The Three Greatest Challenges That Entrepreneurs and Business People Face

For the past decade we've worked with hundreds of thousands of entrepreneurs and business people helping them grow their businesses and invest their wealth. Over that time we've both watched so many of these intelligent and hard-working people get stuck by the same three pitfalls that once upon a time trapped us in the stressful, underperforming, frustrating world of being self employed.

The first challenge they had to overcome is what we call the Self Employment Trap™. You see, most entrepreneurs don't build a business; they merely create a job for themselves. They have achieved the satisfaction that comes along with their own businesses, only to find that this freedom has its price: Daily attendance is mandatory in order for the business to succeed and be profitable. In a sense, rather than creating their own business these entrepreneurs have instead created their own jobs, with all of the responsibilities that go along with it.

If you've ever felt this way about your business, we have a way out. In fact, in this book you'll learn the concrete strategies and techniques you need to build a business that succeeds without you needing to be there every day to run it. You'll learn to build a business that works for *you*, not one you have to work for. We've both used the ideas you're about to learn to build multimillion dollar businesses that live on to this day with minimal input on our part.

You *can* have the freedom and financial success you desire from building your own business, and in Part One of this book, we'll show you exactly how to go about getting it. You'll learn how to use your business to tenfold your net worth and massively increase your cash flow. Most important of all, you'll learn how to build a business that isn't dependent on you, the business owner, showing up each day to run it!

The second challenge successful entrepreneurs face is that while they have developed the business skills they need to grow their business, very few of them have cultivated the personal wealth skills they need to build wealth *independent* of their business. This is extremely shortsighted and risky. Not only do they have all their economic eggs in the single basket of their business, but they also lack the financial fluency to intelligently and effectively manage their wealth and invest it wisely.

For this group, a lack of financial fluency often leads to poor decisions after they no longer have their businesses. They wake up one day without their business, and with nothing to show for their years spent building their business.

To create the wealth you truly desire you must understand that your business is a piece of the puzzle, an important piece, but not the only piece. You must develop your wealth skills in parallel with your business skills. Part Two of this book will show you how. You'll learn how to speak the Five Languages of Financial Fluency™ and how to create your own personal Wealth Map™. You'll also learn how to understand the 10 causes of investment risk, and how to maximize your returns.

The final challenge you face comes years into your successful business when you wake up one day and ask yourself the painful question: Is this all there is? To truly be successful your business must be about more than the money. You must find a deeper meaning, and to have a sustainable business, you must help your employees and customers find that deeper meaning. In Part Three of this book you'll learn how to do this by tapping into your single greatest competitive advantage.

Why This Book Is Different From Every Other Business Book You Will Ever Find

Most business books tell you how to grow your business. They teach you how to focus on your business and grow it over time. Make no mistake, we'll share our best ideas and strategies on doing just that.

Some business books even show you how to build your business to be independent of you the business owner. You'll learn that, too. In fact, we'll share with you the four keys to turn any business into a thriving independent business where you, the business owner, don't need to show up each day. In essence you'll learn how to move from being self-employed to being a passive business owner.

But what makes this book unique is that we won't just show you how to build your business, you'll also learn how to use your business to grow your personal fortune. You'll learn why you must grow your wealth independent of your business' success, and exactly how to do it.

It's so easy to think about wealth as one-dimensional ("How can I make more money with my business?"), and completely overlook the skills you need to grow and sustain that money. It's those skills—what we call the Five Languages of Financial Fluency—that we talk about in the second half of this book. It's those skills that will keep you from putting your financial future at risk by being one-dimensional from a wealth perspective.

Much of what you're going to learn in this book is unconventional. We're warning you about that up front, and we make no apologies for it. If conventional thinking was the answer, wouldn't the logical conclusion be that every business owner would be happy, wealthy, and successful? What we're going to share with you took us decades to learn, and many painful mistakes to finally "*get*."

Our goal is to cut your learning curve by 90 percent so that you can build your personal fortune in a 10th of the time. But to do that we need you to sit up, pay attention, and wrestle with the ideas and strategies we share in this book. This is no time to sit back, passively ingesting what we have to share. If you want these ideas to make the difference then you've got your part to play. The ideas work—we've already proven that in our own business lives, and in the business successes of our Maui Millionaire clients. The only question is, will you do what it takes to apply these ideas to your business and to your personal finances to accelerate your wealth building? The choice, and rewards or consequences, is all yours.

FREE Millionaire Fast-Track Program! ($2,150 Value!)

We've designed a powerful online training program to help you turn the ideas in this book into tangible results. Best of all, we've made this training course, called the *Millionaire Fast-Track™ Program*, available to readers like you for FREE! For full details see the Appendix or go to **www.MauiMillionaires.com/book**.

PART ONE

INVEST IN YOUR BUSINESS

CHAPTER 1

The Single Decision that Leads to Financial Failure or Financial Fortune

Let's get something clear here at the start: Most of what you've learned about business, wealth, money, and investments is wrong. It's skewed, warped, twisted, bent, and at best, middle-income advice. But, unfortunately, that's the best that most people will ever have.

Think of this book as the graduate program on how to build a truly successful business, grow your personal fortune, and in the process, become a Maui Millionaire™.

Your Wealth Model
Directs Your Financial Results

Our decisions are often determined based on something called models. A model is an internal construction that we make up in our brain to help us make sense of the world around us.

Sometimes models are expressed in language, often metaphorical language. For example, we might say love is a game or we might say that love is a battlefield, like the old Pat Benatar song. What difference would it make in your life if you believed that love is a battlefield? How would that belief impact the way you interact in your relationships? What about a belief that says life is a joy or that life is a gift? What impact would that have on your life?

Once it was common knowledge that the world was flat. During the time of the grand explorers, this was a limiting model. The belief that the world was flat stopped people from going out and exploring. They were afraid they'd sail over the edge of the world. That fear kept people in a much more closed and smaller environment.

Today, the flat-world model has changed. The belief that the world is flat is now a model for how close our world is. We now think in terms of a global economy and how connected we are, personally and through the Internet and other means of communication. In a sense, we have reclaimed the belief that the world is flat.

So models can be positive, or they can be negative. But what's more important is their power. Once we believe in a model, it doesn't matter

---

Is More Money the Answer?

Winning the lottery might seem like the ultimate American dream— money for nothing and rags to riches in an instant. But what really happens to the big winners?

- A New Jersey lottery winner won twice for a total of $5.4 million. Now, 20 years later, she is completely broke and living in a travel trailer. A Pennsylvania man won $16.2 million in 1988 and now barely subsists on Social Security payments of $450 and food stamps. He also has a serious heart condition. He has been sued by a girlfriend and family members, and one of his brothers even hired a hit man to kill him to try to collect some of the money.
- A Virginia woman won $4.2 million in 1993. She's now "upside down" with more loans than assets. She borrowed against the future payments without considering how she would pay back the loans as she upgraded her lifestyle.
- A Michigan machinist won $1 million. He went into business with his brothers and within five years was bankrupt. His brothers say the early conversations regarding their business were centered around buying planes and luxury cars as "perks."
- Another Michigan man won $3.1 million, and within two years he was broke and charged with murder. The money went to a bitter divorce and crack cocaine.

whether that model helps us or harms us. Once we believe, it is accepted as true. We no longer think about it. The model leaves our conscious thought and enters into our subconscious and our unconscious. It impacts how we deal with the world, and it codes the way we experience the world. We completely ignore the fact that the model is in there, running, and maybe ruining, our lives.

As much as we try to stick to just the facts, there is no such thing as perception without interpretation. We perceive things only by having our brains think about them. We don't know anything about an experience or object until our brain experiences and codes that experience. Our perception is our reality.

This is why it is so important to have an effective wealth model. The wealth you create is dependent on what your current wealth model lets you have.

Money isn't the answer. Your wealth model determines your success or failure with money. We call this model your Wealth Operating System™ (WOS). Your WOS is the sum total of your emotional associations and your belief system about money and wealth and your ability to earn, enjoy, sustain, and share it. Curious about what your current WOS is set for? Just go to **www.MauiMillionaires.com/book** and take the free Wealth Factor Test™ available there. In less than 10 minutes you'll discover *exactly* where your current WOS stands.

Money alone doesn't solve money problems!

The Traditional Wealth Plan

So what goes into the traditional wealth plan of the average person? In the traditional plan, security is paramount, and the four-step path is clearly defined.

1. Get a good education.
2. Get a good job.
3. Save and build up your nest egg.
4. Retire at age 65–70.

This is probably the model your parents followed; it may or may not be your model, and it may be the model you're preparing your children to follow. There's just one problem: It doesn't work very well today. In fact, it may never have worked very well.

Did you, or anyone you know, get caught in the dot-com downturn, either directly or indirectly? Were you one of the people working really hard for a company, buying into the idea of delayed gratification by way of stock options, and thinking about the day those options would become worth a fortune? Or were you on the outside, listening to stock promoters, and sinking pension fund or mutual fund dollars into rapidly rising stocks, hoping to ride the wave and cash out at the absolute peak of the market? How much did you lose when it all fell apart?

Maybe your loss was less dramatic. Let's take the traditional model at face value for a minute. Perhaps you are one of those who worked hard for 45 years or so, paid into the company pension plan, and have now retired on somewhat less than what you were used to earning. You don't work anymore, so you've got less security. Perhaps your medical costs are rising, or you live in an area where your property taxes have increased so much you're feeling squeezed. Maybe you're considering a part-time job just to give you some financial breathing room. Maybe you're just feeling plain worn out.

And yet this is the traditional model that most people use, and it just doesn't work. Did you know that in the United States the General Accounting Office estimates that 96 out of every 100 Americans will either have to retire with a greatly reduced standard of living or live with family? Only 4 in 100 will be able to sustain their current lifestyle. So we have a model with a 96 percent failure rate, and yet we buy into and perpetuate this model because it's the conventional plan. (And this failure rate is even higher in most other parts of the world!)

Okay, now, putting the failure rate aside for a minute, even if things all went as planned, is the end goal really something we want? Is it really something to strive for? Do you really want to put off living and enjoying ourselves for 45 years until you turn 65 or 70, and then and only then finally have the opportunity to break free or as free as your financial constraints will allow? Do you really want to pass this model along to your children as your financial legacy?

Personally, we don't think so. We want amazing freedom *now*. We

---

Maui Millionaires Have "Money Plus"

They have money *plus* the time and freedom to enjoy it.

They have money *plus* the people to share it with.

They have money *plus* the health to fuel it.

They have money *plus* the meaning to magnify it.

They have money *plus* the peace of mind to sustain it.

want to be Maui Millionaires and enjoy Money Plus™. And we want to share this model with our children, and our children's children, and so on for generations to come. In fact, that's one of our driving reasons to write this book—to share a better plan with readers like you.

Back to the traditional model. Step One is education. What is the mantra we tell ourselves and our children over and over again? Get a good education. Why? Because that's how the traditional model works. The traditional model tells us that the more formal education we get, the more value we have as an employee. This rolls us right into the second step: Get a good job.

What qualifies as a good job depends on two things. First is security. How "safe" is your job? How likely is your career to be outsourced or made redundant by technological advances? Why spend the time and money educating yourself in a field that is rapidly being flooded with others who are younger, hungrier, and often willing to work for less?

The second part of this equation is, of course, money. A good job equals a good income-earning opportunity. The more money you earn the more money you have. That allows us to grow our lifestyles: bigger house, multiple cars, and the ability to pass that along to our children by giving them the opportunity to get a good education.

Having more money also allows for Step Three in the traditional model: Save. Save a lot. Save for the future, save for your children, save for your golden years, save for emergencies, save for weddings, save for . . . the list goes on and on. Those savings go into your savings accounts, employer-sponsored 401(k) retirement accounts, the equity in your home, certificates of deposit, government bonds, high-grade corporate bonds, mutual funds, and stocks.

Now you put in your time. Lather, rinse, repeat for, say, the next 40 prime years of your life until you hit Step Four, where you. . . .

Retire. That's right, you're off to enjoy your golden years in the sun. The traditional plan has focused on this as your end goal: getting that nest egg built—that magic number representing how much you'll need to see you through to the end of your life.

And that's it. That's the four-step traditional model. Figure out what we have to do to save enough money so we die before we run out.

Yikes! Is this really the life you want to live? Does this plan really inspire you?

The Times We Live In

We are living in a time of unprecedented opportunities. Technology is changing at a pace never before seen. Globalization has removed barriers to growth. The smallest company can become a multinational overnight.

There is more money to be made, by those who understand how, than at any other time in human history.

Did you know that today's world is creating millionaires and billionaires faster than at any other time in recorded history? In 1958, for example, there were about 40,000 reported millionaires. By 1975, that number was 350,000. In 2006 (depending on whose numbers you believe), there were between 2.9 and 8.9 *million* households in the U.S. alone that report a net worth of $1 million or more. In 1916, John D. Rockerfeller was the only reported billionaire in the world. The first Forbes billionaire ranking (done in 1986) found 140 billionaires around the world, and by 2006, this number had increased to 793. The number of millionaires in South Korea, India, Russia, and South Africa is increasing 15 to 21 percent per year!

It has never been easier for you to become wealthy than in today's world. You have never had so much opportunity. But that's how we see it. How do you see it? Is wealth scarce, or is wealth abundant?

Maui Millionaires believe we live in an abundant world—a world in which you can build a fantastically successful business and use your business as the foundation for your personal fortune. And you can do it in a way that generates great value in the marketplace and effects powerful good in the world.

Step One: Don't Just Get an Education, Get the Right Education

The traditional education system prepares you, at best, for a trade. For example, if you go to college for four years (more or less) and receive a pre-med degree and then go to medical school, serve the requisite internship, declare a specialty and serve a residency, eventually you'll be a well-trained physician. But, how well prepared would you be to start a *medical practice*, a real business, of your own? In 2001, the American Medical Association reported that out of some 550,000 doctors in private practice, approximately 65.5 percent were self-employed, either on their own or with a couple of other doctors. But while doctors know how to treat illness and disease, they aren't so skilled in business. Industry estimates show that about 70 percent of doctors have been embezzled from at least once, and 60 percent have been embezzled from two or more times!

Attorneys have problems, too. The California Bar Association wanted to know why, out of a total of 350 complaints made against attorneys, 68.5 percent of those complaints were made against lawyers in solo practices, 26.1 percent were made against attorneys practicing in firms of 2–10 lawyers, and only 5.4 percent of complaints were made against large firms. What they discovered was that solo practices and small firms got into trouble because (a) attorneys were overworked to the point they were missing deadlines and not returning client calls, (b) they had serious money concerns that sometimes led to *"borrowing"* money from client trust accounts, (c) they lacked sufficient support staff to manage administrative and clerical tasks, and (d) they often had insufficient documentation to defend themselves against client complaints.

In other words, without the business training to understand how to put systems in place to protect themselves or to make sure their offices functioned properly, these attorneys put themselves at risk.

Education is important, but it needs to be the right *kind* of education. Unless you're a business major, or more specifically, an accounting major, you will probably never learn anything about accounting, taxes, or financial matters in college. But how many accounting majors also study economics, or sales and marketing, or negotiating, or any one of the hundreds of business skills needed to succeed?

A traditional education prepares you to make a living, not a life. The Maui Millionaires plan focuses on getting the education you need to become financially fluent and speak the Five Languages of Financial Fluency. Given a choice, why be merely literate, when you can be fluent?

Financial fluency doesn't mean knowing enough to get by, that's financial literacy. To be financially fluent, you need to be able to speak five languages fluently: the Language of Money, the Language of Business, the Language of Wealth, the Language of Cash Flow, and the Language of Leadership.

Step Two: Don't Just Get a Good Job, Create Good Jobs!

People talk about affluence as though those who have it, hoard it. But successful businesses and business owners circulate a ton of money through the economy. Think about it: Businesses have vendors, clients, customers, employees, advisors . . . for every dollar a business receives that business may circulate two to three dollars through our economy. That's how our economy is built. That's how it keeps going.

Here's something to think about: You don't necessarily need to have employees working for you. You can create jobs and have no employees. How? By getting people to spend money on your business and then spending some of that money yourself on other people's businesses.

Circulating money always increases its velocity, which, in turn, increases our society's wealth.

Step Three: Don't Just Save, Invest!

There are two very different philosophies in play here. In the middle-income world that is using the traditional four-step plan, wealth is built through income. More specifically, wealth is built through saving and conventionally investing your leftover money over an extended period of time. Discipline and consistency are the keys. It's very sound advice as long as you want to be middle class.

The second philosophy, the Maui Millionaires philosophy, is to build wealth not from income, but from your assets. You use your wealth to create more wealth, and you eventually transition a portion of your wealth into cash-flow-producing investments. We'll go into great detail about this fundamental wealth distinction in Part Two of the book, but for now what's essential for you to get is that the wealthy approach wealth and investing in a totally different way from the middle income.

There's an old saying that goes, "The first million is always the hardest." Why is that? It's easy to say, "Because I have no assets," but the truth is different. The truth of why it's harder to make your first million is partly because you don't know how to do it, but mostly it's because you are scared that it's not possible for you to do. Once you've achieved that goal, though, things get easier. You know the way now and how far it is. It's like walking back to the car after a long walk somewhere else. It's *always* faster to walk back, because you've been the distance, and you know exactly how far you have to go and the exact route to get there.

Step Four: Don't Focus on Security, Focus on Freedom!

The problem we have is that security in retirement is so often a fallacy. Retirement turns out not to be about security but more about trying to stretch the nest egg far enough so we don't run out before we die. Having to take on a part-time job to augment your retirement benefits seems to defeat the purpose of retiring in the first place.

With the Maui Millionaires model, the goal is freedom, complete and sustainable freedom. It encompasses your lifetime and perhaps leaves a legacy, either for your children or for causes you feel passionate about. There is no uncertainty or insecurity here, only the need to keep a current passport on hand.

So what's it going to be for you? Door No. 1, or Door No. 2? The traditional plan or the Maui Millionaires plan? Will you choose the door marked "security" or the door marked "freedom"? Are you ready to become a Maui Millionaire? Mark your answer below.

❏ I choose the Maui Millionaires Plan! (Go on to the next chapter.)

❏ I'm too scared to let go of the traditional plan yet, maybe after a few more chapters I'll gather up the courage to let go and dream. (Go on to the next chapter, too. There's still time to change your mind!)

SECRET #1: Build a Level Three Business and Get on the Millionaire Fast-Track

CHAPTER 2

The Three Levels
of Building a Business

hat does owning a business mean to you? Is it a way to create job protection for yourself so you can never be downsized or made technologically redundant? Or is it a way to follow your dream or passion, or is it a way to get on the Millionaire Fast-Track and make yourself free?

And what does being an entrepreneur feel like to you? Does it feel risky, like you'll have to step outside of your comfort zone and launch a new, untested business idea? Does it mean long hours, employee hassles, and lots of risk? Do you think you'll find yourself wondering if you made the right decision, or whether staying in the W-2 workforce would have been a better choice?

If you have found that running a business isn't freedom at all, that it's even more work and hassle than a regular job, chances are your past experiences have all been with Level One or Level Two businesses.

A Level One business is a fledgling company. It's really the beginning point of a business. There is nothing wrong with a Level One business, provided you only use this level as a temporary launching pad where you put together your business plan and get into action. Any business that stays at this level is probably more of a hobby or a fantasy than a real business.

A Level Two business is nothing more than owning a job. If you don't show up to work, there is no money. It's really not business ownership, so much as it is self-employment. You've got all of the long hours and feelings of lack of control you had as an employee, but you don't have just one boss you're trying to please anymore; you have a whole bunch of them. Only now you call them customers. Plus, all of the decisions, all of the risks, all of the responsibility—all of it—rests on your shoulders. Every day you have to prove yourself and keep going because if you stop, it all ends. That's what having a Level Two business means.

Contrast this to a Level Three business. A Level Three business is one where your business runs without you needing to be there each day. In fact, the criterion of a Level Three business is that it operates smoothly, efficiently, and profitably without needing the daily input of the business owner.

Why do these three levels matter? Because, as you'll learn in this section of the book, when you build a true Level Three business, not only will it make you wealthy, but it will help set you free.

But before we go into all of the rewards you get for building a true Level Three business, first let's dive deeper into each level in the progression of building a Level Three business.

Level One: The Dream (The Conception of Your Business)

Focus: Planning Your Business

Leverage Point: Building on Your Passion

A Level One business is really a business in its infancy. This is the level where an entrepreneur dreams, plans, and perhaps even steps out and sells a promise that she must then rush out and build the product or service to fulfill.

All Maui Millionaires understand that the single most important ingredient in the real success of their new venture is passion. Does the business somehow, in some way, meaningfully tap into a deep passion of the entrepreneur? Without passion you have no fuel to sustain the hard work involved in turning a raw dream into a concrete reality.

David's Story

Most people don't know this but I failed in my first business. It was a weight loss company. When I was 21, I dropped out of college to work to open up an established company's product line in San Diego. At the time I didn't understand it, but in retrospect I can see that my motivation to

(continued)

David's Story (continued)

do the business was all about making money. I had no real passion for the industry. Is it any wonder that within a year I was dead broke and out of business?

Fast forward to today. My current business passion—and passion is an accurate word to describe it—is Maui Millionaires, LLC. Our mission of helping generations of entrepreneurs and investors create, grow, enjoy, and share great wealth inspires me. And tying in the business with regular charity events, which have raised millions of dollars so far, makes it a lot more than just a business.

Now after having launched, grown, and sold several multimillion dollar businesses, I get a lot of new entrepreneurs who bring me their business plans to look at for input (I think that they secretly hope that I will be so enamored of their idea that I'll either fund it or jump on board or both). The most important question that I ask them is why they are starting that business. Not why are they starting *a* business, but why are they starting *that* business. If their answer doesn't show me how that specific business somehow meaningfully connects with what is most important to them, I tell them to pick a different business. Life's too short to build a business you aren't passionate about.

Level Two—Early Stage (The Infancy of Your Business)
Focus: Launching the Business by Getting Your First Clients
Leverage Point: Your Ability to Change and Adapt

An early stage Level Two business is fresh in the marketplace. It's just started actively marketing and selling its products or services. At this juncture it's critical that you as the owner listen to the marketplace—will it embrace your product or service in a profitable way for your business?

Now, we say to listen to the marketplace, but don't count on being an immediate hit. Instead, listen to the marketplace first as a place to fine-tune your marketing and sales message. Are people buying? If not, why not? How do they perceive your offerings? Can you shift, tweak, or re-vamp your marketing to get people to buy?

Notice how your early focus in launching a business isn't on building the perfect product or service but rather on first seeing if you can get people to buy. Too many entrepreneurs get caught in the trap of making the perfect gizmo but never proving that they can actually *sell* that gizmo to the market at a profit.

Once you've proven that the market will buy, which in turn ensures your economic viability as a company, then and only then are you ready to move to the next step.

Level Two—Middle Stage (The Teen Years of Your Business)

Focus: Establishing Your Business's Foundation

Leverage Point: Maximizing You, the Company Founder

As a middle stage Level Two business owner you are scrambling to do two things. First, you need to bring some organization to the chaotic world of your new business. Second, you must impose this order in a way that not only doesn't kill sales but instead *enhances* sales.

You can always spot a thriving middle stage Level Two business by the way the business efficiently hums around the business owner who consistently does quality work. For example, think of a doctor's office, often the perfect example of a middle stage Level Two business. (Notice we say "often," because we know several Maui Millionaire doctors who have taken their medical practices and their ancillary businesses well beyond this stage.)

You check in with a receptionist who whisks you into a small exam room. Next, a nurse comes in and takes all your vitals, records them on your chart, and makes the room ready for the doctor to appear. A moment later the doctor steps in and after a minute or two of polite rapport-building chit chat, she gets right down to discussing your health issue. Within 10 minutes she's diagnosed your problem (or ordered more tests), written your prescription, and sent you back out to the front desk to schedule your follow-up appointment. Then she's off to the next exam room, wherein waits another patient ready for the doctor to do her 10 minutes of magic. One after the other. The staff lines them up, the doc swings on through and does her thing, and the staff cleans up after.

Herein lies the trap. That doctor is efficient in her business. In fact, she's consciously designed that business to maximize her every minute so that she can generate maximum revenue. But what she never sees, or at least never sees the way out from, is that her whole business revolves around her. She is the hub around which her middle stage Level Two business revolves. Without her it all comes to a screeching halt.

It's at this point that most entrepreneurs get caught in what we call the "Small Time Bubble." No matter how hard the business owner works, she can never get past a certain size business if the business is designed solely to maximize the business owner. Your goal is not to be the producer for your business. Your goal is to build a business that produces results for your clients without being dependent on you.

So let's move on to the transition point between a Level Two and a Level Three business.

Level Two—Advanced Stage (The Young Adulthood of Your Business)

Focus: Building a Business that Thrives Independent of the Owner

Leverage Point: Systems, Team, Technology, and Outsourced Solutions

An advanced stage Level Two business is the bridge between a Level Two business that needs you to work in it and a Level Three business that works so that you don't have to.

You have radically shifted your attention from working *in* your business (middle stage Level Two) to working *on* your business (advanced stage Level Two). We'll go into great detail later in this section of the book as to exactly how you make this transition in 36 months or less, but what is crucial for you to get deep in your entrepreneurial, freedom-loving bones, is that the goal of your business must be to build a business that works independently from you, the owner of the business. That doesn't mean you won't continue to work in the business. After all, we've already gone on and on about how you need to choose a business that you are passionate about, and if you listened to us then you probably love working in your business. Good! We're all for it. Just make sure that work is out of choice and *not* necessity. And also make sure that you raise a strong business, one that isn't weakened by a crippling dependency on you.

Level Three—The Entrepreneurial Promised Land (The Mature Years of Your Business)

Focus: Determining Your Next Deep Passion

Leverage Point: Making the Time and Space to See What's Next for You

You've reached it! Congratulations! You have built a Level Three business. Now what? For many entrepreneurs this is the point at which they sell the business. Others choose instead to own it, but as a passive business owner rather than as an active self-employed person. And some entrepreneurs who've made it to this point decide to take their Level Three business and make it big time.

Which is right for you? All three choices are great. The key is to give yourself the time and space to tap into your heart and decide what you truly want to do next. Let's face it, at this point, provided you follow the advice you'll learn in the second half of this book about building the wealth skills you need to shepherd your wealth, you'll be financially free forever. So this becomes a chance for you to reinvent yourself and your life.

Diane's Story

In my life, I've built a number of different businesses. Most of the businesses I start are either sold or turned into automatic cash machines.

Take the example of Tax Loopholes, an online tax strategy and education company, I founded in 2001. At that point, I'd been a certified public accountant for almost 20 years and found that my clients often had the same type of questions. Rather than charging them $250 per hour to explain the same thing over and over about tax loopholes that save thousands, business structures that protect assets, and strategies that legally avoid income tax altogether, it made more sense to package my best how-to information into affordable courses that people could purchase for a fraction of the cost of hiring me. Tax Loopholes has now become an almost automatic cash machine for me. I have additional researchers and writers that I meet with every month as we create cutting-edge tax strategies, but, other than this, I don't do the day-to-day work.

The Powerful Perspective Shift
Necessary to Build a Level Three Business

The critical perspective shift that leads to true financial freedom and security and ultimately to a Maui lifestyle, is to see yourself not as a producer for your business, driving sales or fulfilling the purchases of your clients, but rather to see yourself as a business builder who is growing a business that will one day work without you needing to be there to run it. You are only a temporary producer until you can build the business that can replace yourself. In essence, you are the engineer, designing and

Target of Your Business

To build a business that consistently creates value in the market and thus earns you a healthy profit without you needing to be there to run it.

building a profit machine that consistently kicks out cash flow each and every month.

Keep this goal firmly in mind and let it influence all the decisions you make and the actions you take.

Remember, the real reason you are putting in all the energy and time to build a business isn't so you can make more money, although that will happen. The real reason to go through the effort of building your business is so that you can gain your freedom. You don't want to spend all your time stuck managing and running your business. Yes you can make a ton of money doing this, but why not make the money *and* have the freedom too? Personally, we think that the only way you can really be secure and know that your income streams are secure is to have the business infrastructure in place to run it over time.

In many ways, building your business is the most exciting time of all because not only is your business working to consistently make you money, but you're starting to reap the benefits of having reliable systems and team members to handle the parts of the business that either stress you or that don't interest you. This means it is easier for you to take time away from the business because you have reliable teams and systems to ensure that the business gets done while you are away. It also makes the business more fun as you're able to let go of the work that you find mundane or unpleasant and instead focus your time on growing your business. Can you imagine how satisfying it is to watch your fledgling business mini-empire grow and blossom? Each day as you enter your office you feel a directed sense of energy, of purpose, which guides your efforts as you build your business for you and your family not for some faceless corporation or conglomerate.

The Three Pitfalls of Building Your Level Three Business

Pitfall One: You struggle to let go of the control of the details

As you empower your team to take over whole sections of your business, you may find yourself like many entrepreneurs, struggling with the desire to keep control. You are going to need to develop the delegation muscles that allow you to let go of your business—piece by piece—as you bring in key team members to take over. As long as you build in simple score-cards that let you track your team's performance on a daily, weekly, and monthly basis as you hand off areas of your business, you'll be able to ac-curately assess the performance of each business area and celebrate your team members' successes and coach them through any rough spots.

Pitfall Two: You are a great producer but a lousy leader

At a certain point the only way your business can make the jump to the next level is for you to have key staff that you have recruited, groomed, and developed to take on the responsibility and challenge of running your business. But how do you empower talented people to run your business if you don't understand the difference between managing and leading team members?

Managers focus only on executing for bottom-line results. They are fo-cused on effective ways to get their team to perform. The struggle is that most managers don't grow their team's abilities to self-manage. And what is even more, very few managers ever develop the next generation of leaders on their team or know how to set the big-picture vision and di-rection for a company.

Leaders have their focus not just on getting results, but on getting re-sults in a way that develops and grows other leaders on the team who can lead and get results. The ultimate form of leverage is to develop leaders on your team who are committed, capable, and utterly reliable. It's not just about making a leader better, but about upgrading the knowledge base of your entire team and unifying the vision they hold of exactly what you are all working to accomplish.

Pitfall Three: You grow impatient to get to Level Three and let go of key areas too early

Now this pitfall probably sounds like a direct contradiction to pitfalls one and two. And it is. Yet, that's life for you, full of seemingly insolvable paradoxes. We want to caution you about leadership by abdication, which is an all too common costly mistake we regularly watch entrepreneurs make. Leadership by abdication is not the same thing as strategically de-veloping your business systems and team to take over and own parts of your business. It usually happens when entrepreneurs grow impatient with the slow pace of growing their business systems and teams, and they want to speed up the process. But some things take time, and developing people and systems are two of those things. Most entrepreneurs who rush this don't delegate, they dump. That is they walk into the office of the new team member and dump projects and responsibilities on her desk. It just doesn't work to throw the keys to a part of your business at a new team member who hasn't been trained or where no real business system exists. That's a recipe to set them up for failure.

Instead, hand off small pieces of the business to your team one at a time. Be sure to arrange the time to coach them during the transition, and check in on them regularly over time until they are truly ready to take complete ownership.

It's a delicate balance, this incremental handoff of your business. On the one hand, many entrepreneurs hold on too tight, and on the other hand, some entrepreneurs let go too soon. You'll have to feel your way through this dynamic balancing act as you go.

What Stops Most Business Builders from Putting Their Profits on Autopilot

We're sure you've flown on an airplane before. Just think about how amazing planes are nowadays. As they take off they have a highly trained pilot getting the plane up into the air and on course. Then they turn on the autopilot system. This system maintains their course and manages long stretches of the flight with the pilot keeping an eye on the instrument panel to troubleshoot any problems that might arise. And when the plane gets close to the destination airport, the pilot again takes over and lands it.

We think this is a lot like how you'll build your business. You'll have systems that generate leads for new business and close sales, which is like the takeoff of the airplane. Once you close the sale, your business' systems and team will manage and fulfill the orders or services you sold, with you there to just keep an eye on their progress over time. This is like the autopilot on the plane. And finally, when you come in for a landing and strategically evaluate the directions of your business's growth, you will take a more active role in the decisions to make sure you're comfortable about the new destinations you fly to next.

Now you don't need autopilot to fly a plane, just like you don't need a business infrastructure of a team and systems to make money in a business. But you need to understand that without an autopilot, flying a long distance is exhausting and uncomfortable. Can you imagine the strain of having to focus on flying the plane for four to six hours at a stretch? It's not like you can just pull off the road for a quick pit stop!

It's the same way with your business. When you don't have the systems and team (your business autopilot), you can make a ton of money, but the strain—and lifestyle cost—is too great. We've seen many entrepreneurs who make $1 million or more each year with their businesses, but they live, breath, and die by their businesses. They can't get away from their business for more than a long weekend here or there. That doesn't feel like success and wealth to us. Real wealth—Maui Wealth—is when you have money *and* freedom, money *and* quality of life.

Now we don't want to make building a Level Three business and becoming wealthy sound too easy, because it's not. It will take work, it will take sacrifice, and it will take a deep commitment. But it is a very real possibility for you.

Is it worth it? Well, you'll have to decide for yourself. As we see it, having built thriving Level Three businesses before, it's worth every ounce of the time and effort needed. You get five main rewards.

First you get the freedom of time that comes from having a business work for you instead of you having to work for the business. No more clock to punch or calendar that you are a slave to. You choose what you want your life to look like and how you want to spend your days.

Second, you enjoy the passive, residual cash flow that comes to you as the owner of a thriving Level Three business. This money funds your lifestyle and your giving projects. This money provides the financial base for you and your family, sometimes for generations.

Third, your Level Three business becomes the platform from which you get to impact the world. We didn't start Maui Millionaires because we needed the money. We launched the company because we believe it's the vehicle through which we can touch and better the lives of millions of people.

Fourth, because the business works so well, you get to pick and choose the parts of the business that you are most passionate about and spend your time there. For example, one Maui Millionaire we know still runs the engineering department of his Level Three business. Why? Because he loves tinkering with design and production processes. For him it's all one great big puzzle to figure out. Nothing says that a Level Three business owner can't still work in his or her own business. The critical distinction is that you don't *have* to work in your business in order for the business to work.

There is one more reward you'll get when you build a Level Three business—you'll increase your net worth tenfold—or more! This reward is so central to the theme of this book that we want to take our time and show you exactly what we mean step-by-step.

Level Two versus Level Three Business Values

A Level Two business is typically valued based on a multiple of the gross sales. Depending on the type of business, you can generally expect to receive a sales price of somewhere between 50 percent and 100 percent of the business' total gross sales. So, if you have a business that grosses* $100,000 per year, it will be worth somewhere between $50,000 and $100,000.

You have a very small market when you sell a Level Two business. The person who would buy a Level Two business is someone who is looking to buy a job. Typically your buyer is one person or a couple. It will rarely be a corporation looking to expand operations.

A Level Three business, on the other hand, has a higher sales price, typically five to eight times net income. You also have many more prospective buyers, because the business is no longer a job. It is now an investment. Your buyer is looking for a return on his investment not trying to create a job for himself. The decision of whether or not to buy becomes much more matter of fact. It's not an emotional, *"Oh, I've always wanted to own a . . . ,"* but rather, *"What is the return on my investment?"* The numbers and decision-making process are supported by financial statement analysis.

You'll make more money, a lot more money, selling a Level Three business than you will a Level Two business. However, you'll also need to further hone your financial fluency because when it comes time to talk to the buyers, you'll be in another league.

Let's walk through the numbers involved in turning a current Level Two business into a Level Three business. First, you'll have to hire your replacement. And, of course, the business will need to be able to pay for the cost of your replacement plus still provide you with a return on your investment. That's good, because it means your business will grow. In fact, it will have to grow in order to fulfill the Level Three business commitments.

In Chapter Three, you'll learn the 12 characteristics of the ideal business opportunity. You'll see that one of these characteristics is that a business is scalable. In other words, the business model must allow for it to grow. Without scalability, all you're doing is building a job for yourself. And, if

---

*The gross sales figure is the total amount of sales, before any expenses, including the cost of goods, are deducted. If a business grosses a certain amount, it takes in that much in sales. Accounting terms like this are covered in more detail in Chapter 11, The Language of Money.

you do it as a Level Two business, you're just working yourself into an early grave as your business grows beyond your capabilities to get the work done. That is definitely not a Maui Millionaire plan.

We'd like to show you a three-stage example of a Level Two business transitioning into a Level Three business. As we go through this example, please note that the actual numbers for your business will vary a great deal based on the sales price and valuation techniques for your industry as well as the gross profit margins.

In the example that follows we've used a consulting business. Typically, a business in this industry will sell for 100 percent of gross receipts and the net profit is 30 percent. So, if the company makes $100,000 per year, it would sell for $100,000. Meanwhile, if you do all the work, you can expect to make $30,000 per year from your full-time work with the business.

Stage One (Level Two Business): Value: $100,000 Income: $30,000

Let's assume that you replace yourself with an employee who will make $40,000. If the business doesn't grow, you will actually lose money every year. So, you need to grow the business. But, instead of working *in* the business, you can now work *on* the business as a business builder.

Imagine you are able to grow your business sales to three times their previous amount. (By the way, this is a very reasonable assumption for a business once you stop being the primary source of fulfillment within the business.) The business now makes $300,000, with a gross profit of $100,000 less $40,000 for your replacement.

Having a gross profit of $100,000 less your employee's $40,000 salary means you've doubled your income from $30,000 to $60,000 per year. Your business isn't big enough to attract the interest of a Forbes 400 company yet. But, let's see how taking that step to Stage Two changed your net worth and active income.

Stage Two (Level Two Business in Transition): Value: $300,000 Income: $60,000

Wow! Your net worth has tripled and your income has doubled. You're now a believer, and you're ready to really knuckle down and get the business growing as a Level Three.

Level Two to Level Three Game Plan

- Replace your fulfillment role in the company.
- Create systems to ensure quality doesn't suffer as you pull out of your current role.
- Work on the company, not just in the company. Where is your leadership needed?
- Increase the sales and reach of the company.
- Continue refining the Level Three model for your business.

Now imagine it's 36 months later and you've done it. You have a Level Three business with a gross revenue of $1,000,000. We'll assume the gross profit percentage stays the same (although the reality is your gross profit percentage will most likely go up. That means you'll be making even more money than this example will show. But, let's stick to the same gross profit percentage.) That means you now have a profit of $300,000. You'll need a higher level replacement for yourself than your previous $40,000 per year manager, but you'll easily be able to afford this more experienced team member out of your $700,000 in additional gross sales. We've accounted for the higher salary as part of your increased gross sales and the associated cost margin, so you'll still personally earn $250,000 or more from your $300,000 net profit. Wow! That decision that was so hard in the beginning probably now seems like the smartest thing you've ever done. Your method of valuing the company has changed as well. The value for Level Three businesses is based on the net profit of the company. Now we're looking at a value of somewhere between $1,300,000 and $2,080,000 for your company.

Stage Three: Value $1,300,000 to $2,080,000 Income: $250,000 or More

Of course it's not going to be as easy as just snapping your fingers to build a Level Three business. But as you've seen, the rewards are so great that it's worth the effort.

Diane's Story

My first business was a CPA practice in Reno, NV. I worked very hard to build a Level Two business. In the first five years of business, each year doubled the gross income of the year before, but it was still a Level Two business, and that meant I had to show up every day for it to work. After five years, I was exhausted and sold the practice. I was very proud when I talked to a business broker to discover how much the business was really worth. I had created an asset that I sold within a month for almost $400,000!

About a month later I read a story about someone I had known in college. He was an accounting major as well, but he didn't go the traditional path to become a CPA. All of us CPA-types were sure he'd made a really bad decision. You can only imagine all the comments we had when he started a payroll preparation company. Why would he get into something that was so much like bookkeeping? After all, wasn't he an accountant? He should act like one!

Well, his business was just a few years older than my CPA practice when he sold it. Besides having a business just a little bit older, there was one more difference. He had built a Level Three business with some very unique intellectual property attached. In fact, his company, Computing Resources, had contacted Intuit (maker of QuickBooks™) with a request to get into the source code so that they could link their innovative payroll preparation program directly with QuickBooks. Intuit wanted more information and in the end, they told him he couldn't have the source code. Instead, they made an offer to buy his company. He sold his business for $200 million!

That was the moment for me when I truly got the difference between a Level Two business and a Level Three business: $400,000 versus $200,000,000. The choice is yours.

When you build a Level Three business you'll increase your net worth tenfold or more (in our example from $100,000 business to a $1 to $2 million company). Plus, you'll enjoy the deep satisfaction of building a great company.

It's time to roll up our sleeves and get to work on exactly *how* to build your Level Three business.

In the next chapter you'll learn about the five pillars of a Level Three business and how to make sure your business is built on a solid foundation.

CHAPTER 3

The Five Pillars
of a Level Three Business

There are five key areas of any business. These five pillars hold up the structure of the business. As you expand your business, you need to make sure your business can stand up to the additional load. Think about an old house with a half-full well out back. Because the well isn't full, the water pressure is never too high. Everything works okay, but not great. Then the city brings in a new water line and suddenly the old house is on the city water system. The homeowner excitedly looks forward to having plenty of water to wash clothes, take a shower, and even water the yard, all at the same time. Now comes the critical moment when the house is hooked up and the valves turned. Next thing you know, water starts pouring from the walls. The pipes couldn't hold up to the new increased pressure.

It's just like that with a Level Two business as it makes the change to Level Three. It's possible that your old systems and practices worked okay, or even great at Level Two, but what happens when you step up to Level Three? If you're not there to make all the decisions or to troubleshoot problems, can the business stand up to the increased pressure?

Let's take a look at the five pillars. First, there is the operational area. This is the part of your business that fulfills the promises that the sales department makes. Next is the sales and marketing area that is responsible for generating sales. Third is the financial area that deals with the accounting

and payment of bills. Fourth is the human resources part of your business that deals with the team that works in and with your business. Finally, there is the leadership area of your business that is responsible for the big-picture vision and strategy of your business.

Pillar One: Operations

The operations pillar of your company fulfills promises made, creates the products or delivers the services your business offers, and performs the general and administrative back-end functions of your business.

No company can stand the test of time without having an effective operations department. You might be able to make some quick sales to fill the coffers, but it won't last without a solid operations department. At the other extreme, it's possible to become too obsessed with operations. Every possible new project could be shut down because it would mean some uncertainty for operations. The best businesses find a way to balance the stability needs of operations and the dynamic needs of their sales and marketing teams. It's in this shared dance between sales and operations that you'll face the greatest test of your growing business.

Typically, a Level Two business owner has the hardest time letting go of the operations portion of the business. The desire and habit to keep all 10 fingers in the pie can be very hard to break! But one of the signs of a good Level Three owner is his or her ability to walk away from the day-to-day work of the business, while still keeping a finger on the pulse. The best way to do this is by reviewing statistics on a regular basis.

Some examples of statistics you might want to review regularly from your operations team:

- Shipping or service delivery time (from order to the product being shipped or the service being delivered).
- Client satisfaction rating.
- Referral rates.
- Profit per client.
- Cost per product.

Ultimately, operations is all about two things: keeping the back office function of your company working and fulfilling on the core product or service that you've promised your client when she bought from you.

How Well Does My Business Fulfill Its Promises?

The best way to ask your clients how satisfied they are with your product or service isn't a fancy 20-question survey. Instead, you can measure how your clients really feel about your business with one simple question: "Would you refer a friend or family member who needed this product/service to do business with us?" Any answer other than yes is a clear indication that your product or service did not live up to expectations.

David's Story

One of the ways Diane and I knew we were on the mark operationally was the number of referrals we get from Maui Mastermind participants bringing their friends or family members to Maui events. For example, at our last two-day "Mini Maui" wealth weekend (a two-day wealth workshop where the proceeds go to various charities), roughly 50 percent of the attendees found out about the event from a direct referral from a Maui grad.* I can't think of a higher compliment your customers or

(continued)

David's Story (continued)

clients could ever pay you than this. Do you get consistent referrals? If not, what changes could you make to your operational systems to both wow your client and empower them to refer you new business?

*To find out more about attending one of the Mini Maui Wealth Weekend workshops, go to **www.MauiMillionaires.com/book**.

Pillar Two:
Sales and Marketing

The sales and marketing pillar of your business is the part of your business that is responsible for finding clients, making sales, and generating revenue. This is the part of your business that makes it rain cash flow.

Too many entrepreneurs only focus on this area of their business because they have to, not because they want to. They are intimidated by the idea of selling. But understand this—in the early and middle stage Level Two of your business, it is crucial for you, the company founder, to focus a great deal of your attention and energy on generating profitable sales. If you don't, your new business will not survive let alone thrive. It is only as you grow your business that you can replace yourself in this area of your business. To do that, it becomes critical for you to create a profitable selling *system*.

In the earlier stages of your business you need to make sure sales are happening. Often this will mean you will meet with clients and close deals to generate sales. Later, however, your focus needs to shift to creating repeatable and scalable selling systems that aren't dependent on key staff.

For example, imagine you have a new software start-up. A lot of your early effort as the company founder will be in landing the key joint venture relationships with more established players in your industry to market through their client relationships and split the revenue. As your software company grows, rather than focusing on meeting with new joint venture partners, you might instead focus on finding and hiring the talent to do that for your company. Later, you'll focus on making sure your business is creating the systems that consistently find and hire new sales talent for your team.

Or imagine you have a contracting business. Early on you will meet with prospective clients to give them estimates and close sales. But this is only a Level Two solution. To create a Level Three business you need to build the *system* that generates those sales. This might mean creating the advertising systems to generate leads, hiring and training new estimators to go out on sales calls and generate business, and at some point hiring on a sales and marketing manager(s) to take over leadership of this area of your contracting business.

This focus on selling systems is crucial for you to build a Level Three business. Your selling systems include the following components:

- The marketing and lead-generation systems to consistently generate the lead volume your business needs to generate sales.

- The lead conversion systems and team to consistently convert leads into thrilled clients.

- The tracking and reporting systems for you to reliably measure the effectiveness of your marketing and sales efforts so that you can optimize your selling systems over time.

Since many sales systems use live sales agents to close sales, your system might also need to include the processes you use to find, hire, and train new sales agents.

It is important to build your sales systems to be independent of any key team members. There is a temptation to build the sales and marketing pillar of your business by relying on superstars. While it's great to hire sales superstars, it is not a smart business move to have a company that is reliant on a single person who generates all the companies sales—whether this is you the business founder, or a sales person you hired in the second year of your business—unless you have a dependable means of replacing your superstar if he decides to leave your business.

You must find ways to generate sales that aren't dependent on your superstar. Or you need to develop a dependable system for finding, hiring, and training sales superstars, in which case your business is not dependent on any one superstar but on the *system* that finds or creates these superstars.

None of this is easy, but the rewards are huge.

> ### David's Story
>
> One of the companies I built originally was dependent on me and my partner to generate all the sales. And sell we did. The two of us generated several million dollars of sales each year. But it required long hours and even worse, at least from my perspective, lots of travel. In those days I spent 10 days out of every month on the road selling and closing new business. I was making a lot of money, but this sure wasn't the dream I had for myself.
>
> We finally got smarter and began building the sales team and systems that didn't need us to close sales. We built up our online sales to half a million per year. We built a network of independent sales reps who sold another $2–$3 million per year. And we created a whole new selling channel with joint venture partners that generated several million dollars of annual sales for us, which we split 50-50. All told, it took us 36 months to build and optimize these selling systems. In the process, we tripled our company's sales volume and radically reduced our dependence on me and my partner to generate sales. Best of all, I cut my travel time to 3 days per month!

Active Sellers and Passive Sellers

When you have found a selling mechanism that consistently closes sales, congratulations—but you are not done yet. Most selling mechanisms are what we call "active sellers," that is, they take a live sales agent to close the sale. This could be an outbound sales call, a live sales agent at your store, or an outside sales rep who visits clients at their place of business. The key is that making the sale requires someone to actively sell the product or service. Every business needs active sellers. But the real leverage comes when you transform an active seller into a passive seller.

A passive seller is an automatic sales process that doesn't need a salesperson to close the sale. The best part of a passive seller is that you can instantly scale it up with minimal cost or risk. For example, when you develop a display ad that prompts clients to call in and order at a profit, you can scale up on your ad buy. The real freedom and scalability for your business happens when you are able to turn an active seller into a passive seller.

How do you do this? You need to first identify your best active sellers and offers and then find a way to capture your most compelling offers in

What are the top five lead generators for your business?

1. _____
2. _____
3. _____
4. _____
5. _____

What are five ways you could automate each of those lead generators?

1. _____
2. _____
3. _____
4. _____
5. _____

What are the three best active sellers for your business?

1. _____
2. _____
3. _____

How could you turn one or more of those active sellers into a passive seller?

_____
_____
_____

What are the top three passive sellers you already have in your business?

1. _____
2. _____
3. _____

What are five ways you could massively and profitably scale up on one or more of your passive sellers?

1. _____
2. _____
3. _____
4. _____
5. _____

What is the single most promising idea you just generated, and what is your specific next step to implement this idea *fast*?

_____
_____
_____
_____

FIGURE 3.2   The Strategic Seller Audit

print or other recorded media. For example, you could turn your best tele-marketing script into a direct-mail piece. You could record a live sales presentation and have that viewable on your web site or sent out as a DVD to prospective clients. Or you could outsource your sales offer to an outside company that has its team follow up and sell to your leads. Or you could create an automated e-mail sequence that prompts your exist-ing clients to re-order. Or you could. . . . We think you get the idea.

Figure 3.2 is a powerful audit to help you begin the process of turning your active sellers into immensely profitable passive sellers.

Pillar Three: Team (aka: Human Resources)

When we talk about starting a business at the Maui Millionaire workshops, there is one reaction we can always count on from someone in the audience: absolute horror at the idea of having employees! Yet, most businesses take a team to run them. Sometimes business owners attempt to build a business solely with independent contractors. This will often provide much better tax breaks for both the business owner and the person providing the services. In fact, it's one of the strategies that we recommend later on in the book. But, it doesn't make the challenges of having a team go away. You still need a "team department" for your company to help hire, orient, train, assess, and if necessary, let go of, people who work as part of your business.

The problem is that Level Two business owners tend to feel overly pro-tective about their businesses. They have created something unique and something that is very important to them. For these Level Two business owners, their resistance to the idea of hiring employees stems from a be-lief that because no one else could possibly care about the business the way they do, no one else is to be trusted with their business.

And yet there is no other way to Level Three! In fact, done right, when you build your team you'll find the ultimate source of leverage—other people's passion and skill.

So how do you make sure your team works the right way together?

From our experience, the key to creating the team with which to build your business is to clearly articulate three things to *everyone* you work with: your business' vision, mission, and values. That includes your ven-dors, customers, clients, joint venture partners, and especially the inde-pendent contractors and employees that perform work directly for your business. We'll talk more about these three critical elements of building a cohesive team and culture in Pillar Five: Leadership.

The bottom line is that any growing business will need team members to help support that growth. Whether it be adding on sales team members to increase sales, or engineers to design products, or accounting staff to keep track of the money, your business' greatest source of leverage is your company's ability to attract, hire, integrate, and empower talented, committed people to play on your team.

Pillar Four: Financial

The financial area of your business comprises all the essential functions of collecting, tracking, distributing, and reporting the flow of money in and out of your business. It includes your billing procedures, collection practices, and accounts payable processes. It also includes all your financial reporting from simple profit-and-loss statements and statements of cash flow, to more sophisticated reporting that helps your business team make smart decisions.

Cash flow is the lifeblood of your business, and it is your financial pillar that makes sure your cash flow volume and health is always closely monitored. The financial area also monitors and fine-tunes your business' use of debt as you finance growth or capital expenditures.

A Level One business has no one looking at the financial area. An early stage Level Two business generally has the owner handling the bookkeeping and financial area. A middle stage Level Two business has a bookkeeper keeping the books with a CPA preparing the tax returns. An advanced stage Level Two business typically has a full-time controller working for the business monitoring and handling the financial area. A controller is generally a college graduate with either a CPA or Certified Management Accountant accreditation. And most true Level Three businesses require a big picture chief financial officer in addition to a controller and possibly an accounting clerk or two.

Diane's Story

One of the benefits of being a CPA for over 25 years is that I get to see what works and what doesn't for small business owners. Without a doubt, the biggest mistakes are always centered on their accounting, or lack thereof.

Accounting provides a scorecard for your business. You can tell what you want more of and what you want less of. And, the accounting provides the raw material for a tax strategist. Without

(continued)

Diane's Story *(continued)*

good financial statements, it's pointless to try to even design a tax strategy.

When I first began my accounting practice years ago in Reno, NV, I had two clients that I'll call Tom and Bob for purposes of this story. When I first met them, they were very similar. They both were contractors and both used the old "shoebox" method of accounting. In other words, sometime in March, they each showed up with a box of papers and wanted to know how soon their tax returns would be done. Both of them reasoned that they wouldn't have to pay much in taxes because they didn't have any money in their checking accounts.

Well, after weeks of work sorting through all the papers, I had an answer for them. First, I had to present my accounting bill. Let me tell you both Tom and Bob had the same reaction and it wasn't pleasant! Then, I had to tell them how much taxes they owed. Both made about $50,000. Tom was furious. He blamed me. He blamed his wife. He blamed the government, and he went away mad. Bob was upset. too, but he then asked the question that would change his life. He asked, "What do I have to do so I never have to go through this again?"

That's when Bob learned about the importance of accounting and frequent reviews of financial statements. And that started Bob down the path of turning his early stage Level Two business into an advanced stage Level Two business, and eventually into a Level Three business. Ten years later, Tom still made about $50,000 per year and Bob made $1,000,000 per year.

The second mistake that Level Two business owners make is trying to do all the bookkeeping themselves. In the beginning, that might be a good idea so they can understand how the money flows and how financial statements work. But, to be honest, if you don't plan to be a bookkeeper, is this a skill you really want to learn? Instead, hire a good bookkeeper (preferably an outsourced bookkeeper) and learn how to talk to her in her language.

Your Financial Information is Your Business' Lifeblood

Your business' financial information is probably the most important aspect of its function. If you don't know, or can't find out where your business is financially, then the best business plan, business product, and sales team in the *world* won't make your business' heart beat. And yet, time and time again we meet people at seminars and other events who insist on doing their business' bookkeeping because they either don't see the value in hiring a bookkeeper to do that work, or they don't trust a bookkeeper to get it right.

It's hard to hear those words coming from someone who isn't a trained bookkeeper or accountant. It's frustrating to see people nodding their heads in agreement about the need to take themselves out of the business in order for it to grow and then dig in their heels on this issue. But here's a truth we both firmly believe:

Your business will *never* reach Level Three if you hang onto the bookkeeping.

Accurate and timely bookkeeping is critical to your business' success. It's also time-consuming, detail-oriented, and, as the business owner, a complete waste of your time. Those hours you spend trying to enter receipts and balance the checking account are hours you aren't spending growing your business. And, in all honesty, unless you're a trained bookkeeper, you'll probably do something wrong.

We're not suggesting that you bring someone in to handle your business' financial side and completely withdraw. What we are suggesting is that you:

- Bring someone in to handle the books or outsource that work to a contract bookkeeping service.
- Have at least a working knowledge of bookkeeping.
- Understand how to read basic financial statements and information.
- Establish strong financial controls.
- Implement the systems you need to keep your business' financial information secure.

Perhaps one of the best educational steps you'll ever take is a night class in bookkeeping and basic accounting. Just having an understanding of double-entry bookkeeping (for every amount entered on the debit side, there is a corresponding amount entered on the credit side), and what each of the three main financial statements (balance sheet, profit-and-loss statement, and statement of cash flows) represent, can put you miles ahead. For those of you who don't have the 150–200 hours it will take to

learn basic bookkeeping, check out some of our financial fluency products at our web site, www.MauiMillionaires.com. Get yourself in a position where you can knowledgeably monitor your business' financial records
without being bogged down in actually doing them.

We are going to go further into reading financial statements in Chapter
12. Again, learning how to prepare them isn't the lesson. Learning how to
read and interpret the story behind the numbers is.

At the advanced stage Level Two, most business owners move away
from an outsourced bookkeeper and hire a full-time controller. The controller generally has more education and experience and has the ability to
design systems and see the story behind the numbers. And, finally, at
Level Three, it's time to get a CFO. The CFO is able to forecast the intri-
cacies of multiple businesses and investments and how they relate to the
owner's personal financial statements. It's like the bookkeeper knows
how to play checkers, the controller can play chess, and the CFO can play
three-dimensional chess. The differences have to do with perspective and
ability, along with talent.

The final element of your business' Financial Pillar is systems and financial security. This is the place where you can create the safeguards
that will allow you to let go of the financial record keeping and still sleep
at night. Yes, it is reasonable to have concerns about an unscrupulous
controller or CFO raiding your business' finances. However, the answer
isn't trying to control the risk by doing all of the financial work yourself.
The answer is creating, implementing, and maintaining financial controls
to protect yourself.

For example, even the smallest business should make a distinction between who writes the checks and who signs the checks, and between who
creates the deposits and who makes them. As the business owner, signing
checks and (at least in the early stages) making deposits are two things
you should be doing personally. Separating the money-handling tasks is a
key to preventing fraud and embezzlement.

As your business grows you will reach a point where it is necessary
to bring additional people on board to assist with the financial area.
Again, as people come in, you will want to separate responsibility for
looking after money coming in from responsibility for looking after
money going out. By always separating the process so that at minimum two different people would have to collude to steal, you are
minimizing the chance of that happening. You add a second layer of
defense by establishing consistent audit procedures and other financial
checks and balances. These are standard financial practices and safeguards, so a great way to find out how your business should be structured in this aspect is to talk to your CPA, or, better yet, have your

CPA work with you to design and implement your business' financial safeguards.*

Pillar Five: Leadership

Your business will never be able to reach its true potential without quality leadership lighting the way. Leaders set the vision for your company. Leaders create meaning for your team and transmit your company's values throughout your organization. Your biggest job inside your company as you grow from a Level Two to a Level Three business is in the area of leadership.

When you own an early or middle stage business, leadership is your job. As you grow to an advanced stage Level Two business, your job is to hire and grow leaders who can lead your business. As a Level Three business owner, your job is to remain involved enough in your business to make sure that your company never strays from the vision, mission, and values that you have imbued in your business. In a way, your role is that of a compass, which keeps your company pointing north, even in rough seas or cloudy nights.

Your executive leadership is responsible for the most important functions of your business. Of these, the most important role is the clear creation of your business's vision, mission, and values.

Let's take a closer look at what makes up a business' vision, mission and values.

Vision: Why Are We Here?

Great companies understand that people are inspired by meaning, and that businesses must be about more than just making a profit. Your business' vision should convey noble purpose and higher value, always pointing toward the future.

Your business' vision is the most fundamental reason for its existence. For example, Walt Disney's vision was not to make cartoons, it was to

---

*Would you like to get a simple one-page list of the top five financial controls your business *must* put into place to protect yourself? You can download this list for free at **www.MauiMillionaires.com/book**. See the Appendix for details.

make people laugh. 3M's vision is to solve problems innovatively. Merck's vision is to preserve and improve human life.

Maui Millionaires' vision is to put the humanity back into wealth-building.

This vision is why we get up every morning and run one more seminar, write one more book, and create one more online course. How can you stay in bed or just be a couch potato all day when you have your vision to fulfill?

There is one more hint for writing your company's vision statement. Challenge the reader! Write it aggressively to spark interest and stimulate creativity. More than anything a vision must inspire. It must move. It must call the reader into action.

Mission: What Do We Do Here?

The second key is your business's mission statement. A mission statement defines your business' real purpose. There is an element of the vision statement in it, but the mission statement is more specific, as it defines exactly what your business does.

Your business' mission statement should define what is the essential work of your business.

For example, the mission of Maui Millionaires is simple: We are the founders and guardians of the world's premier wealth-building community. We help generations of wealth-builders create, maintain, enjoy, and share great wealth.

Values: How Do We Do It?

The third key is your business' value statement—the statement that sets out *how* you get things done. They reflect what you find most important.

> Where your vision and mission inspire and define, your values help align. Your values are the critical piece that helps you align behavior with what truly matters to your business. What is acceptable? What is not acceptable? Your business's values are the filter through which your team evaluates decisions and behaviors.

At Maui Millionaires our values statement is:*

We believe in dreaming big, giving back, and supporting each other's highest good.

The mission is *always* more important than the money.

We do what we say we will do.

We keep the business fun, energizing, and engaging.

Your business's leadership must also establish the bridge between its vision and mission, and the actual work of the company. What is your business' profit model? What are the specific goals and targets you have set for it in each of the key areas? What strategies will you employ to reach these targets? How will you monitor progress and troubleshoot as you go? This, too, is the responsibility of leadership—to bridge between the lofty vision and the daily work.

The Only Thing that Makes a Business Work

In business you get paid for one thing and one thing only: bringing value to the market. That value is determined *entirely* by the buyer. It has nothing to do with your perceptions, or with your actual costs, nor even with the effort that went into your product or service. It has to do with perception of value by your buyers.

Lest you think this is strange, or that you can convince your customer that your widget has value that it really doesn't deliver, remember this. It's not just the initial perception of value from your customer that matters, but the *long-term* perception of the value that your widget helped them achieve that really counts. No business thrives or even survives that doesn't deliver exceptional value to its clients, with that value determined over the long term by its clients. As the saying goes: You can

---

*Please see **www.MauiMillionaires.com/book** for a free online workshop on creating your own Vision, Mission, and Values for your business.

fool 'em in the short term, but in the long run you'll end up dead and in the dust.

So how can you apply this insight to make your business more successful? Think about going to see a CPA. If your CPA is a tax strategist who is familiar with Preemptive Tax Strategies™, she may very well develop a strategy for you that will immediately reduce the amount of tax you pay by $10,000. How much would you pay for this strategy that will save you an additional $10,000 off your tax bill, year after year, for 10 years? Essentially, your CPA has helped you to create a cash flow of $100,000. How much is this result worth? Wouldn't it be worth $5,000 for a clear tax plan to help you get that result?

Now compare that with going to visit a CPA who merely bills hourly and who hands you a bill for $3,000 (10 hours at $300 per hour) to prepare your tax return.

What is the value of that CPA's time? It doesn't matter what result he got for you. He wants to be paid for time and effort. The first CPA earned $2,000 more because she created more value for you probably with a great deal less work. How is this possible? Because the first CPA didn't focus on billing for her time, she focused on producing a clear, demonstrable value for her client. And here's the secret that will make you millions: When you can clearly, unambiguously, and convincingly demonstrate the concrete, tangible benefit or result your clients will get when they buy your product or service, your clients will pay you in relation to that value and not in relation to the time or effort or cost you invested to get them that result or benefit.

Hallelujah! This secret is how you escape the tyranny of commodity pricing and commodity competition. It is what allows you to move up the value chain and have throngs of thrilled clients pay a premium to do business with you. And this secret is one of the most important tasks of the leadership in your company—to establish your value model in the marketplace.

Enjoying Your Journey to Level Three

Too often, when we grow our business from a Level Two to a Level Three business, we focus solely on the scramble and day-to-day activity, and we forget to regularly step back and savor the growth and journey.

We both have grown several multimillion-dollar companies in various industries, yet for us the most exciting and special time in a business remains those years of struggle when you move a Level Two business to Level Three. So don't forget to look around as you go, someday you will miss the rush and challenge.

Diane's Story

A number of years ago, when I lived in Reno, NV, I went to a country-western concert. The featured band was the Desert Rose Band and the opening act was Garth Brooks. It was one of those concerts where if you test drove a car or bought a pair of jeans, you could get a free ticket, so the place was packed. (Nothing brings 'em in like free stuff.)

The interesting thing was that the acts had been touring for a while and Reno was just one more stop on the trip. During this time, Garth Brooks had started to get a lot of radio air play. His song, "Friends in Low Places" was all over the airways, but he'd been on the road and had no idea what was going on. Or if he'd been told, it hadn't all sunk in yet. In his mind, he was still just the opening act for someone else.

The crowd knew him and went wild when he came out on stage. When he played "Friends in Low Places," the entire stadium sang along. Garth was completely dumbfounded. In fact, he'd commented on an earlier song how much he liked the Reno audience. But at the end of his popular song, he had tears running down his cheeks. He still didn't quite get that he was famous yet though. He said to the crowd, "If I had known that Reno was like this, I'd have come here years ago." At that moment, he attributed the response just to Reno. He didn't understand yet that was how he was viewed by a much larger audience.

I wonder if Garth Brooks remembers that night in Reno. I saw him a couple of years later and he had grown into his fame. Still, I will never forget how he looked, and talked, that night when he first came face to face with his new reality.

When your reality shifts to Level Three I hope you look back and savor your nights in Reno with an audience that gave you your first taste of successes to come.

The five foundational pillars create the structure for your business. The stronger the foundation, the bigger your business can grow. Without a foundation, the business will never be able to survive in the long run. In the next chapter we're going to look at specific steps that your business needs to take to move to Level Three as quickly and painlessly as possible.

CHAPTER 4

The Four Keys to Turn Your Business into a Thriving Level Three Business in 36 Months or Less

I t's time to get into the details of just how you can transform your Level Two business into a thriving Level Three business—fast! Now of course it's possible that you might say that 36 months seems like a long time, but let's look at it another way. In just 36 months, you can create an asset worth $1 million or more. Plus that asset will be producing thousands of dollars of cash flow for you, month after month, year after year. Isn't that worth the effort it takes to make the Level Two to Level Three leap?

There are four keys that make all the difference between Level Two and Level Three businesses. Let's take a close look at each in turn.

Key One—Systems

Repeatable Results You Can Count On

A *system* is any repeatable business process that allows your business to get a consistently great result.

The key words are *repeatable* and *consistent*. The systems you build need to reliably get you a predictable result. The very best business systems can be used by any member of your team who has undergone the proper training, and ideally that training is also a systematized part of your business.

Systems can be everything from the scripted sales process you have your call center use, to the spreadsheet your operations manager uses to sort out staff scheduling, to the monthly reconciliation checklist that your controller uses to make sure your financial records are kept in order. In other words, systems are used in each of the five key areas of your business so that you can build a business that is never dependent on any one person and that consistently produces superior results.

Building Blocks to Great Systems

- Scripts.
- Worksheets.
- Spreadsheets with built-in formulas.
- Other software that automates a process for you.
- Databases of key information.
- Templates and samples.
- Common question-and-answer sheets.
- Step-by-step instructions.
- Predictable problem areas and how to deal with them.
- Camera-ready artwork.
- Pre-approved forms and contracts.
- A timeline or master calendar.
- Online communication tools that help you effectively share information.

We now have a list of the building blocks of successful business systems. Again, remember the goal of any business system is to allow your business to produce a consistently great result in some area of your business.

Let's talk about how you build a business system.

The Seven Steps to Building a Business System

Step One: Clearly define the outcome or desired result for the system under construction.

What do you want the business system to do? What is the result you want it to consistently produce?

Step Two: Find the best person in your business (or outside your business if you have access to someone better) to model your business system on.

Who is the very best of the best at consistently producing the result you want to achieve? Can you model their process and replicate their success?

Step Three: Observe this person producing the result and stop him as he progresses to write down each steps he takes and the order in which he takes them.

Whether it's yourself or some other person, follow the progress as a highly skilled person produces the result you want the business system to produce and list the steps this person takes and the order in which he takes them.

Step Four: Repeat step three a few times to make sure you have all the steps and the exact order.

With complicated business processes that involve interactions with other people you'll usually need to run through it several times to get all the steps down accurately. Each time you go through the process you are fine-tuning your documentation of the process and procedure.

Step Five: Teach the system to someone new and see if they can use the system to get the desired outcome.

Nothing shows the weaknesses and holes of a system better than getting a new person to try out the system. By watching the new person use the system it is very easy for you to spot the steps that you didn't notice and write down earlier. You'll also be able to spot the steps that need more explanation.

Step Six: Make the system even easier to use by filling in the gaps with checklists, instructions, worksheets, scripts, samples, and so on.

The best way to see where the gaps are is to pay attention to the questions and struggles of the team members you are training to use the system. It's their fresh, new perspective that will give you the most accurate feedback on where you need to beef up the system.

Step Seven: Simplify the system and refine it over time.

See what steps of the system could be automated by building the right software or worksheet. How could you eliminate or combine steps? Is there a better way to get the desired result that is simpler? You should not only be building systems over time, you should also be *pruning* your existing systems over time so that they stay fresh, healthy, and vibrant. Your goal is to get more from less.

Now that we've talked about the importance of building systems, and told you how to do it, you still need to know where to start.

Start with the master system. This is the system for your systems. This is a written document that says what the systems will look like. The document will tell everyone where the individual systems for the company are stored, how they are maintained, and the format you use for writing them up.

Caution! Don't try to build your systems all at once. Companies that do this take their focus off of the active selling and fulfillment that is the lifeblood of their business. Instead, build your systems as you go. Improve and refine them as they are used.

Sticky Note System Builder

For those of you who can't imagine ever enjoying building systems, we have another technique for you to use that is guaranteed to be fun (or at least a whole lot less painful than the formal process we laid out above). It's called the Sticky Note System Builder. This works really well whenever you have a project or task that you just can't figure out how to hand off.

You will need to assemble a pad of sticky notes, a pen, and a piece of tag board. Think through the task for which you want to create a system. Write down each part of the task on a separate sticky note. Peel the note off the pad and then slap the note on the tag board. Neatness doesn't count here. The point is to come up with all the individual steps that go into the task. Separate out the individual steps into one action per sticky note.

Next, put all of the steps in order on the tag board. Run through the process again. Do you have all of the steps? If not, add the additional ones.

Now, put an initial or name on each step. If you feel you're the only one who can do some of these steps, that's okay. But ask yourself for each step if there is someone else who could do this task. If you have to hire someone for that just put down a general job title so you can keep track of the people who would be responsible.

List out the sticky notes and you have the steps of the system for your process.

The process of writing down the systems for everything you and everyone on your team does can feel overwhelming at the beginning. That's another reason it's a big mistake to build all of the systems up front in one massive process. You and your team will feel overwhelmed and it often takes the focus off of the business. Watch out for that—your business could go broke during this process!

We recommend that you create a plan to spend three to four hours each week specifically on creating systems. Map out the overall flow and then work on the individual systems. Have each member of your team follow the same regime: three to four hours each week building another system. The key is to regularly review and share the systems as they are being created. If you don't do this critical step you'll find your systems are gathering dust in a binder with no one using them!

Key Two—Team

Leveraging the Passion and Talent of Other People

No great Level Three business is ever built without key team members. Great team members are the secret ingredient to growing your business exponentially. Here's the challenge most Level Two business owners face: They hold tight to each of the five key areas of their business and in so doing strangle its growth. The Level Two entrepreneur thinks he is spending time leading each area, but in reality he is focusing 70 percent of his time and energy in the area he likes best, 25 percent of his time in the area that is crying out the loudest and most urgently for his attention, and the other 5 percent of his time wondering if he'll ever get a chance to take a deep breath and regroup.

The key is to get people to incrementally take over areas of your business so that you get 100 percent of their energy and talent focused on that key area. Plus, because you'll hire people whose passion and talent is for the specific area of the business you hire them to run, they will more likely than not be much better in this area than you.

For example, if you are primarily a sales and marketing person, your first critical hire is an operations manager. This will free up so much of your time that your business will get an immediate boost in sales. Or if you are primarily an operations person or producer for your business then your first key hires will be in sales and marketing. This will again give you a quick boost in sales. Ultimately, the right team members will not cost your business; they should raise your business' bottom line and make you more profitable. If not, you didn't bring on the right people at the right time.

Which leads us to an interesting point: At different points in its evolution, your business will need different types of people on its team. The operations leader in your business' infancy may not be the leader you need when you grow to become a $10 million company. The controller that worked so well when your business was generating $700,000 a year in sales may not be the CFO you need when you reach $22 million in gross annual sales.

Your team will change and grow over time, which is the best reason we can think of to make sure that everyone's job includes building systems as they go so that the knowledge is captured in your systems and not just in the brains of your team.

Key Three—Outsourced Solutions

Building a Scalable Business with Fewer Employees

If you want to grow fast, you'll need to be both flexible and scalable. One of the hardest things for a growing business to do is to staff up fast enough when it hits the wild ride up the growth curve. We want to let you in on one of the best-kept secrets in the business world—outsourced solutions.

Every business has core functions that it needs its own team to handle. But most businesses would do much better outsourcing a great deal of their non-core business functions. Why? Because they get instant scalability in that area. Plus they benefit from the greater expertise the outside company brings in that area. Finally, they get the additional benefit of knowing up front exactly what their costs will be because they are paying for a result, and they have the ability to increase or decrease those expenses as needed to maintain proper cash flow levels inside their business.

For example, you might hire an outside call center to take your customer service calls. Or you might hire a PEO (Professional Employment Organization) to handle your human resources functions. Or you might hire an outside financial company to handle your accounting functions.

We believe in outsourced solutions wherever you can lower your *real* costs and create a better, more scalable result. On the surface, hiring an employee may seem cheaper, but it often isn't true. That's because of the hidden infrastructure costs of hiring an employee that go far beyond a salary. For example:

Payroll Taxes

Social Security	7.65%
Unemployment (Avg)	3.0%
Worker's Comp	0.35%

Medical Insurance	$400.00
Office Space	$200.00
Computer, Telephone, Desk, Etc.	$2,500.00 (one-time cost)
Technology Support	$50.00
Phone line and long-distance service	$50.00

We pulled these averages from our business. What it means though, is that for every employee we hire who makes $30,000 per year, our actual cost for their first year of employment is $44,200. (And that doesn't include the costs of other benefits you might add in other than basic medical insurance.)

Outsourced solutions are a lot cheaper. You don't usually have a training curve, and it is much easier to adjust job descriptions and roles once you've determined exactly what it is that you need. For example, you might find that by creating an effective system you really don't need as many people as you thought you would.

The question then becomes: "How do you intelligently hire outside vendors and leverage them when you find them?"

All the normal recommendations for hiring come into play. Check references, do background checks, and work with a standard written contract that your attorney has drafted for all your contractors and vendors. Make sure you have both nondisclosure and noncompete agreements signed by all independent outsourced service providers. And verify that you own any intellectual property that you pay them to create by specifically referencing their work as a "work for hire" in your contract with them.

Review your vision, mission, and values with each new hire, outsourced vendor, or independent contractor. We filmed a short video of us explaining these in a small in-house workshop. Each new team member gets a DVD to watch before they do anything else. They also sign an agreement stating that they understand the values.

You must also consider the tax issues of hiring an independent contractor versus an employee. If you have an employee, you have to pay payroll taxes. If you have an independent contractor, you don't. But it's more than just saying, " She's an independent contractor" when it comes to the IRS. The IRS is actually looking at 20 separate factors in determining whether someone is a contractor or not.* Another strategy we've used

---

*For the complete list, along with strategies to pass the independent contractor test, please go to our web site at **www.MauiMillionaires.com/book** for a FREE Special Report of this important area of scaling your business.

> A growing business doesn't have to worry about starving for lack of opportunities. The biggest risk it faces is choking on too many opportunities.

effectively at Maui Millionaires to grow our business is to partner with others as new opportunities come up. For example, we've partnered with several of the guest stars at Maui Mastermind to create valuable niche courses or resources for our clients. Take the area of real estate investing. We know that our clients need real estate contracts that are specifically created to protect them as the investor. But we are not attorneys, nor is creating a CD-ROM of real estate contracts and agreements our core business. The solution? We partnered with Michael Schinner and Michael Powlen, two of the top real estate attorneys in the country, who are also guest stars at Maui, to create *The Investors Contract Library*, a multivolume, downloadable collection of the contracts and agreements designed for people who invest in real estate. This is one of the best-selling resources on our web site.

The problem that successful businesses face isn't that they will not have new opportunities. Without fail, the problem is always too many opportunities. You can't effectively manage a new business plus take on new opportunity after opportunity and do it all well. Why not exercise some synergy, share some profits, and spread resource costs out by forming a partnership* or joint venture to handle it?

Key Four—Technology

The Power of Virtual

The world of business has changed dramatically in the past few decades. A lot of our ways of structuring, running, and leveraging our businesses have changed as well. Technology lowers costs and provides more flexibility, mobility, and freedom to businesses.

Once upon a time launching and growing a business required massive outlays of capital for the purchase or construction of needed facilities, equipment, and infrastructure. This is rarely true today, at least at anything approaching the scale it once was. Today companies can use technology to create massive value to the marketplace with very little cost.

---

*You can find our FREE Special Report, "30 Key Questions to Ask Before You Partner," on our web site, **www.MauiMillionaires.com/book**.

Compare Ford Motor Co. to Microsoft. In 2006, Ford had $143.3 billion in gross sales with a net *loss* of $12.6 billion. That same year, Microsoft had $11.8 billion in gross sales, with a net profit of $2.8 billion. That's the opportunity in today's world, to build a company leveraging technology that is immensely profitable and requires much less capital outlay to launch.

We want to focus on an emerging trend and opportunity for you and other entrepreneurs to leverage to create your Level Three business—building a virtual company. A virtual company is a business with no all-encompassing bricks-and-mortar building in which all the team members perform their work for the company. Instead, a virtual company consists of a network of remote team members who work out of satellite offices, often their own homes. Not only does this unleash a huge amount of capital that no longer must be invested in paying for the fixed expense of office space, but it also frees you up to find talented team members virtually anywhere in the world. With no office or plant where everyone must show up to work, your virtual company will use the Internet, phone, and fax both as the method of commuting to work and as the place where all the communication flows.

David's Story

Over the past decade I've built a number of virtual companies and have loved the ease of building them, the lower risk involved, and the flexibility to run them from anywhere I want to be. For example, one company I built provided investment education for more than 100,000 clients around the world. I ran that business with the help of 45 key team members located in over a dozen cities in the United States. At its peak, the company generated more than $3 million of net profit off of $7 million in annual sales. Yet we did this with no office and no employees. Our "office" was a rented mailbox. Our orders came through our outsourced call centers and our company web site. Our products were shipped by an outsourced fulfillment company. Our client consultations and trainings were lead by a team of independent contractors we brought in to give our clients an amazing experience. The backbone that held this company together was a sophisticated company intranet and tech team that tied all the parts of the business into one unified and organized whole. Nowadays, when I build a new business, I look for ways to make most or all of the business virtual.

It's important to be aware that a completely virtual business can also be problematic. You lose something when your key players don't get together for synergistic idea creation and to build relationships on a regular basis. Plus, if you have any employees or independent contractors who work on a time-and-effort basis (rather than a pay-for-a-completed-project-or-result basis), there is always the concern of whether they are really working. Here are 10 quick tips that we had to learn the hard way about using an independent contractor team.

Ten Tips to Lower Your Exposure Using Independent Contractors to Staff Your Virtual Company

1. Pay a flat fee versus an hourly wage. This eliminates the overtime issue and allows you to know exactly what your team costs will be month by month. Also, this eliminates the need for your independent contractors (ICs) to track their hours for you to pay them. How do you know they are working? Because they are responsible for getting certain results. If they get those results in an amazing fashion, then who cares if it takes them 20 hours a week or 40 hours? If they aren't getting great results, then you have to decide whether you have the right people on your team.

2. Pay them enough so that they can buy their own benefits. ICs don't get benefits, so you'll have to factor this into the amount you're willing to pay your team each month. To get the right people, you'll need to pay them enough so that they can buy their own benefits and still feel like they are getting a great deal.

3. Encourage your ICs to incorporate. Not only will this save them several thousand dollars on their taxes,* but it will also greatly reduce your risk of them ever being reclassified as employees by the IRS.

4. If appropriate, hire your ICs to work for more than one of your companies. One of the IRS criteria for IC versus employee is whether they in fact operate a business. One way to strengthen your case that an individual is an IC and not an employee is the fact that he is contracted with more than one company. In other words, your IC has more than one client of his business.

---

*Diane has prepared a special report that sells your independent contractor team on the benefits they'll enjoy simply by incorporating, and what the next step would be for them to do it. You can download that special report as part of your FREE Millionaire Fast-Track Program. Just go to **www.MauiMillionaires .com/book**. See the Appendix for details.

5. Pay them extra so they can pay their own office costs. You are not able to pay for an IC's phone, Internet connection, and other ordinary business overhead costs. However, like any smart business, your ICs should charge you enough to cover their costs and then some. We suggest you consider adding $100–$150 per month to their contracted payments to allow them to cover their own costs and nominal incidentals.

6. Establish a clear written contract with all of your ICs that lays out what they are responsible for accomplishing and the exact nature of the relationship.

7. You must control all phone numbers, fax numbers, and e-mail addresses they use while doing business on your company's behalf so that if they ever leave your company you can simply point the stable number or e-mail address to another team member at any time.

8. Make sure they have a clear, simple, consistent way to self-score their own performance on a regular basis. To keep doing great work they need to be able to track their results, see progress, and correct as they go. One of the key parts of making a virtual team work is to make sure every team member knows exactly the standards they must live up to and the results they are accountable for daily, weekly, monthly, and quarterly.

9. Find ways to daily and weekly draw your IC team into the mainstream of your business. That's the only way they will really buy into your company's culture, understand your company's focus, and have real access to the information they need to do a great job.

10. You must find ways for them to find meaning in their work with you. You won't get and keep great talent in today's competitive world unless you help your team feel a part of something greater than themselves and to clearly see how they personally make a difference in your business. (See Secret Five in Chapter 22 for several ways you can super-size this within your company.)

Technology can also be difficult to manage. For example, it's imperative that you have some kind of central server or intranet through which all your company's documents, records, and e-mails flow. It's too easy to simply build files of documents, spreadsheets, and vital e-mail communications on individual laptops. If that happens, time can be wasted trying to track down who has what and oftentimes there is duplication of effort as documents are created and re-created. Plus, a centralized Web-based system allows your team to share their work and avoid duplication of effort.

We call this centralized system our UBS, which stands for our Ultimate Business System. In our company, UBS is both a noun as in, "Did you add that form to the UBS?" and a verb, as in, "Did you UBS that project?" In essence, your UBS becomes the institutionalized memory of all the process, procedures, and knowledge of how your company operates and creates value in the market.

To make this centralized system work, it's essential that you organize it in an intuitive way that makes it easy for your team to find what they need, when they need it. Otherwise you spend thousands and thousands of dollars on a procedures manual that just sits gathering dust. For your UBS to work, you must make it fun, easy, vibrant, and relevant. If it helps people get things done faster, it will get used. If it creates extra work but produces little value, it will be ignored.

The Danger of E-Mail in Your Virtual Company

Most people have a love/hate relationship with e-mail. They love the ease with which they can keep connected, dash off a note or request, and have a permanent record of a conversation. But they hate the way it can consume so much of their day and feel so overwhelming and well, bottomless.

E-mail is a great way to give quick information, but it has some significant limitations for your virtual business. Your company must balance the utility of e-mail with the way it can proliferate and drown your team.

There's another inherent problem with e-mail: it can be misread. Since e-mail is a communication stripped of the emotional color of body language and tone, with no way to see how your communication is landing on the other end, it's too easy to misread and see something in the comments based on your mood at the time. E-mail is a useful tool that must be used consciously.

The Future of Virtual Companies

Virtual companies are here to stay. Yes, they are a relatively new phenomenon, but they are becoming more mainstream everyday. There are huge benefits for cost savings, scalability, and mobility. But there are risks as well. The regulatory rules are changing almost daily in regards to spam, sales fulfillment, and taxes. This is one area in which you will want to have good advisors who stay current on the latest rules and trends particularly regarding the legal and tax issues. It's our belief that the top Level Three businesses in the next decade will be increasingly virtual.

In the next chapter you'll learn the 12 characteristics of the ideal business so that you know exactly what to look for in any business you start. For those of you reading this book who already have existing businesses, which of the 12 characteristics does your business have? How could you tweak your existing business to tap into the power of the missing elements? When you're ready to find out just flip the page!

CHAPTER 5

The 12 Characteristics
of the Ideal
Business Opportunity

Now that you've learned the five
pillars every business is built on and the four keys to build a Level Three
business, it's time to focus on a different question: What business will
you build?

Of course if you already have one or more businesses you are building
then the question for you is really: What elements of the ideal business
are you missing that you can work to build into your business to improve
its ease of operation and profitability?

But what about those of you who don't yet have a business you are
building? What follows are the 12 characteristics you should look for
when choosing your next business opportunity.

David's Story

When I sold my last company, MFG, I thought I was
going to retire and take it easy, at least for 6–12 months. Yes, I
was only 35 at the time, but I thought I'd love to just relax and
take things slow for a while. When I told my wife Heather this,
she just smiled as if she knew something I didn't, which,
considering how things turned out, she must have.

(continued)

David's Story (continued)

One month into my retirement I was bored and bouncing off the walls. Two months into my retirement I was talking with Diane about ideas for businesses to start down the road. Three months into my retirement I had retired from my retirement and was back in business.

But this time I sat down with Diane and she helped me consciously design my ideal business. What were the parts of business that I loved? What were the parts of business that I wanted to eliminate? What was I most passionate about? What would my new business really look like?

From this conversation, which we conducted over e-mail and rambling phone calls, I came up with a concrete list of the elements of the ideal business I wanted to build. In case you're wondering what that business looks like and if I ever succeeded in building it, the company is called Maui Millionaires LLC. And it's everything I could have hoped for and much more.

1. Something You Are Passionate About

The starting point of any ideal business is, was, and will ever be *passion*. What are you truly passionate about? What do you love so much that you'd do it for free?

Don't worry, we recommend that you get paid, and handsomely, but if you wouldn't do it for free, then you shouldn't be doing it just for the money. You'll never have true wealth, defined as money plus all the intangibles, unless you are doing what you love. Besides, your passion is what fuels you to tap into deep parts of yourself that you never knew existed as you grow your business and serve the world.

Life is too short and there are too many other important things to do to spend your time building a business you really don't care about. If you want to really harness all the creativity that you and your team have, then make sure the business you're building has a meaning to you that is more than just about the money.

2. Specific Market Niche

Find a niche in which your business can be top dog. Don't try to be a jack of all trades. Remember the rest of that quote is ". . . and master of none." Pick something and stick to it. After you've mastered that niche, then you can grow it or shift focus to tackle another niche. The danger is in trying to do too much and be too much at the beginning.

The critical question to ask yourself is: Can you become known in your niche as *the* business to turn to for your product or service?

3. Low Start-Up Cost

Having a low start-up cost means you can use your own money to start the business and then bootstrap business growth out of business income. You won't have the cost of financing weighing you down, plus you don't have to worry about pleasing investors. A low start-up cost gives your business a chance to grow with the highest degree of control at critical points. Plus you own all the growing equity of your business.

Some of the biggest business success stories come from bootstrappers:

- In 1975, 20-year-old Bill Gates read an article in *Popular Electronics* about a new computer made by MITS, the Altair 8800. He and his partner, Paul Allen, contacted MITS to tell them they were working on a software platform for the computer. In actuality, they didn't even have an Altair computer yet. They created a demonstration, sold the idea to MITS, and Micro-soft was born with an idea and little money. Later that year, they dropped the hyphen and registered their new company, Microsoft, with the U.S. Patent and Trademark Office.
- Michael Dell, founder and CEO of Dell, Inc., started the company with $1,000 in 1984. Annual sales for his company have reached $50 billion and, in 2005, he made the *Forbes* list as the fourth richest person in the United States.
- Larry Page and Sergey Brin started out with a doctoral project and ended up billionaires with Google!

4. Low Fixed Costs

There are two types of costs in a business: direct (or cost of goods) and indirect (fixed costs). Direct costs are the type of costs that occur when you sell the product or service. If you didn't have any customers, you wouldn't have this cost. For example, when Maui Millionaires puts on a seminar, the cost of the room, the handouts, the staff travel, and other costs associated with just that event are direct costs. If your company manufactures scooters, the costs associated with making those scooters (materials, parts, and labor) are direct costs.

Indirect or fixed costs are costs that occur no matter what. As long as you have a business, you'll have these costs. Examples might be the office rent, copier cost, office staff expenses, and the like.

Fixed costs can bury a company. The higher the fixed costs, the more you have to sell before you can break even on your costs.

5. Deep Funnel

Picture a vertical funnel—wide at the top, narrow at the bottom. The top of your funnel is where your prospective clients enter. They get some great taste of your business (information, special introductory offer, trial period, etc.) for free or very inexpensively. Once they've experienced the value you deliver they can buy from you an increasingly richer and richer selection of products or services. Each time they step to the next offering it's like they're stepping deeper into your business funnel. As clients progress down through the funnel their numbers diminish, but the products or services they buy are increasingly more expensive and have larger and larger margins. Ultimately, your clients decide for themselves at which level of your business they want to operate. Of course, your job as an entrepreneur is to entice them to keep journeying deeper into your business funnel by creatively creating richer offerings that deliver more and more value to your clients.

Now, contrast the funnel idea with the way most businesses operate. They create one or more products and then go out to the market and try to sell those products to as many people as they can. Rarely do businesses work to build a real connection with their clients and take them deeper and deeper into their business funnel. In fact, most businesses don't even *have* a business funnel.

Another problem we have observed in many businesses is that they go for one big sale with one "yes" or "no" answer from prospective clients. The big-ticket sales strategy loses and often alienates clients. It's like walking up to a stranger and asking her to marry you. No courting, no dating, just popping the question!

We prefer the funnel approach because you create more clients, provide more value to those clients, and fundamentally build a stronger connection with those clients.

For example, you might hear a lot about the Maui Mastermind events we hold twice a year for our elite clients. These events are definitely high-end big-ticket affairs. But most people don't walk in off the street, plunk down their credit card, and ask to sign up (actually because everyone selected to attend that event has to go through two interviews this would never happen, but hey, give us a break, we're trying to make a point here). Most people have gotten some other product or service of ours first (read one of our books, attended one of our workshops, taken an online course of ours, etc.) *before* they ever stepped up to come to Maui. They can do that because we have a deep funnel. The Maui Mastermind events are part of the funnel but not the *only* part.

6. Recurring Sales to Your Clients

The easiest sale you'll ever make will be to an existing happy customer. That's why selling a consumable, recurring product is better than selling a single item that never has to be replenished or augmented. With the sales theory of one sale once, you're always looking for more customers. This gets tiring and this costs a lot more money in marketing dollars.

Our ideal business has a product or service that regularly needs to be repurchased or updated. Done right, a recurring sale is an opportunity to build a lasting relationship with your clients. Personally, our favorite type of consumable is information. It's cheap to reproduce, infinitely expandable, and because our world is so fast changing it has a shelf life measured in *months*!

For example, one of the services we offer to our clients is called Maui Mastermind Online. It's an online community where each week they get updated workshops and special reports on building businesses, investing, tax strategy, and financial fluency. Because we have a large membership base we can spread the costs over a large pool of members and hence any one member only pays a nominal monthly fee that automatically applies on their credit card.*

---

*As a reader of this book you qualify to receive a FREE 30-day trial membership to Maui Mastermind Online. For more information see the Appendix or go to **www.MauiMillionaires.com/book**.

7. Collect Money *Before* You Fulfill Your Product or Service

Did you know that the reason most businesses fail is because they don't have enough cash to keep going? That makes sense when you consider how a typical product-based business works. The business pays to manufacture or purchase a product and inventories it until customers buy its goods. Buying that inventory ties up the business' cash and increases the business' risk (e.g. damaged inventory, obsolescence when you upgrade, etc). Wouldn't it be better if you could get paid *before* you manufactured or purchased your product wholesale? This isn't always possible, but in our ideal business we'd have this element present.

Collecting fees up front also makes sense with service-based businesses. Far too many service providers wait 30-90 days to be paid. If the service also involves some out-of-pocket costs to fulfill, the business has now paid for costs out of its cash flow, performed the work, and then must sit and wait around to get paid.

The best business model is one that collects cash up front as a deposit or retainer or full payment before the product or service is performed. Not only does this help with cash flow, it saves your company all the time and energy of collection.

8. Power of Pre-Eminence

There are two ways to make your mark on the market: (1) by being the best, or (2) by being the cheapest. Being the best means you make more money with less stress. It also means your clients value and appreciate you more. Best of all, your clients will actually listen to you and use your products and services as you advise them to maximize their results. This allows you to feel great about the positive impact you are able to make in your clients' lives.

However, the one challenge with this approach is that eventually someone will try to rip off your ideas and compete with you on a "we're almost as good as your company—and we cost less" basis. When that happens, celebrate! You know you've got the Power of Pre-eminence. Aim to be the highest value, premium quality, and often most expensive player in your market.

9. No Perceived Competition

The next element of an ideal business is closely related to the Power of Pre-eminence. It's the element of having a clear, distinct position in the marketplace that jumps to your clients' and prospective clients' minds.

We prefer our market position to be one of pre-eminence. However, your market position can be that of the value provider (i.e. you're the best-buy-for-the-money people). Or it can be that you are the cutting edge, techie-cool leader in the market.*

It's almost impossible to go up market with a brand. If you start out as a discount shop, no one really takes you seriously at the high end. On the other hand, it's fairly easy to go down market with the huge advantage of having the highest-end aura. There is no perceived competition as you go down market. You are the high end just a little more affordable.

The key is to have a strong, distinctive, and *protected* brand. Besides the legal protections of copyright, trademark, and patent registrations, you can also protect your brand by being first and foremost, the market leader in your niche.

Any ideal business must have a strong brand that clearly and distinctly identifies its core position to the marketplace.

10. Maximize the Unique Talents of You and Your Team

What do you do best and absolutely love doing? Spend your time doing that and you'll find that you are much more effective and interested in the role you have in your business.

Just think of what can happen when your team members do the same thing. When you are building your business you want to make sure you get talented team members on board who are focusing on the things they do best and in the areas they are most passionate about. If you are able to do this the sky is the limit for your business! Plus, you'll have team members who are willing to go beyond the norm to make things happen.

---

*There are several great books that we highly recommend on this topic. In fact, we've put together a list of the business and financial books you *must* read. You can download this list for free at **www.MauiMillionaires.com/book**.

11. Scalability

One of the hallmarks of a Level Three business is that it can grow fast. A scalable business has systems and a universal feel that means the model can grow into other areas or fully within a niche. The business must be able to scale up with minimal pains. Ideally that scalability will be via systems, technology, and outside vendors versus just through hiring more employees, because this makes it much easier to grow fast and to scale down if your sales revenue drops for a period.

Ideally your business will be Web-based so you can provide all or more of your product or service via the Internet. This will give you the ultimate in flexibility, scalability, affordability, and power. Plus, you have the unique advantage of being able to have a distributed team that can work anywhere. Your fulfillment to clients is instantaneous and easy to support.

And, as if that weren't enough, you are able to run your Web-based business from anywhere in the world.

12. Create Intellectual Property

The final quality of the ideal business is that the business consistently generates valuable intellectual property (IP) that you can sell or license. IP is weightless and costs virtually nothing to reproduce and distribute. In a real way it's the ideal product.

That doesn't mean your business is solely revolving around IP, but ideally your business should generate proprietary IP that it transforms into a significant profit center. For example, one of our Maui Millionaire clients, Kerry, has a bathroom shower glass franchise. The business has a very high profit margin and opportunities for him to grow his business. To help him do this he invested in an integrated software solution to help him optimize all aspects of his business. Now, most people would see that as an investment to help him more effectively run his business. Kerry sees it also as an opportunity to license to the several hundred other franchisees in his business. They win by improving their businesses, and Kerry wins by getting paid handsomely for his IP.

We hope that you look for the IP inside your business. Perhaps you can bundle your systems and franchise your business to others to expand your brand. Or perhaps you can sell your expertise and get paid a royalty. Your business IP includes your software systems, your client base, your business systems, your trademarks, your patents, and your copyrights. Because you developed your intellectual property as a part of developing your business, it costs very little to turn it into a saleable commodity, which means it has a very high profit margin. Best of all, it pushes you to make your business better so that you have better IP to potentially sell. You win twice!

So there you have the 12 elements of an ideal business. How does your business or business idea stack up? How can you modify your business so that it increases its value by taking on one or more of the missing elements? And finally, if you were starting over again today from scratch knowing what you now know, with zero investment (mental, emotional, financial) in this product or business, would you build it again?

This final, "If I were starting over again from scratch," technique helps overcome the tendency we all have to hang on to "sunk cost" economic models. You can't get back spilt milk, nor can you get back sunk cost.

In the next chapter you'll learn how to avoid the 10 biggest business blunders. These mistakes can literally cause your business to fail and yet are so easy to avoid when you know how to identify them.

CHAPTER 6

The 10 Biggest Blunders (and How You Can Avoid Them)

ou're about to learn the 10 most costly mistakes that we commonly see so many entrepreneurs fall prey to. As you read this chapter, ask yourself how many of these blunders are you making right now? And more importantly, what are you going to do about it?

Time to confess: Both of us have at one time or another made *every single one* of these embarrassing business mistakes. In fact, to be perfectly frank, we've made some of them more than once!

Still, it's our hope that you can use this chapter to sharpen your thinking and avoid these painful pitfalls.

Let's get started!

Blunder #1: Taking Your Eye Off of Your Cash Flow

The number one reason that businesses fail is lack of cash. Period. End of story. Some of the issues that can bury a new business are:

- Under-funded growth.
- Lack of adequate record-keeping.

- No review of financial statements.
- No control over business assets.
- Unnecessary infrastructure.
- Having to wait for payment for sales.
- Sacrificing short-term cash flow for long-term growth.
- Thinking that because they have a sale they have cash.
- Spending on inventory.

Strategy: Watch your cash flow and do whatever you can to protect it. In each of the previous examples of mistakes that cause cash flow problems, there was simply a lack of consideration about cash flow. You wouldn't grow too fast if you didn't have the cash, *if* you knew to watch the cash. You'd have good financial statements and review these on a regular basis. You would practice good control and make sure you weren't overspending when you couldn't afford it. And, you'd make sure you first had the cash flow automatically working before you took on any more projects or expansion. Cash flow is the lifeblood of your business. The next five blunders are closely related to blunder one.

Blunder #2: Improper Management of Accounts Receivable

Accounts receivable are the amounts that your customers owe you. The best way to handle accounts receivable is to not have them! Get paid in advance or get paid at the time of service.

David's Story

I have this guy who comes over to fix my computer. I'm not the most computer-literate person in the world, so he comes pretty frequently. He does great work, and I appreciate him. But here's the thing. He never gives me a bill when he's at my home or my office. He's so uncomfortable with his own value and asking for money up front that he'd rather go back to his office

(continued)

and bill me via e-mail. And the really crazy thing is I'd pay him on the spot if he'd just ask, because I *know* how valuable his service is. Let this be a lesson to you—the faster you ask for payment the sooner and more reliably you get paid.

Strategy: If you must have accounts receivable, front load your collection effort. The longer you wait to collect the money, the less chance you have of getting it. Collection agencies know this. After all, that's why their businesses exist in the first place. Yet, most businesses only put their energy into collection after 60 days have passed. Imagine how much more effective it would be if that same effort was put into collecting that money at the beginning, as soon as the service has been provided. (We'll go into greater depth on this subject in the next section of the book.)

Blunder #3: Over Expansion

If you're a forward planner, over expansion can be a real danger. You know there is more business coming and so you staff up and invest in inventory, capital assets, and additional space. The problem is that all this growth is done without the revenue to cover the additional cost. The new business, if it indeed does come, might be too little, too late. Your business is now vulnerable.

Strategy: Plan for just-in-time growth. Remember to outsource and watch your cash flow during expansions. It might be best to take out small, short-term loans in the beginning to make sure you have enough cash to handle all the other aspects of growth.

Blunder #4: Too Much Time Setting Up Instead of Getting Business

There are some business owners who like everything planned out and organized before they start. It's a great skill, but it can be death for a new company. Often it's an excuse to hide behind instead of going out there and asking for the sale.

Strategy: Sell first! Get money in the door, otherwise, you don't have a business. You need to collect money and have cash before you can start organizing anything.

Blunder #5: Selling by the Hour

If all you sell is your time, it's hard to build a true Level Three business. If you sell by the hour, you are operating in the commoditized world competing against everyone else. Find a way to capture your value in a comprehensive solution, or a project result, or a value proposition, so that you can create and charge for your value independent of your personal time involved in fulfilling. It's also a much easier transition from a Level Two to Level Three business, where you are transitioning away from day-to-day work in the business.

Strategy: Look for the unique value you create with your ideas and work. If you have a successful Level Two business, or Level Two skills, then you can transition easily to Level Three once you let go of the need to sell by the hour. Begin by charging a flat fee for the service and then systemize and optimize the service so your team, technology, and systems fulfill your promise in a way that creates more value for your client with lower cost to your business. And finally, turn your knowledge into an information product and sell this as an additional revenue stream.*

Blunder #6: Giving Your Expertise Away in a Way that Has No Perceived Value

This is a challenge for many professionals. Prospects call and want to meet with you for a free consultation. You want to dazzle them and give

---

*For any professionals out there who are stuck in the "hourly trap," make sure you check out the Millionaire Fast-Track Program offered in the Appendix. In it you'll learn powerful ideas on how you can restructure your professional practice (be it as a CPA, a chiropractor, an attorney, or consultant) to make more money while working fewer hours. You'll also learn about a unique course we offer specifically for professionals who want to turn their professional practice into a Level Three business.

them tons of good information in the free consultation. Yet this one-on-one time is the most costly time you have, because you've got no leverage on it and you haven't been paid for it. Plus, you have no guarantee that you'll even get a client out of the deal!

Strategy: You've spent a career lifetime learning the skills to ask the right questions and look at your client's situation and challenges in a systematic way. Charge for this expertise and structure that you bring to the table. Not only will it make you more money because it will be an additional revenue stream, but it will also dramatically increase your closing ratio in converting prospects into paying clients. Best of all your new clients will benefit from the extra value they'll receive now that you help them understand and appreciate the tangible value your expertise delivers to them.

Blunder #7: Requiring Payment Before You Give any Value

Okay, this might sound like a contradiction to Blunder #6, but it's not. Be willing to give value first to start the relationship, but do it in a virtual way that minimizes any one-on-one time of your own. Giving value is often a great way to invest in a new business relationship that can pay great dividends. Just do it consciously and not out of habit or fear of asking for payment.

Strategy: Give prospective clients some huge benefit that has just a one-time cost and requires no ongoing time of yours. For example, we've created the "Millionaire Fast-Track Program," a $2,150 free bonus for people who register their copy of *The Maui Millionaires for Business* (to register just go to **www.MauiMillionaires.com/book**). While it costs us over $100,000 to create and maintain this valuable bonus, we know that over time it will generate millions of dollars of value for our business. How? Because it is a simple and easy way for readers to start doing business with us after getting an incredible free gift that shows them the quality of the information we offer. We used this with our last book, *The Maui Millionaires*, as well, and thousands of our readers let us know their appreciation for the book bonus we used in that case by choosing to enter into a long-term, mutually profitable relationship with us and our companies.

One hint: Your free content needs to have real value. It shouldn't be just a sales pitch. Instead, gracefully and tastefully offer your products or services in your free content in a way that makes the experience a positive and valuable one for your new clients.

Blunder #8: Ignoring Window Shoppers in Favor of Customers

A lot more people will visit your brick-and-mortar shop or your virtual business than will ever become customers. Don't make the mistake of concentrating on the customers only and ignoring the visitors. Your visitors are people who contact your company through an inbound phone call, in-store visit, or someone who buys your book, or visits your web site. Far too many businesses ignore these unrecorded guests even though your business may be spending hundreds of thousands or millions of dollars in marketing costs just to get them to come by. You must find automatic, systematized ways to get your visitors to tell you who they are.

Strategy: Offer your visitors such great value (for free) that they choose to enter into a relationship with you in a way that lets you know who they are. The special book bonus you get with this book is a powerful example of this. You'll find several more examples of prominently placed free offers at www.mauimillionaires.com. Each of these offers requires our guest to let us know who they are in order to receive this free information. We each get something of value in the exchange. This same strategy can be used in a retail store (e.g. offer them a free gift certificate), in a service-based business (e.g. script out how your phone team will offer your callers a free e-book, gift, or upgraded service), or in any other business. All it takes is a little imagination.

Blunder #9: Hiring "Warm Bodies"

When the rush of new business happens, it's really tempting to hire any and everyone. The problem with doing warm body hiring is twofold. First, you may or may not be getting quality employees. And second, you could very well experience a sales slump and be stuck with a big payroll.

Strategy: Use outsourcing to fulfill staffing needs rather than hiring employees. When you do hire employees, always make sure you do background checks, verify references, and get signed non-disclosure and non-compete agreements.

Blunder #10: Failure to Fulfill Sales Promises

In Blunder #4 we talked about the danger of spending all of your time and effort in building the infrastructure and systems and ignoring the sales component. That's a complete non-starter for a successful business. Without sales and cash flow coming in you *have no business*.

But the extreme opposite is a problem as well. In this case, you make lots of sales, but don't have a good operations system to fulfill the product or services. In the short run, you're fine because you have cash. But, in the long run, you don't have a business that is sustainable because the only referrals you are getting are tepid at best and negative at worst. And, taken to the extreme, you might even have a lawsuit if you fail to fulfill or make a mistake because your internal documentation is out of order.

Turn the page to perform a performance audit on your business. (See Figure 6.1.)

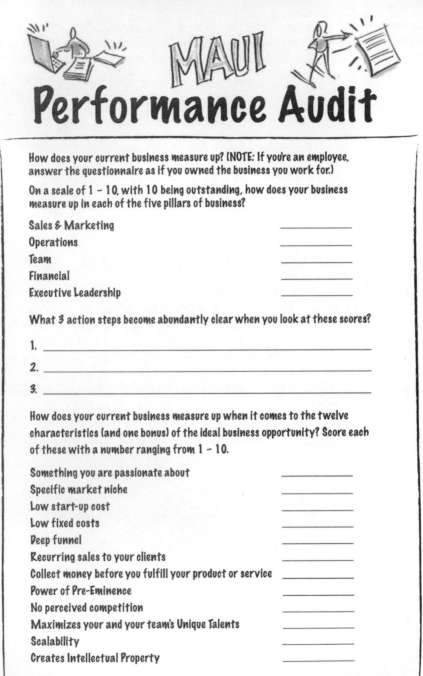

MAUI
Performance Audit

How does your current business measure up? (NOTE: If you're an employee, answer the questionnaire as if you owned the business you work for.)

On a scale of 1 – 10, with 10 being outstanding, how does your business measure up in each of the five pillars of business?

Sales & Marketing   _____
Operations   _____
Team   _____
Financial   _____
Executive Leadership   _____

What 3 action steps become abundantly clear when you look at these scores?

1. _____

2. _____

3. _____

How does your current business measure up when it comes to the twelve characteristics (and one bonus) of the ideal business opportunity? Score each of these with a number ranging from 1 – 10.

Something you are passionate about   _____
Specific market niche   _____
Low start-up cost   _____
Low fixed costs   _____
Deep funnel   _____
Recurring sales to your clients   _____
Collect money before you fulfill your product or service _____
Power of Pre-Eminence   _____
No perceived competition   _____
Maximizes your and your team's Unique Talents _____
Scalability   _____
Creates Intellectual Property   _____

FIGURE 6.1   Maui Performance Audit

What 3 action steps do you want to take after you look at these scores?

1. _____

2. _____

3. _____

Based on this review, what 3 action steps do you want to take to maximize your business value?

1. _____

2. _____

3. _____

Rate your company with a 1 – 10 for each of the four keys to take your business to Level Three:

Systems   _____

Team   _____

Outsource solutions   _____

Technology   _____

What 3 action steps must you take to take your business to the next level?

1. _____

2. _____

3. _____

Take the Right Steps!!

FIGURE 6.1   *(Continued)*

SECRET #2: Leverage Your Business Assets and Triple Your Cash Flow

CHAPTER 7

The Five Most Important Business Multipliers

Cash flow is the lifeblood of your business. It pays your bills, feeds your growth, and rewards you for your investments of time, talent, and money. In essence, you need cash flow to fuel your business dreams.

In the last section, you learned how you can build a Level Three business and get on the Millionaire Fast-Track. The focus was on building your business, which in turn massively increased your business' value and your net worth.

In this section, we're going to look at 72 techniques to leverage your business in a way that increases cash flow. First, we'll focus on the five most important business multipliers. These are the five universal leverage points you can use in *any* business, in *any* industry, in *any* marketplace, in *any* country, to make your business succeed faster.

Then in Chapter 8, you'll discover 35 hidden business assets you can tap into to increase your cash flow. Finally, in Chapter 9 you'll learn about 32 often overlooked techniques to *immediately* boost your business cash flow.

Let's begin with the five business multipliers.

Business Multiplier #1: Mastermind Power

One of the secret strengths of Maui Millionaires is the power of the mastermind. A mastermind group is a group of two or more people who come together to work on a common goal in the spirit of focused harmony and trust, where all members benefit. The skill of masterminding is so essential that we devoted an entire section of our last book, *The Maui Millionaires*, to it (pp. 125–164).

Level Three business owners have learned that they don't have all the best answers or ideas. But they have cultivated a huge advantage in the marketplace—multiple mastermind partners in various areas that they can turn to for ideas, input, accountability, and support.

We recommend five mastermind groups to maximize the growth for your company. They are:

1. *Within your company*. This is your inside team. The mastermind principle is how you unify, focus, engage, and unleash your team to accomplish the work of your business. For a small company, this may include one group of all team members. For a large company, this may entail multiple groups in various areas of the business, each trained in how to use the mastermind principle to get great results.*

2. *With key industry players*. Form a mastermind group with people outside your company who are in your industry. This could include your vendors, companies that provide complementary services or products, or perhaps even competitors. Just think of the range of ideas and potential joint ventures that you could get from a mastermind group like this!

3. *Outside board of advisors*. Successful business owners know they need input from quality business people outside of their industry and outside of their immediate financial world. Consider forming a mastermind group with like-minded achievers to help each other succeed and live at your best.

---

*Would you like to learn more about how to use the mastermind principle in the business world? Register now for your FREE Millionaire Fast-Track Program and get immediate access to an online workshop that shares with you five key steps to put the power of the mastermind to work in your business. Go to **www.Maui Millionaires.com/Book**.

Diane's Story

Don't immediately dismiss forming a mastermind group with your competitors. One of the most fulfilling mastermind groups I've ever had has been with other CPAs and tax attorneys. We discuss new tax strategies and future legislation at a very high level. We all know that there is far more work in our specialty field, and potential clients as well, than any of us could ever serve. So, we don't come into the group with a thought of scarcity.

These meetings often help influence policy for tax laws. That's one reason my companies, DKA (a CPA firm), and TaxLoopholes (an online tax education company), are able to consistently create innovative strategies that are legal and ethical. Our group contributes to setting the rules for what works, and what doesn't, when it comes to tax strategies.

Look within your professional organizations for like-minded individuals in your field and try out a mastermind group. You might be surprised at how great the results will be!

4. *Your family.* Bring your family into your business life by master-minding with them on a regular basis (perhaps monthly or quarterly). Not only will they understand better the things you are experiencing in your business life, but by involving them in your business goals they will feel a part of what you do. This means they will support you and also, when needed, hold you accountable to not let your business grow out of proportion to the real values that you hold.

5. *Your hired team.* Finally, every entrepreneur needs a team of talented professionals (CPAs, attorneys, insurance agents, brokers, etc.) who can advise you as you build your business. Use the mastermind principle to more effectively get the input and guidance you need from your hired team.

Business Multiplier #2: Your Client Base

Your client base is probably the most valuable business asset that you have. Does your business treat your client base with honor, respect, and integrity? If the answer is yes, then over time your business will grow and thrive. If not, your business will never last over time.

Yet how do many businesses treat their most valuable asset? Like a database to be strip-mined for maximum value. The people and relationships you've built are more than just data. They are the heart and soul of your business.

One clue as to how a business views its clients is what it calls them. Are they called "customers" or "clients?" Do they end up in a database or a client base? While this may seem like a minor distinction, in our experience the mindset behind it makes a huge difference. A customer is someone to sell to; a client is someone to care for. Databases die, go stale, or move on. Client bases grow as communities thrive. If you remember to always put your client's needs in front of yours, you'll find you have the secret ingredient to build that client relationship.

David's Story

Early on, Diane and I made the decision to treat our clients as a community, not a database. We wanted to source and serve the community by teaching its members ways to become wealthier, get involved with giving projects, and live the life of their dreams.

For both of us, being part of Maui Millionaires is one of the most important things we will ever do, and it's the relationships we've been blessed to build with our clients that keep us engaged to do more.

We love getting e-mails and letters from people about the changes that have occurred in their lives since getting the Maui message.* That's why we do this; we don't *have* to do this business, we *get* to do this business.

Has this attitude affected our relationships with our clients? We believe it has made all the difference in the world. For example, when we first came up with the idea of Maui Mastermind, *the world's most exclusive wealth retreat* in 2003, we had no idea how people would receive it. So Diane and I sent out a heartfelt 16-page e-mail detailing exactly what the event was, why we had

(continued)

David's Story *(continued)*

created it, and who we would select to attend. And the phone started ringing off the hook before the e-mail was even completely sent out to all our clients. There was no way we could have created such a successful annual event if it weren't for the deep and valued relationships we had spent the prior decade developing with our clients.

How do you think about the people who buy your products or services? How about your team, how do they think about them? The answers to these two questions will have a dramatic impact on your company's future.

*If you have a story or experience you'd like to share with us, we'd love to hear from you. Just send us an e-mail at DavidandDiane@mauimillionaires.com.

Business Multiplier #3:
Creativity

Creativity is that priceless ingredient that can solve any problem, turn around any business situation, and enhance any business. It's one of the most underutilized business multipliers, yet the creativity you harness in your company literally can take your company to the top of your industry overnight.

Consider eBay® for a minute. It began in September 1995, and the very first item sold was a broken laser pointer for $14.83. That's when founder Pierre Omidyar knew he was on to something. Over the past decade, by tapping into its teams' and its clients' creativity it has become one of the most powerful marketplaces in the world. In fact, it's now the 17th largest world economy!

Creativity is what made that all happen. Creativity is what can exponentially grow your business. You don't need more money, you don't need the perfect marketplace, you need to unleash the creative genius held idle in your company. How best to free it up? Combine your creativity with the mastermind principle.

Business Multiplier #4: Character

Your character magnifies you. It helps you be your best self and it's an essential ingredient in leading and influencing others. In essence, your character is that part inside you that keeps you moving toward your dreams even after the blush of the initial excitement has worn away.

There are four parts of your character we want to highlight. First is integrity—the way you honor your word. Since all business relationships are predicated on trust, you will never succeed on the scale you dream unless you are impeccable with your word. Also, to build lasting success means you live your life in accord with your most deeply held values and principles.

Second comes passion—the fuel that takes you to your dreams. We've already shared how we believe that every entrepreneur must find a meaningful way to connect his or her passion to their business in order to be wealthy. But understand that passion is also the fire inside you that warms your team, your vendors, and your clients to your business' vision. And when it burns brightly it is a contagious source of exponential power.

Third comes courage—the steel that keeps you moving forward even when you are scared to death. And all entrepreneurs reach multiple points when they are scared to death. Yet it's your job to learn to act in the presence of your fears.

Finally, there is faith—the gossamer quality that brings deep meaning into your business. Understand this: If your business exists only for the money you will never be wealthy. You may become rich but never wealthy. Enduring wealth comes from deep meaning and that takes faith. Faith is also the secret to enduring peace of mind. It's the real foundation for business and life success. And, just as you do with courage, you also have a faith muscle that expands with exercise and use.

Business Multiplier #5: Your Business Skills

There are certain skills that may generically be applied across any business, which when mastered, will create real value in your business. Here is a list of six skills that we think are essential to business success.

1. Leadership—Your ability to create a coherent business vision, inspire others to join you over time, and empower your business to willingly accept and embrace change.

2. Negotiation—Your ability to uncover complementary needs and reach mutually profitable agreements.

3. Time mastery—Your ability to maximize your time, to manage priorities and conflicting demands, and achieve a harmony in what you do (and choose not to do).

4. Salesmanship—Your ability to influence the way people perceive a given situation and to sell a dream, a product, a service, an opportunity, or a course of action.

5. Financial Fluency—Your ability to speak the five languages of financial fluency and move in the world of money, wealth, and business with grace and ease.

6. Emotional Fluency—Your ability to understand emotions, yours and other peoples', and to be able to connect, engage, and, when needed, manage emotions.

So there you have the five business multipliers. Remember you can apply these universal leverage points in *any* business, in *any* industry, in *any* marketplace, in *any* country, to make your business succeed faster.

In the next chapter you'll learn about the 35 hidden business assets you can tap into to dramatically increase your cash flow.

CHAPTER 8

35 Hidden Assets You Can Leverage in Your Business

How can you create more cash flow from your business' hidden assets? Several months ago we asked ourselves this very question. We spent hours going back and forth via phone and e-mail conversations—brainstorming, arguing, explaining, and imagining. The answers you are about to read have been loosely grouped into 10 categories. We suggest you don't use this list as a checklist of items to build your business. Rather, we suggest you use the list as an artificial spark to help you spot hidden opportunities in your business that you can immediately use to increase your cash flow.

Client Base

Here is a list of nine ways you can tap into your client base to increase your cash flow. It's important to note that you must make sure that you always sell to your clients by creating real value and honor your relationship with them.

1. *Upsell:* An upsell is a richer, upgraded offering with which you move a percentage of your clients to purchase. For example, imagine

a payroll company that normally offers to just take over the proper processing of employee paychecks. This company could offer its clients a complete outsourced personnel services package. Even if only 10 percent of the company's clients upgraded to this full-service offer it might double the business cash flow. What can you upgrade your clients, or a subsection of your clients, to something that would better serve their real needs at a healthy profit?

2. *Cross sell:* When a client buys from you what else do they need that your business could sell to them? For example, a home furnishing business just sold a client new tile for her master bathroom. A cross sell would be for that business to offer the purchaser grout, tools, or other bathroom fixtures at the time of purchase. What else can you offer your clients at the time they buy from you?

3. *Refer out:* What other types of products and services do your clients need that you don't provide? You can refer out on a fee-for-referral basis, on a profit split (see joint venture), or simply within an informal reciprocal relationship where a small network of businesses help each other generate business and serve clients.

4. *Referrals:* When you give great value to your clients ask them for referrals to other people they know who would benefit from your products or services. For example, at a typical Maui Millionaires workshop roughly half the people in the room originally became clients from referrals. Not only is the cost for a referral incredibly low, but you've got immediate trust transferred from the referring client over to this prospective client. This means that you'll have a much higher conversion rate of referred prospective clients who end up buying from you.

5. *People who said no:* How much money did your business spend on its average lead? Yet how many businesses never market to a prospective client once they say no. Instead, ask yourself what else could you offer them to get them to say yes? Could you turn these types of leads over to a special sales team in your company that you authorize to make an irresistible "gateway offer" (see below)? Or perhaps you could team up on these leads with another business, or even a competitor, on a joint-venture basis? Or maybe you can just keep them coming back to your business knowing that over time enough of them will eventually buy (proven out because you've tracked this via your client base).

6. *Stale leads:* Every business has a large number of leads that responded once to inquire about a product or service (either via phone, mail, Web, in person, etc.), but then just faded into the background.

How could you contact these stale leads and entice them to become clients? Perhaps you could write a letter apologizing for letting their valuable needs slip between the cracks and offering them a special gift when they contact your office. Or maybe you could have your sales team create a special script and sales process to work just with these types of leads (see selling systems below). The key is that you've spent a lot of money and energy to get these people to raise their hands once, how can you capitalize on that now?

7. *Empower your clients:* How can you make it easier for your clients to get increased value from you in a way that decreases your costs? Can you get your clients to support each other? Can you set up self-service options for your clients online so they can find the answers they want without waiting in line? For example, our Maui Mastermind Online clients help each other. Sure they get answers from David and Diane and other Maui Stars, but much of the value they get comes directly from the vibrant community we've collectively created where people help each other.

8. *Content and product ideas:* Get your clients to share with you their problems and pains, their ideas and desires. Let them beta test new products or services at a reduced fee or even free. Their feedback and buzz will more than pay back your investment. Also, every business needs cutting-edge clients. For us, our Maui Mastermind clients keep us on the leading edge. We have to scramble pretty fast to serve their needs and often work together to test our new business ideas or investing models. The winning ideas then work their way down to our other Maui Millionaires clients through our books, online courses, and live workshops. Your cutting-edge clients can be demanding, but they are worth their weight in gold. No business can hope to stay fresh and sharp unless it has a group of cutting-edge clients.

9. *Testimonials:* When you combine great value with simple systems for reliably asking your clients to share how your product or service benefited them you get irresistible stories. And stories sell. How can you get compelling stories of the results your clients gained from investing in your products or services? And how can you share these stories in ways that compel your other clients or prospective clients to do more business with you?

Competitors

10. *Joint venture with your competitor:* If your client would be better served with a competitive product or service, arrange to provide

that product or service to your client at a profit. You could do this by licensing your competitor's product or service and private labeling it as your own. You could buy your competitor's product at a steep discount and sell it at a profit to your client. Or you could refer your client to a competitor for a referral fee or residual percentage. You could also arrange to do the reverse, selling your product or service to your competitor's active clients in a mutually profitable and healthy way.

11. *Buy your competitor's dead, stale, or sated leads:* Your competitor surely has leads that said no, or have gone stale, or that have already purchased all your competitor has to offer. Help your competitor turn these leads into an additional revenue stream(s) by selling them to you.

12. *Reciprocal lead exchange with competitors:* Mutually trade dead, stale, or sated leads with your competitor. Or, if it makes sense, trade your active clients with each other, too.* Catalog companies do this all the time. They create a collective clearinghouse that helps them share names among several dozen catalog companies. How can you work together with your competitors to help each of you get more clients and create more options and value for your clients? A crazy question we know, but one that pays to ask.

13. *Model your competitors:* What can you learn from modeling your competitors' best practices? How can you avoid the things your competitor does that are bad business? What do your competitors have to teach you that could immediately boost your cash flow?

Joint Ventures

14. *Form a joint venture with providers of noncompetitive products or services your clients need:* What other products or services do your clients need? Create a joint venture with a partner to create an easy sale because you've already done the work to gain the

---

*Every business must have its own client information policy, which is clearly communicated to every client. In some industries, such as the direct mail industry, it is the industry standard to rent out their client list. In other industries this would be both unethical and totally inappropriate. At Maui Millionaires, we have a very strict policy that we will never rent or sell our clients' information. Only David- and Diane-led companies will ever have access to our valuable client list.

trust and confidence of your client base. Your joint venture partner gets a new client, you add a new income stream that is almost pure net profit, and your client is better served. Everybody wins.

15. *Reciprocal lead exchanges with noncompetitor:* Instead of doing joint venture projects, how about just exchanging leads? This can be a formal lead exchange program or an informal program. Examples include trading Web banners, ads, or links, cross promoting each other through each other's marketing materials, putting signs or flyers in each other's place of business, training each other's sales or client services team to refer out to each other when appropriate.

Vendors

16. *Infusion of specialized expertise:* Your vendors are experts in their niches. Tap into them to get their input and ideas to make your business more profitable. What ideas do they have to help you lower your costs? How have their other clients set up their businesses to be more profitable or provide more value or generate more sales? What ways would they suggest you better maximize their services in your business? Turn your vendors into your partners using the mastermind principle. After all, it's in their best interest for you to be more successful so that you can purchase more of their products and services.

17. *Referral of new business:* Since your vendors rely on you for business, they have every reason to want you to succeed. How can they help you get more business, knowing that the more business you get the more that you'll buy from them? For example, does your attorney know of other people who might benefit from your contracting business? Or does your wholesaler know of other people who might want to hire your design team?

Your Network

18. *Doors opened:* Who do you know who can help your company get in the door to find a new client, a new referrer, or a new joint venture partner? Ask them for an introduction.

19. *Endorsements:* Do you have any relationships with key industry players that you can respectfully leverage into powerful

endorsements? In any industry there are influencers whose acceptance carries massive weight with the mainstream.

20. *New ideas:* Oftentimes, the best ideas come from relationships
you've cultivated outside of your industry. Who can you mastermind with to share ideas back and forth to help each other?

Your Selling Systems

21. *Gateway offers:* A Gateway Offer™ is a special offer that your
sales and marketing team has perfected that has the highest odds
of leading a new client along the most profitable pathway with
your company. It's the first sale that leads to all the other sales.
Most businesses let random chance dictate the first sale. That's
sloppy and bad business. Instead, over time by properly strategiz-
ing and tracking your clients' behavior, determine which offer you
can make that will draw a new client onto the richest purchase offer pathway with your company.

22. *Makeup offers:* The next time you have a client complaint or a
canceled order is a prime chance for your company to make a
profit and deepen a client relationship at the same time through
the use of a makeup offer. Here's how it works. Joe calls in and
complains about his order arriving late. In fact, he says he wants
to return it. You have a special sales script to handle just these
types of calls. "Joe, thank you for telling me about how we
messed up. Forgive us for our mistake. I don't blame you for
wanting to cancel your order just to teach us a lesson. If I were
you I'd have been even angrier and more upset than you are. May
I make it up to you?" When Joe says yes, offer him some special
gift such as a discount or certificate valid toward his next purchase. The key is to try to both close this sale (the most expensive
thing that could happen is that Joe cancels and never orders from
you again) and put Joe on the path to making his next purchase
from you. That's the power of a makeup offer that has been systematized for your team to use.

23. *Reactivation offer:* Go back to old clients who haven't bought in a
while to spark them to buy again. This should be a formalized
sales system that happens automatically and regularly versus just
a haphazard, random decision. Here's the best part: You'll typically have three times more success selling to old clients than you

will going after new clients. They just need to be asked and given a compelling reason to buy again.

24. *Unconsummated transactions:* An unconsummated transaction is any client interaction that started with the client ordering, but then before the transaction closed the process got derailed. It could be a dropped cart from a website order, or a phone order that didn't go through, or a sales call that got interrupted. The key is to have a formal process in place, ideally technology driven and automatic, to follow up with that client. For example, you could have your system automatically send an e-mail that says: *"I'm writing to apologize that we dropped your Web order earlier today. I want to personally take responsibility for this mistake and make it up to you. Please call my office at 800-555-1212 and not only will I see to it that you get 10 percent off your order, but I have instructed my staff to have a special gift waiting to send to you. This is my way of letting you know how much I personally value you as a client."*

25. *Referral systems:* Does your company have a formalized process to encourage satisfied clients to refer you more business? Does it have more than one? If your answer is no to either of these questions then you have a real opportunity to increase your sales.* Start off by looking at where your current referrals come from. Is there a way to super-size and formalize what your business is already doing? Look at other businesses, especially outside your industry. Is there anyway you can apply and layer in their referral systems to increase your sales volume?

26. *Convert active sellers into passive sellers:* You already learned about active and passive sellers in the last section of the book. This a powerful strategy to immediately boost your company's cash flow, because you can easily scale up a passive seller with minimal cost, which, in turn, will boost your cash flow. What active sellers do you have in your business that you could convert into passive sellers? What passive sellers do you already have that you could expand?

---

*We've put together our favorite list of courses and books on business and financial success. On that list we've included the single best audio program on creating referral systems for your business. To download that list, just go to **www.MauiMillionaires.com/Book.**

Duplication

27. *Add another location:* Is your business one where adding an additional location would be a smart way to expand cash flow? The key ingredient to make this one work is a Level Three business model that can easily be copied over to another location at a healthy profit.

28. *Franchise:* One of the most powerful ways to duplicate yourself is to franchise your business. If your business systems could be replicated in other markets, and if you have a strong brand that would be successful in other markets, franchising your business is a powerful way to grow.

29. *Affiliate programs:* One of the most successful ways we've duplicated ourselves with Maui Millionaires has been through our affiliate program. Our program generates thousands of dollars in extra revenue for our affiliates and us. Best of all it is automated, scalable, and we only pay for results! Look at your business. How can you use an affiliate program to automatically expand your sales?

30. *Optimize your sales process:* Continue refining and improving your sales process. Test and improve your print and online ads. Script your sales team. Can you turn a great sales script for the phone into a sales letter? Or try turning your sales letter into a sales message. Check your statistics. What works? What can you do better with?

Your Fulfillment Systems

31. *Reengineer your core value process:* Every service-based (and many product-based) business has a Core Value Process™. This is the series of stages you take a new client through to help them generate a specific result. Go back to your company's Core Value Process and create ways that you can massively increase the value to your clients in ways that radically reduce the costs or time (or both) needed to fulfill it. If your business has more than one Core Value Process then you're lucky; you now have multiple opportunities to increase your value and lower your costs.

32. *Leverage your time:* If you're like most Level Two business owners, you probably waste 70 to 80 percent of your time doing lower

value tasks. Focus on the things you do in your business that truly create value. If you have a Level Three business, help your key team members do the same thing.*

Your Intellectual Property

33. *License your intellectual property as a side venture:* Your intellectual property includes your proprietary systems, custom software, copyrights, trademarks, patents, and much more. If your business is geographic specific, consider licensing it to a competitive business outside your area with clear agreements on the terms of that license. Or perhaps you can license it outside your industry altogether. One of the easiest income streams to add to a Level Three business is often the sale or license of your intellectual property. What proprietary know-how has your business created that you could sell or license for a residual income stream?

34. *Offer your Core Value Process for sale as your main business:* Once upon a time, David was primarily an entrepreneur and real estate investor. Now he gets paid millions for teaching his Core Value Processes to other entrepreneurs and real estate investors. Once upon a time, Diane was primarily a world-class tax strategist who had created an efficient and powerful way to consistently create legal and ethical tax strategies that saved her clients as much as $100,000 per year in taxes. Now she sells that Core Value Process as a comprehensive system to other CPAs.

Your Team

35. *Unleash your team's passion, creativity, and ownership:* Too many businesses never tap into even a fraction of the true talents of their teams. It's a catastrophic loss that these businesses will never even understand. Your business must be different. How can you connect your team to your business' vision and mission in a way that truly enlivens your team? We've discovered a simple yet

---

*We designed a special online workshop to help you reach Level Three. It's available as part of the Millionaire Fast-Track Program. See the Appendix for details or go to **www.MauiMillionaires.com/book**.

powerful secret to make this happen in *any* business, in *any* industry, and in *any* country. In fact, this secret is so powerful and
makes such an amazing difference in any business that we've devoted the final section of this book to it! Because we don't want to
leave you hanging, what you'll learn is how to connect your business to a powerful mission of giving and doing good in the world
beyond the day-to-day activity of your business. This may seem
naïve, but we've watched it transform businesses. For example,
with Maui Millionaires, it's helped our team feel part of a major
mission that goes well beyond helping an individual client become financially free. Our team puts in plenty of time on their off
hours to further the giving projects we as a company take on. And
the sense of mission and engagement carries over to the daily
work they do for our company. You can do the same thing for your
company. The results will astound you.

So there you have 35 business assets that most businesses never tap
into. Below is a worksheet for your use.

Strategic Session #_____	Idea to Leverage	Next Step
Client Base	_____	_____
Competitors	_____	_____
Joint Ventures	_____	_____
Vendors	_____	_____
Your Network	_____	_____
Your Sales Process	_____	_____
Duplication	_____	_____
Your Fulfillment Systems	_____	_____
Your Intellectual Property	_____	_____
Your Team	_____	_____

In the next chapter you'll learn 32 specific techniques to immediately
boost your cash flow.

CHAPTER 9

32 Often Overlooked Techniques to Immediately Boost Your Business' Cash Flow

We've both spent years buying, building, and selling businesses. We've coached, consulted, and trained hundreds of thousands of business owners. And one simple, unadulterated, undeniable observation comes clear: The overwhelming majority of businesses do dumb things that cut into their cash flow.

There, we've said it. We've admitted that the emperor doesn't have clothes. What follows is our abridged course of 32 simple techniques that you can use to immediately boost your business' cash flow. Any one of these techniques might mean an extra $10,000 or $100,000 or $1 million or more in extra cash flow in the next 90 days.

Sound too good to be true? Well, a close friend of David's who is a key marketing person for a growing Internet business shared how she used one technique (technique No. 22) to save her company $1 million in a 12-month period. That's $1,000,000 of pure profit—additional cash flow—with no real extra work, with no extra risk, with no extra effort. Or take the example of technique No. 14. This very simple strategy was used by a service business to help the owner cut his overhead by $22,000 per month in less than 30 days! What both these people show is that they had the willingness to question the status quo and test out a new way of doing business to see how much extra cash flow it actually meant for their business.

Is your business willing to let your team suggest and implement techniques like these? If so, we suggest you don't just read this chapter yourself, but that you get a copy of this book for everyone in your company and get them to read this chapter and brainstorm ideas as a mastermind team.

Let's dive right in with this list by considering the ways your company asks for and collects money.

Client Billings

1. Consider the timing of your bill. Collect up front. If you can get paid before you fulfill your product or service you can eliminate a whole lot of hassle and additional cost chasing down payment later.

2. Don't wait to bill. If you can't bill before you fulfill, at the very least, give your customers a bill at the time the services are rendered. Remember, the longer you wait to bill, not only the longer before you get paid, but the more likely you are to have collection problems.

3. Get your clients to prepay an entire year by providing a terrific incentive to do so. This will help your cash flow plus eliminate the need for the entire accounts receivable collection process. Incentives might include a special add-on bonus or a discount.

4. If your business model must have accounts receivable, front load the collection process. Send statements out right away and start your follow-up procedures right away, not after 60–90 days have passed. Put that energy in upfront when your odds of collection are highest and payment means more to you.

5. When you ask for money, make it easy for your clients to pay you. Include a self-addressed envelope. Make sure the invoice clearly says who to make the check out to and for how much.

6. Build a "cost" for your clients into your standard contracts. If you are going to be financing your clients' purchases then you should get paid for your trouble. Make sure your contract includes a monthly financing charge for all accruing bills. Make sure it also states that they are responsible for all reasonable costs of collection. Finally, where possible, get the business owners of your clients to sign individually and not just use the name of their business.

Payment Options

7. Make payment automatic through auto-debit of their bank account. Or, if appropriate, use auto-payroll deduction. Not only will you get your money with no thought or effort on your client's part, but you'll also immediately know when you have a collection problem so you can get your team right on it. The best part is that you can leverage technology to make this process automatic and to make the accounting easier. You just may find you can reduce your staff cost at the same time.

8. If appropriate, take credit cards. Yes, you'll have to factor in the 1.5 percent to 3.5 percent transaction fees your merchant account bank will charge you. And yes, you'll have a percentage of your clients who will dispute the charges. But the bottom line for most businesses is that you'll raise your cash collected by at least 50 percent.

9. Let them finance the purchase. Sometimes you can create an additional profit center by financing your client's purchase.

10. Break the sale down into two or more payments. For example, you could collect half up front and half upon completion of the project. Or you could let them pay one-third at the signing of the contract, one-third at initiation of work, and final third at completion of work. If your business now waits for payment after completion, this simple idea will increase your cash flow and lower your collection costs immediately. But many businesses that already collect payment up front find that by adding payment plans they increase their sales so much that the net effect is a boost in profitability.

11. If you do offer a payment plan, make sure to incentivize your client to pay in full. This can be through a discount, an extra bonus, or some other added value they get for paying in full upon purchase. We suggest that you structure your payment plan option high enough to make it easier for you to offer an attractive discount for payment in full.

Inventory

Building inventory is problematic for a growing business for a couple of reasons. First, it ties up cash. Second, even though it's a very real cost of cash for the business, it's not a deductible expense for the business until the inventory is actually sold. It's possible for a company that is growing to have absolutely no cash at the end of the year, but still owe a huge tax bill. That's what happens if a business aggressively grows inventory. Here are some suggestions to maximize cash flow if your business model includes inventory.

12. Consider creating just-in-time inventory processes. Wal-Mart® has been the industry leader in this strategy of managing inventory. The retailer doesn't hold a lot of inventory. Instead it tracks inventory carefully and buys just in time. Wal-Mart takes this savings in capital and uses it to fund growth.

13. Go digital! If you have information products (and you should, even if you are primarily a service provider), don't make big, lumpy products that cost money to ship. Instead, consider delivering your audio, video and print products electronically. Invest your savings in creating more value for your clients. For example, the savings that Maui Millionaires enjoys paid for the heavy investment we made in technology to create a better client experience for people who take our online workshops.

14. Remember you have an inventory made up of staff time if you provide a service. Move to "results billing" for the people who do the work. This is where you pay your team (or part of your team) based on producing a result and not simply for logging hours. For example, you can pay per completed client assessment, or per completed account reconciliation, or per completed project milestone. That way you don't pay people to sit around. You simply pay them when you get a good result.

Taxes

One of the most expensive line items for a business is the amount of tax it pays. And, while it's hard to keep Diane to just a couple of line items on the subject of saving taxes,* she's given it her best, brief shot below.

---

*Actually, we've worked out a compromise. In order to keep this chapter to under 200 pages, David had to promise to let Diane teach a comprehensive tax strategy workshop as part of the free online Millionaire Fast-Track Program. All kidding aside, Diane put together an amazing one hour online workshop walking you through the 12 most important tax strategies for entrepreneurs. To get immediate access just go to **www.MauiMillionaires.com/book**.

15. Timing of tax deposits. Watch when you pay your personal taxes. If you're getting a big refund, all you've done is give the government an interest-free loan. (And, they didn't even say thank you.) One thing you don't want to mess with, though, is employment taxes that you withhold from your employees' paychecks. You must remit those to the government on time. If you get slow on these payments, the IRS can come in and seize all of your company's assets . . . and they will.

16. Identify your personal and business deductions. There are literally hundreds of categories of tax reductions available.

17. Good record keeping. The most common reason that business owners miss deductions is that they don't have timely bookkeeping. If your idea of bookkeeping is to throw everything in a box and give it to someone else to figure out at the end of the year, it's guaranteed that you're missing deductions.

18. Pre-emptive tax strategies. The best way to not pay taxes is to build net worth and cash flow from your wealth, not as after-tax income. For example, use forced appreciation that you access as unrealized income to legally avoid taxes. Or, invest in your business and real estate through pension plans to defer or completely avoid taxes. These are more sophisticated strategies that require an advanced Level Two or Level Three business and accounting system to maintain. Diane has put together a detailed special report called *Preemptive Tax Strategy: Why the Rich Legally Pay Less in Taxes than the Poor and Middle Income*, that you can get for free just by going to **www.MauiMillionaires.com/book**.

Cash Flow Management

19. Create a systematic way to manage both your cash in and your cash out. If your collections of accounts receivable are slow, now is not the time to be adding a lot of expenses. Manage your cash flow both ways and in relationship to all aspects of your business. Be willing to quickly dial down your expenses if revenues slow.

20. Watch your business sales cycles and make sure you're not building up assets, inventory, or staffing at a time when business is about to slow down.

21. Consider *not* prepaying too many expenses unless you are given a business reason to do so (e.g. a meaningful discount). Sometimes

it is better to pay monthly to guard cash flow rather than pay annually up front.

22. Consolidate your purchases and negotiate better pricing. This is especially important for companies that have gone through a recent burst of growth. Too often we see companies paying prices based on purchase volumes that they far exceed.

23. Get competitive bids from vendors. Even if you plan on staying with your current vendor the very fact that you know and they know that you're getting outside bids will keep their pencils sharp and help ensure you get better pricing.

24. Train your staff to ask for and get discounts. A short training course on how your team can get discounts, plus consistent recognition for people who do this for you, pays off handsomely in increased cash flow. This one idea alone could reduce your variable expenses by 5–10 percent!

Debt Management

The intelligent use of debt is one of the greatest secrets to increasing your cash flow. Here are several ways you can protect your cash flow when using debt.

25. Negotiate better interest rates with your lenders. Our best advice here is to get your lenders competing for your business. It's a critical shift, but one that takes you out of the applicant role and transforms them into the sales people working to earn your business.

26. Negotiate better amortization schedules. The longer you take to pay off your loan the lower your payment will be. If the loan amortizes over five years your payment will be lower than if it pays off over three years. Ten years is even better. You can always pay extra principal, the key is to minimize your required payment to guard your cash flow if you have a short-term down turn.

27. Negotiate better payment terms. Ideally you'd have your interest and principal accrue. If that isn't possible, what about paying interest only? Again, your goal is to make your minimum payment as low as possible to give your business the maximum flexibility to protect its cash flow.

28. Negotiate away the hidden "gotchas." Fight hard when you're negotiating with your lender to avoid or minimize hidden costs and

penalties like loan origination fees, or payment processing fees, or automatic rate increases. Pay attention to the small print, it often has a way of coming back to haunt you if you ignore it.

Sales Strategies

29. Raise your prices. Consider a bump in the fees or prices you charge. Be careful about this though if you haven't followed our earlier advice about creating a pre-eminent position in the marketplace first.

30. Lower your prices. Run the numbers and see if you could maximize your profits by lowering your price in return for increasing your sales volume. Again, you need to be cautious about applying this technique, although we've both used it to get an immediate boost to cash flow. Our best advice to lower your prices is to give your prospective clients a limited time only gift certificate valid toward the purchase of your product or service. This lets you keep your price high, while in effect discounting it for an increased sale. Notice also the urgency created by an expiration date on the gift certificate.

31. Create a bundled offer. One of the best ways to increase cash flow and profitability is to get your client to buy a larger volume of your goods and services. By bundling several of your offerings together into one package deal you can often increase both your unit of sale and your net cash flow from the sale.

32. Bring on more sales team members. It never ceases to amaze us how companies cut sales staff just when they need them most—during a cash crunch. Instead, shift your sales team to a commission structure that lets you pay only for results.

So, there you have 32 techniques for immediately boosting your business' cash flow.

In the next section of the book we'll be making a major shift away from techniques and strategies to build your business, to ideas and insights on how you can build your wealth independent of your business' success.

PART TWO

INVEST IN YOURSELF

SECRET #3: Become Financially Fluent and Guarantee Your Future!

CHAPTER 10

The Five Languages of Financial Fluency

The "Cashing Out" Myth

Too many entrepreneurs only look and plan as far ahead as selling their business and retiring. Oh, they have detailed dreams of the beaches they'll lie upon and the cool waters they'll bathe in, but they seldom think past that fantasy to the functional reality of navigating the world of wealth.

And this is the trap that far too many entrepreneurs find themselves caught in. They've made the money by building up an incredibly successful Level Three business, but they never learned the key wealth skills along the way to build their *personal* wealth in parallel with building their business. And that means that most of them are totally unprepared when they "cash out."

David's Story

I dropped out of college to start my first real business when I was 23 years old. I invested $2,300 and all my energy into making it a success. Less than six months later I was broke. Over that time I had learned some of business' hard lessons: Gross income is not the same thing as net profit; sometimes business people lie, and you need clear contracts and

(continued)

David's Story *(continued)*

disciplined due diligence to protect yourself; effort is not enough to guarantee success, you need knowledge too.

I took those lessons to heart and two years later began building my second business. This time I invested the hours studying the books and taking the courses; I interviewed the top 10 people in that industry and picked their brains clean; I enlisted smart attorneys and other professionals to protect my interests as my business grew. The result? Within 10 years I was a multimillionaire with a business earning me a seven-figure income.

And then I sold that business. And while I got a very healthy wire transfer with lots of zeros for my efforts, my steady income stream was radically diminished. It was then that I started up the second steep phase of my learning curve—understanding what to do on the other side of "cashing out" of your business.

Impossible as this is for many people to imagine, a lump sum of millions of dollars does not end your money needs for life. It just shifts you into a new challenge—how to intelligently steward that money to grow it, sustain it, and, most importantly, convert it into passive, residual income.*

I really had to scramble mentally to catch up to this lesson and I've had some incredible mentors along the way as I've moved into the world of the wealthy. The question for you is are you *really* prepared for this next phase of wealth or are you currently out of your depths?

*Those of you who read our last book, *The Maui Millionaires*, will be very familiar with the concept of passive, residual income. For those of you who haven't read it yet, we heartily recommend you get a copy and read it, especially pages 167–209, which deal with the concept of passive, residual income.

The Five Languages of Financial Fluency

To become financially free in today's competitive world it is not enough to be financially literate (able to get by in the world of money and personal finance); instead you must become financially *fluent*.

Financial fluency is what allows you to move in the world of money, finance, and wealth with grace, confidence, and ease. In fact, the only way for you to truly take charge of your financial life is to become financially fluent. Otherwise you'll always be dependent on outside agencies that directly or indirectly control, shape, or coerce your economic behavior.

Your goal is to use your financial fluency to build Level Three wealth. Level Three wealth is when you have secure, independent, hands-off income streams that flow to you without your actively having to work to keep them flowing. It's the wealth you build that lets you have the money *and* the freedom. And it's the foundation of true financial freedom.

The problem is that this is not an education that you were ever taught in school. In fact, we have one Maui Mastermind participant who graduated from the Wharton School of Business, arguably one of the top five business schools in the world. She shared with us how her two years there prepared her to build someone else's business not to be wealthy. In fact, she told us that it took her experiences at Maui to teach her *how* to be wealthy. And we've heard the same thing from dozens of our other clients who've attended Wharton and other top business programs.

It gets worse. This is an education you never learned on the job, whether you were working for someone else or you were working for yourself.

Diane only picked up bits and pieces of this education in her work as a CPA. She had to learn the overwhelming majority of it on her own. And

---

The Language of Money: It's spoken in the vocabulary of accounting, debits and credits, assets and liabilities. It is the foundation of financial fluency.

The Language of Business: It's spoken in the form of contracts and agreements. It's the legal medium in which all your financial moves take place.

The Language of Leadership: This is your ability to move, inspire, influence, and lead other people (and even yourself) to create, build, defend, grow, and share.

The Language of Cash Flow: This is composed of two pieces: the offensive game of investing to create cash flow and the defensive game of using Preemptive Tax Strategy to legally minimize your taxes.

The Language of Wealth: It's the distinctive ways that the wealthy view money and financial matters. At its core are 21 key distinctions that separate the Level Three people from Level One and Two.

David, as a serial entrepreneur with no formal business training started out even further behind and had to scramble to figure this out for himself.

Ultimately, this is one of the strongest reasons we felt we had to write this book. It's the wealth manual that we *wished* we had ourselves when we were building our wealth.

And the foundation of this manual is The Five Languages of Financial Fluency. Here is a quick summary of each of the languages. We'll go into great detail of all five languages in this second part of the book.

We have worked to decipher and translate these mysterious languages for you. We've laid them out visually for you in the Wealth Matrix™ in Figure 10.1. Notice how there are two major lines that we call the Business Wealth Line and the Personal Wealth Line.

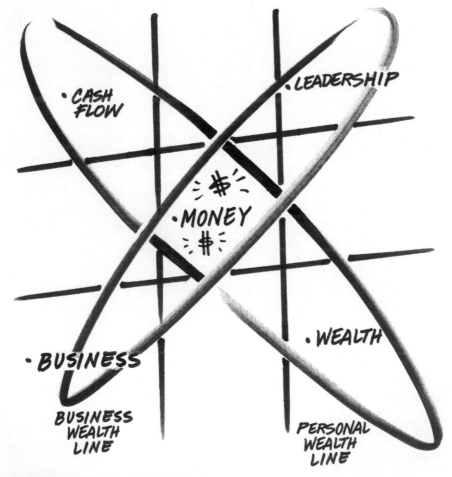

FIGURE 10.1 The Wealth Matrix

Here's the part that most business people miss: it's not enough to master just the Business Wealth Line. To build lasting wealth independent of your active efforts you must master *both* lines.

To us, the most frightening part about not being financially fluent is how vulnerable it makes you. As we walk you through each of these separate languages, you'll discover that each language has a Level One, a Level Two, and a Level Three.

Far too often we observe entrepreneurs who are very experienced with the Business Wealth Line, but haven't even become literate, let alone fluent, with the languages on the Personal Wealth Line. As a result, they make money in their business, but often wonder where it all went when it comes to their personal wealth. It's the coordination of *both* lines that makes the critical difference.

Diane's Story

This story came to me through a colleague who had just finished working with a new client. The client, a successful and wealthy businessman, had come to my colleague with a problem: His nominee officer and bank account check signer had gone out of business, and his company's bank account had been frozen. Thousands of dollars were now locked up until the court decided who the money really belonged to.

My colleague initially thought it would be a fairly simple fix. Install a new nominee officer on record, change the check signers with the bank, and the account would be reopened. But that didn't prove to be the case. When my colleague took a closer look at the client's records, she discovered that the company had been set up with no traceable record of ownership back to her client. Her client couldn't prove, based on the documentation he had, that he owned the company or that the money in the account belonged to him. As far as the bank was concerned, the nominee officer and check signer was also the business owner.

I haven't heard whether or not the money was ever released. It could still be frozen. I'm sure it will get to my colleague's client eventually though.

(continued)

Diane's Story (continued)

So where did the client go wrong? In this case, the client's desire for privacy, combined with a lack of business knowledge, led him to a place where he had absolutely no control over his company or his money. Make no mistake: The client was a great businessman, and very good at what he did. But what he didn't know left him vulnerable. If he had known, he could have accomplished the same thing *and* stayed in control of his money.

My colleague went through all of the business records with the client and showed him how and where he had gone wrong. She set out the steps he needed to take to reestablish control over his company's finances and helped him carry them out. At the same time, my colleague showed the client how to maintain his level of privacy without losing control.

Ultimately as an entrepreneur you need to be fluent in two domains: the domain of business (money, business, and leadership) and the domain of personal wealth (money, cash flow, and wealth).

The next time you hear either of those old sayings, "What you don't know can't hurt you," or "Ignorance is bliss," think about this story! This wasn't a case where a financial neophyte got taken advantage of by an unscrupulous salesperson. This was a successful businessman, who lacked fluency in the language of business and didn't understand the consequences of the agreement he was entering into.

Make no mistake, there is a price to be paid for failing to master each of these five languages. As the famous saying goes, "Pay me now or pay me later."

In the next chapter you'll learn about the center square common to both lines—the Language of Money. It's the most fundamental language of all to becoming financially fluent.

CHAPTER 11

The Language of Money

The Language of Money is spoken in the vocabulary of accounting. It's a language of debits and credits, assets and liabilities. It's communicated through the medium of financial statements.

What all Level Three business owners come to learn is that it is also the difference between sustainable financial success and eventual financial failure.

Do you remember when we talked earlier about the lottery winners who started with a little, won big, and then went on to lose everything? They won a lot of money, but it wasn't sustainable wealth for them because they weren't financially fluent, and they were especially ignorant in the Language of Money.

Let's look at the Wealth Matrix again. There is one language that is essential for both the Personal Wealth Line and the Business Wealth Line. That central point is the Language of Money. Financial fluency in the Language of Money is necessary for both a successful business and a wealthy personal life. If you don't understand the language of money and how money works, you're going to have a really hard time getting to where you want to be.

It's a major flaw in educational systems around the world that we aren't taught the Language of Money in school. If you've graduated with a degree in accounting then feel free to skip this chapter and start learning the other four languages of Financial Fluency. But if you haven't had this kind of rigorous training in accounting, we highly encourage you to bear with us in this chapter as we share with you the fundamentals you need to begin the process of mastering this language.

Now, while we think that every businessperson should understand the fundamentals of accounting (after all, double-entry bookkeeping gave the Dutch a business advantage over the rest of Europe for decades), we don't expect you to cheer about it. But the fact remains that if you can't learn to read the story behind financial statements, both business and personal, then you are at a serious disadvantage. Furthermore, you are at risk of losing everything simply because you don't have the conceptual understanding that will allow you to make progressively more sophisticated and sounder financial decisions.

We promise you that in the medium and long run, your investment of time and energy to learn this language will pay handsome dividends— more wealth, more freedom, and more security. Let's take that first step together.

Level One—Level Two—Level Three

At Level One, people are focused simply on financial *survival*. It's about making active income, paying the bills, and hoping there is enough to get you to the end of the month.

At Level Two, it is about security or comfort. You have a basic grasp of managing your money, and now you have a small surplus each month to begin to *save and invest*. It's important to call attention to the fact that Level Two people invest with that leftover money. They work for income, pay their expenses, and then invest what's leftover. This is how the middle classes of the world do it not how the wealthy do it.

Wealthy Level Three people instead arrange their financial affairs in such a way that they are able to build an asset base that in turns generates their wealth. They don't work to earn income so that they can invest their leftover income to build their wealth. Instead, they build their income out of their wealth. This is a critical distinction and one we'll go into greater detail about in Chapter 13.

For the moment, what's important for you to understand is that there are three levels of wealth building: Level One, Level Two and Level Three. And the definitions we and other people in the Maui community use are different from the traditional definitions of low income, middle class, and rich you hear about in the media. That's because the media's definitions are based on the amount of *income* a person earns. Maui Millionaires know that what level you are at is not a function of your income, but rather it's a function of *how* you earn your income.

If you spend everything you earn and don't have any surplus left to invest to grow your wealth, then no matter what your income, you are at Level One. Level One people work for every dollar they earn and have nothing left to show for it after the month is over.

If you actively work to earn money, pay your bills, then save and invest your "leftover money," you are at Level Two. At Level Two you have begun the process of building wealth, but you're still using the middle-class solution of building any wealth very slowly and with the maximum amount of effort.

It's only when you have assets that work for you, generating passive, residual income in excess of your cost of living, are you Level Three. At Level Three, you use your wealth to create income for you.

Diane's Story

If you were a neighbor or casual acquaintance of Kyle, you'd have been sure he was wealthy. He had a million-dollar house and he drove a higher end luxury car. In fact, if you'd read one of the Maui Millionaire books, you'd have probably said, "Now, that guy is truly at Level Three."

So, one hot Phoenix summer, you'd probably have been puzzled to see his house with a big foreclosure notice on it, and his fancy black car on the back of a repossessor's tow truck.

The problem was that Kyle lived a rich lifestyle, but didn't have Level Three wealth. Even worse, he was at Level One when it came to the Language of Money. He spent more than he made, even though he made a lot of money . . . for a time. His business had started with a brilliant idea and, in the beginning, the money just flowed in. That's when Kyle got trapped by the seductive idea of working in a Level Three business. But he didn't put the time into developing a Level Three business, and he didn't have the personal wealth skills to intelligently invest the money he was making to create passive residual income. He went, practically overnight, from working as a Level Two business to simply not working.

(continued)

Diane's Story (continued)

Eventually the money was gone and soon the trappings of Kyle's life collapsed as well.

I wish I could say that this was the only time I've seen it happen, but, in my 20-plus years as a CPA, I've seen this repeated again and again. Living a sustainable, rich lifestyle is possible, for sure, but not without Level Three wealth skills!

The level you are at is more strongly determined by your financial habits and knowledge base than by your active income. There are a lot of people who earn over $100,000 per year who are at Level One. Why? They spend every single dime of the money they make each month. There are others who make $20,000 or less in taxable income every year who are at Level Three. How do they do it? They have a very simple lifestyle and their passive residual income more than covers their cost of living. So, the next time someone says something about the middle class or another income-based reference, you know that they probably don't have a strong grounding in the Language of Money. The real question that is the starting point for your practical wealth building is where your money comes from (from your efforts or your assets) and what you do with your money once you have it.

With this foundation, let's work on building your Language of Money foundation.

Level by Level Overview of the Language of Money

A huge part of the Language of Money at Level One is the language of accounting: understanding what credits and debits are, what assets and liabilities are, and how to prepare and keep a budget. It doesn't mean you need to be a CPA by any stretch! You just need to be able to talk to one and understand what she is saying.

The key for you at Level One is to learn enough to understand your personal financial statements, which include your personal profit and loss statement (aka: your "P&L") and your personal balance sheet (aka: net worth Statement). We'll go into more detail on financial statements in

What are the main sources of your income?	Probable Level
Active (e.g. W-2 wages, 1099 income)	Level One
Passive income (e.g. capital gains from sale of assets, the distinction is that you aren't actively working for it but you only earn it one time, the income is not recurring).	Level Two
Passive residual income (e.g. dividends, rental income, royalties, passive partnership distributions).	Level Three
What is the relationship of your income to your expenses?	Probable Level
Negative or barely break-even—no accumulation of wealth happening.	Level One
Small, monthly surplus created each month which you save and invest, but you only invest your leftover money.	Level Two
Growing surplus each month as your passive And passive residual income more than cover Your cost of living (aka: your S-Factor™)	Level Three
What is your investment pattern?	Probable Level
I'm going to start investing soon.	Level One
I invest from my income. I use my leftover money to build my wealth	Level Two
I invest from my assets.	Level Three

FIGURE 11.1   Language of Money Test

just a moment, but for now the key is to understand that to escape Level One and move up to Level Two requires that you accurately track your income and your expenses (i.e. your personal P&L) and your accumulation of assets (i.e. your personal net worth statement). Without this discipline it is difficult to get an accurate financial picture and make your move to the next level.

In Level Two you need to unlock the mystery of your business' financial statements, including a third financial statement called the statement of cash flow.

Levels of Language of Money	
	Goal
Level One:	Master Your Personal Financial Statements
Level Two:	Master Your Business' Financial Statements
Level Three:	Master *Other* Business' Financial Statements

Finally, in Level Three, you need to learn the secret of reading the story behind *other* business' financial statements. This lets you invest passively with skill and confidence.

Level One: Language of Money

There is one bit of financial language that you must learn if you're ever going to have real and lasting financial success. If you miss this key part, no matter how successful your business is, no matter how much money just suddenly shows up on your door or no matter how much your investment jumps overnight, you will always be financially vulnerable. You simply cannot create any sustainable wealth without this vital piece of your education.

You simply must understand your own financial statements first. There are two types of financial statements that you need to master at Level One: your personal P&L and your personal net worth statement.

Remember: Money doesn't solve money problems. Understanding money solves money problems.

Your Personal Profit and Loss Statement (P&L)

In the business world, we use a profit and loss statement (also known as an income statement) to track the money the business makes and the money the business spends. When you subtract the expenses from the income, you determine the net income (or loss if expenses are more than income) for the business.

You actually have a P&L as well. Your personal P&L shows the income you make and the expenses you have. Although, most people never actually look at this statement, it's the one statement that determines how well you will succeed financially at everything else, and that's why we start there.

Diane's Story

I just saw another business partnership fall apart. Ironically, the business was doing fine. The problem was that the two partners were not evenly matched when it came to their skills with the Language of Money. Dan had been taking part of his share of the profits and investing for years. Sara had not. She had instead been spending money even faster than she made it. They were equal partners in the business and initially it was the only source of income for both of them. Yet, Sara is on the verge of bankruptcy, and Dan is ready to comfortably retire. They started in the same place and ended up very differently.

The difference between financial failure and success is often based on how the first question on the Language of Money Test* is answered: "Do you have money left at the end of each month?" If your answer is "no" then this is the place to start. Don't start a business, don't invest, don't do anything until you first create Level One money habits of recording, budgeting, analyzing, and saving. Then, and only then, can you move into Level Two.

Creating Your Own Personal P&L

You can use a standard business P&L format during the following exercises or download your own blank personal P&L form at **www.Maui Millionaires.com/book**, we've provided for you there for free.

The personal P&L starts with income. There are three main categories of income to record. In the language of accountants, these three types of income are: earned, portfolio, and passive.

Income: Accountant's Version

Earned: Money you make.

Portfolio: Money your money makes.

Passive: Money your investments make.

---

*Would you like to download the full version of the Language of Money Test? Then go to **www.MauiMillionaires.com/book**. We've arranged for you to get instant access to this and dozens of other powerful wealth tools as our free gift to you. See the Appendix for full details.

These are important distinctions when it comes to tax purposes. In fact, in just a little bit we'll look at the tax ramifications of the type of income you make.

For Maui Millionaires, there are also three types of income. But, in this case, the three types are a little different.

Income: Maui Millionaires

Active Income: Money you actively work to earn.

Passive Income: Money that comes from selling your assets.

Passive Residual Income: Money that comes from your assets, without depleting the asset.

The Maui Millionaire's formula is focused on building wealth. That's why we recommend that you list your income on your personal P&L as the amount you make in each category per month.

Active income includes your job and business that you actively work in such as self-employed work and fix and flip in real estate.

Passive income is income that comes from your assets but that requires liquidation or leverage of your assets. In some cases this income is taxed, and in some cases the tax is deferred.

Passive residual income is income that comes from your assets, without reducing the value of your assets. Common examples are interest, dividends, rent, royalty payments, or Level Three business activities.

Take a minute and consider where your income comes from. On a monthly basis, how much do you make from each of these categories? Now, look at what you've written. Are you a victim of the Earned Income Trap™?

The Earned Income Trap— When Income Isn't Enough

There's more to being wealthy than having a large income. In fact, what we've observed is that earned income is one of the worst predictors for financial success. This is because there is a strong pull on most people who begin to earn more to spend more. The more they earn, the more they spend. It's like they stepped onto a treadmill and the more money they begin to earn the more they turn up the speed of their spending. Five years ago they were able to get by with $7,000 a month of income, but now the treadmill is going so fast they need 10,000 a month just to stay even.

Here's the saddest part. Once they turn up the speed of that treadmill it's very hard for them to ever slow it back down again. They just have to keep running to stay even. If they stop, they'll go flying off the back of the treadmill. This is the financial stress Level One people live with day in and day out. We call this the Earned Income Trap™. But understand this: the Earned Income Trap isn't a function of your income. How many of you reading this right now know someone with a six- or seven-figure income who's up to her eyeballs in debt? Money doesn't solve money problems: understanding the Language of Money does.

One of the biggest surprises for attendees of our Financial Fluency workshop is how many high-income participants in the class are still living from paycheck to paycheck! What's revealing is that over 90 percent of the Level One attendees have no clear picture of how much they are earning and spending each year.

Still, the average person focuses on earning more income, which is not a solution to the problem. The first part of the solution is to first develop the language, then the discipline, to consistently track your income and expenses. It isn't sexy. It isn't glamorous. But it's the start.

The second part of the solution that is essential for you to do to escape Level One is to begin saving at least 5–10 percent of your income. Doing both these two things will take you to Level Two.

Until you have a surplus of money left over to save and then invest, you will forever be caught in the trap of chasing after enough income each month just to get by.*

No matter where you are right now, understand that escaping the Earned Income Trap is something anyone can do. The first step is finding out where your money goes, and learning how to budget it so that you have at least 5–10 percent of your gross income left over each month. The second step is creating cash reserves to stop you from falling back into the Earned Income Trap the first time an emergency comes along.

There is no way out of the Level One money trap unless you are willing to change your spending patterns and develop new ones.

---

*We've included a special online workshop on breaking out of the Earned Income Trap as part of the Millionaire Fast-Track Program. Part of this workshop details a simple yet extremely powerful system to eliminate bad debt. Go to **www.MauiMillionaires.com/book**.

David's Story

While I hired a bookkeeper from day one with all my businesses, it took me about five years before I got up the courage to get one for my personal finances. At first I kept saying that I'd just save the money and do it myself, which is a common Level Two response. But later, after I was earning over half a million dollars a year and I still didn't have a bookkeeper, I knew my time was more valuable than the cost of hiring a bookkeeper. Yet I still didn't hire one right away. Another year passed. Finally, I came face to face with what was really stopping me from hiring a personal bookkeeper—fear.

I was filled with all kinds of fears: The bookkeeper would see how much money I was making and want me to pay her more, she would wonder why I wasn't making more money, I'd somehow see that I wasn't really making as much money as I thought I was, I'd look stupid or ignorant in the bookkeeper's eyes, and the list went on and on.

Well I gathered up my courage and hired one anyway. And I found the reality of having a part-time personal bookkeeper liberating. Suddenly I could see! There it was, laid out in front of me, a clear, accurate, objective picture of how I was doing financially and the direction and speed I was moving in. Besides the obvious benefit of this picture helping me to make smarter financial moves, which became obvious when I looked at my accurate financials, I felt freed from so many of my past money fears. And as if that wasn't enough, once I had clean financials I was able to implement more of the tax strategies Diane was teaching me, which paid me five times over for the cost of hiring my bookkeeper. In essence, for every dollar I paid my bookkeeper it was like I got paid four dollars myself in tax savings I could now comfortably invest!

My advice now to people who are committed to building their personal wealth is to hire a quality bookkeeper as soon as possible, and make it a discipline to review your financials each and every month. It will accelerate you on your path to financial success.

Personal Net Worth Statement

Your personal net worth statement is a snapshot of your wealth. You will list your assets (what you own), then your liabilities (what you owe) and calculate the difference. If you have more value in your assets than your liabilities, you have a positive net worth. Hooray! If you have more liabilities than assets, you have a negative net worth. Unfortunately, many people today are waking up to discover that they have a negative net worth as values went down and credit card debt went up. In Pakistan, for example, consumer debt has increased by 50 percent in less than six years. It's a phenomenon occurring around the world.

Personal Assets

Start off with your assets. When it comes to your personal statement, you get to list your assets at their current fair market value. This is one big difference between your personal statements and your business statements. In the case of a business, the assets are listed at their basis (which is a fancy accounting term for the cost less any accumulated depreciation you've written for this asset).

Some of your assets will likely be bank accounts, investments, pension plans, personal residence, and the equity in the business you own. Be honest here. The fair market value is the amount that you would receive if you sold the asset. So, if you were trying to come up with the value of your designer clothing—you'd probably have to check out eBay first. The value is probably not going to be what you paid originally. And, to be accurate, you need to come up with a value that you could sell that item for in a reasonable time frame. We're sure that someone, somewhere, may actually give you a million dollars for that piece of desert land in Nevada. But, meanwhile, the value shown on your personal net worth statement is what you could get if you sold it today.

Liabilities

After assets come liabilities. The liabilities are the sum total of the debt you have. For example, if you list your home mortgage, you need to list the unpaid mortgage balance, not the monthly payment. The monthly payment would go on your personal P&L. For liabilities, list everything for which you owe: your school debt, your credit card balances, total due on your cars, your real estate, your house, your furniture, and everything else you owe.

> **Level One P&L Action Steps:**
>
> ■ Create and consistently review (monthly) your personal P&L and balance sheet (quarterly).
> ■ Budget your money so that you have a surplus of at least 5–10 percent left over each month that you can begin to invest.
> ■ Invest the time and energy to increase your financial fluency.

You calculate your net worth simply by subtracting your total liabilities from your total assets.

Your personal net worth statement does not need to prepared every month. Most people prepare these every quarter or every year. Keep a copy of your personal net worth statement and compare it to the next period. What trend do you see? (More on this in the next section of the book.)

Level Two Language of Money—Your Business' Financial Statements

After you've mastered Level One habits, it's time to consider starting a business (or investments) and Level Two Language of Money. We'll talk more about other financial fluency requirements for your future Level Three businesses later in this section.

Your business will have three financial statements: the balance sheet, the profit and loss statement and the statement of cash flow. The basic concepts from your personal financial statements apply, but we're going to dig in deeper and approach your business financial statements fresh and with a more sophisticated Level Two eye.

The Balance Sheet

Most people have heard of a balance sheet. It's probably the most well-known financial statement of all. Your balance sheet shows you what you own and what you owe. (For those of you who are new to the world of financial statements, we have additional resources on how to read and understand them available at our web site, www.MauiMillionaires.com).

Your balance sheet contains three things: your assets, liabilities, and equity. *Assets* are things you (or your business) own. *Liabilities* represent money that you (or your business) owe, and *equity* is the difference between the two, which represents your profit or loss. A healthy balance sheet should show more assets than liabilities. A balance sheet going the other way is usually a sign of trouble.

The Accounting Equation

The accounting equation is the basic truth of any double-entry bookkeeping or financial statement and states:

$$\text{Assets} = \text{Liabilities} + \text{Equity}$$

The key is always balance. (See Figure 11.2.) When your assets don't equal your combined liabilities and equity amounts something is wrong, something is missing, or has not been recorded properly. (This is one of the reasons why computer software revolutionized bookkeeping; it eliminated transposed numbers and most math errors.)

Assets

Assets are the things you own, and are typically broken down into current and fixed assets on your balance sheet. Current assets are cash and anything else that will be used up or can be converted into cash within one year—inventory, or prepaid postage for example. Accounts receivable (money people owe you for goods or services they bought but haven't paid you for yet) is another example.

Fixed assets are those with a longer lifespan and are usually tangible things such as equipment, vehicles, buildings and real estate, and machinery.

Liabilities

Liabilities are debts you owe, and, just as with assets, they're broken down into current and long-term categories. A short-term liability would be something that must be repaid within a year, such as sales or income tax and most accounts payable (money you owe for goods or services you've bought but haven't yet paid for). Long-term liabilities are debts that are repaid over a longer period of time such as mortgages and car loans.

Equity

Equity is what's left over after you subtract your liabilities from your assets. As we showed you earlier, it's also called net worth. A negative net worth could be the sign of a business in trouble. Then again, it could also be the sign of a business that is taking full advantage of a good creative tax strategy and shows a loss on paper while putting a profit into your pocket each month.

The second of the three financial statements shows you your income, expenses, and profit for the time period it represents. But there's a very important distinction to be made here between your balance sheet and your

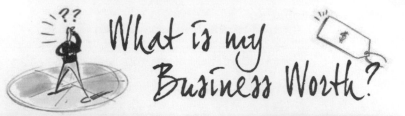

Balance Sheet

ASSETS	$	$
Cash	$75,000	
Accounts Receivable	$35,000	
Inventory	$90,000	
Prepaid Expenses	$16,000	
Equipment	$14,000	
Less: Accum. Depr Equip		$3,750
Computers	$10,000	
Less: Accum. Depr Computers		$2,500
Goodwill	$16,250	
TOTAL ASSETS		$250,000
LIABILITIES		
Accounts Payable		$12,000
Expenses Payable		$8,000
Payroll Taxes Withheld		$1,000
Loans Payable – Short Term		$20,000
Loans Payable – Long Term		$25,000
TOTAL LIABILITIES		$66,000
EQUITY		
Capitol Stock		$5,000
Paid in Capitol		$29,000
Retained Earnings		$150,000
TOTAL LIABILITIES & EQUITY		$250,000

FIGURE 11.2   What Is My Business Worth?

Income Statement at a Glance

Income – Cost of Goods = Gross Profit

Gross Profit – Expenses = Net Income

P&L statement. While they both show you one angle of the picture of your business' finances, they don't show you the whole picture by themselves.

For example, a balance sheet gives you an overall view of your business' financial condition. (See Figure 11.3.) The P&L statement, on the other hand, simply shows you how much income your business earned and how many expenses it had for that same period of time. If you had some large, one-time expenses or a huge sale during that period your P&L statement will be impacted, whereas your balance sheet might not. This is the danger of just reading a single piece of the financial statement—you get a skewed picture. Financial analysts know this, which is why you often see requests for comparative financials, which are statements that compare your current financial picture to other time periods.

Income

Income is the money you or your business receives, and is usually split into two categories, sales and service income (for tax purposes, we have a different split, which we'll talk about a bit later). Accountants like to separate the two income types because it makes it easier to match up expenses. If you have a product that is generating 25 percent of your business' income but eating up 65 percent of the expenses, that may indicate you've got a problem with that product that you need to take a look at.

Expenses

Expenses are payments that you or your business have made or will make. They're similar to your liabilities, although your liabilities actually represent a debt payable, whereas your expenses represent that debt after it has been paid. Before you pay your phone bill it's a liability. After it's been paid, it becomes an expense.

Profit

Your profit is the leftover income after the expenses have all been paid. But you can break this down even further. For service income, take your

How Much Money Does My Business Make?

Profit & Loss Statement

REVENUE	$	$
Net Sales		$750,000
Interest Income		$3,500
Gain on Sales of Equipment/Assets		$0
TOTAL REVENUE		$753,500
COSTS & EXPENSES		
Cost of Goods Sold		$225,000
Selling Expenses		$75,000
General & Admin. Expense		$100,000
Interest Expense		$13,500
Taxes Paid		$40,000
TOTAL COSTS & EXPENSES		$453,500
TOTAL REVENUE		$753,500
LESS: TOTAL COSTS & EXPENSES		$453,500
NET INCOME		$300,000

FIGURE 11.3   How Much Money Does My Business Make?

profit and subtract those expenses directly associated with it (e.g., for a Maui Millionaires seminar we deduct things like travel costs and the costs to rent the hotel for an event). For sales income, take your profit and subtract the costs associated with making that profit (shipping, postage, packaging supplies, etc.), plus what it cost you to buy or create the sales item in the first place (that's your cost of goods sold).

At the end of the day, your net profit is your income less any cost of goods sold less your expenses involved in earning that income. It's your net profit that flows back through the books onto the balance sheet to become a part of your equity.

The Statement of Cash Flow

The last financial statement is the statement of cash flow. The information presented here is quite a bit different than that presented in either the balance sheet or the P&L statement. It's also the hardest to understand, the most overlooked, and the most important.

Your statement of cash flow tells you *where* your business got its cash from and *what* it did with that cash during the period you are looking at. It begins with your business' net income and deducts items that impact your cash. Some of these items affect your cash flow, but don't show up as expenses or income on your P&L. For example, buying a bunch of inventory won't change your net income because it's not technically an expense until your business either sells the inventory or writes the inventory off. But while it's not an "expense," it certainly will impact your cash because you had to spend money to buy the inventory.

Accounts receivable are the same: They often show up on your P&L, when the "sale" happens, even though you don't have the cash until you collect on these receivables.

And if that wasn't enough, sometimes you add things in that impact your cash like depreciation for example, you may have spent cash on a piece of equipment for your business, and yet while you have spent the cash, you are only able to write off the investment in that piece of equipment by "depreciating" it over a period of time. Another example is a loan you are paying back. The principal portion of your payment is not an "expense" on your P&L, but it certainly takes cash out of your bank balance! This is one of the reasons it's so important to learn about the statement of cash flows, because it gives you a critical view of your business' finances.*

---

*For information on more detailed courses on business financial statements, especially the statement of cash flows, please go to **www.MauiMillionaires.com/book**.

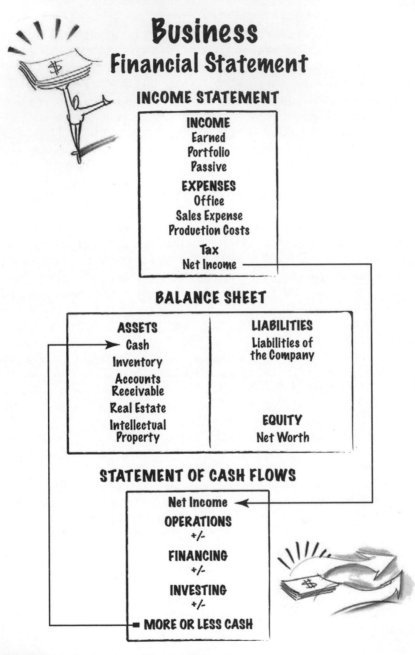

FIGURE 11.4   Business Financial Statement

The Three Business Financial Statements

The three statements aren't independent statements. In fact, they work together to create a pattern that, at a glance, can help you interpret what is happening in your business.

It all starts with the profit and loss statement. Net income (bottom of the P&L statement) flows through to the cash flow statement. There the net income is adjusted by non-P&L cash flow items. For example, depreciation and amortization amounts are added back into the number because these expenses do not take cash flow outflows. Financing and investing also impact cash flow but do not impact the income figure. At the bottom of the cash flow statement, you come up with the change in cash. That new number flows through the asset column of the balance sheet. If the cash goes up, the business' net worth goes up. If the cash goes down, the business' net worth goes down.

We hope this section has helped you to understand at least the basics of reading a financial statement. By understanding and tracking the relationship between your assets and liabilities, income and expenses, you'll be able to identify successful trends and potential problems.

Level Two Financial Vocabulary

Here are some new phrases to add to your growing financial vocabulary:

Cash vs. Accrual vs. Hybrid Accounting Methods. This refers to the way you track your business' income and expenses. With the cash method, you report income when you receive it and expenses when you pay them. This is how most people do their personal finances, but it doesn't always work so well for businesses, especially those that carry inventory or offer credit to their customers, because it can give you a very distorted picture of your business' true operations.

The accrual method means you report income as you earn it and expenses in the year they occur (which is not necessarily when you get paid or when you pay your expenses). In other words, the accrual method allows for accounts receivable and accounts payable. The hybrid method is a combination of the cash and accrual accounting methods. Inventory is reported using the accrual method, while all other items of income and expense are reported using the cash method. Once you choose an accounting method for your business, you can't change it without permission from the IRS.

Prospective vs. Actual. Prospective is a term usually applied to financial statements that are prepared by a business' management. Prospective financial statements represent management's estimates of future business activity over a certain period of time. The term *actual*, is, as you can imagine, applied to financial statements that represent what really did happen over that same period of time, and allow you to compare what management says will happen and what does happen. It's a great way to evaluate how effective the management of a business is. If management is consistently hitting at or close to their prospective numbers, it could show that the business is working properly. (Of course it could also show that management is estimating too low to increase its perceived effectiveness, too). On the other hand, if the projections are wildly different from the actual figures, it could mean that the business is having problems.

Fair Market Value (FMV) vs. Historic. The fair market value of an item is what it is worth today on the open market. The historic value of an item is the original purchase price. Now, here's where things get a little nuts: Businesses record and show historic values, while your personal financial statements record FMV.

Why does this matter? Well, think about this: Say your business bought an apartment building and held it for years. Each year your business took a depreciation deduction, which was recorded on the books and which reduced the book value of the building. What happens when the book value of the building hits zero? Is it worthless? Not at all! But it does present a challenge when looking at financial statements, especially as the building probably has a current FMV that is much higher than the purchase price. Your personal financial statement will record a business value far higher than the business' records show. This is a hole that drives mortgage brokers crazy, especially if you are looking for financing or attempting to sell the business or the building within the business. Typically, the best way around this is to produce your business financial statements showing the book value and also have footnotes that explain the difference in numbers—for example the historic costs are zero, but a recent valuation shows the FMV at $1 million.

That's the unreality of financial statements and why it's so important for you to understand how to read them and how to interpret them, especially as you move from Level Two into Level Three.

Gross Income. Your gross income is the total amount of income your business earns before any expenses or cost of goods sold are deducted.

Gross Profit. As we showed you earlier, gross profit is the income your business earns less the cost of goods sold.

Gross Profit Margin. The gross profit margin is a ratio that is similar to the profit margin ratio we showed you above. However, in this case the ratio is the gross profit divided by the gross income. When looking at this number you want to compare it against the industry standard to make sure your business is making a decent return.

Direct Costs. A business' direct costs are the costs that are directly associated with the creation of a product or the performance of a service. So when we conduct a seminar, for example, the costs of renting the hotel room, transportation, setup and tear-down, staff, food and beverage service, hotel accommodation, and so forth arc all dircct costs. If we weren't conducting that seminar, we wouldn't have those costs.

Indirect Costs. These are your business' other costs, such as the cost to maintain an office, the electric and heating bills, furniture, equipment, photocopier, postage,and so on. In other words, the indirect costs are those costs your business has whether or not you are producing any products or selling any services.

Net Income. Your business' net income is the same as its net profit (which we showed you above), and is what remains of the income after subtracting the cost of goods sold and all business expenses (including taxes). On the personal side, your net income is your gross income, less all taxes, allowances and deductions, and is used to determine how much tax you will owe.

Taxable Income. For both business and personal purposes, taxable income is the portion of your income that is subject to taxation under the laws of your taxing jurisdiction. We'll share with you some powerful insights on effective tax strategy in Chapter 20.

Moving to Level Three

Mastering Level One and Level Two gives you the foundational skills you need to easily transition to Level Three. You'll get better and better at reading the story contained in your personal and business' financial statements, which in turn allows you to make better financial decisions. You'll grow your courage muscles by your willingness to face the exact picture of your personal and business situation through the lens of your financial statements. And through the progress you make in these two levels you'll learn different ways of handling money criscs so you can break the cycle of the Earned Income Trap and gain control of your spending. And you'll begin to build a surplus that you save and invest. These small steps are critical as you journey up the road to Level Three.

Level Three changes are related to your time. Your Language of Money skills will still need to improve, but by the time you've solidly hit Level Two, you have most of the Language of Money skills you're going to need.

Your challenge as you transition into Level Three is to pick up one more skill set. This third skill set is the ability to read the story inside other business's financial statements. At Level Two, you have mastered your own business' financial statements. You have learned how to interpret the numbers, but you had a bit of an inside advantage because you thoroughly understood your business already. You had an instinctual feeling already as to what was working and what was not. That's why Level Two learning is so important. You've learned to ride a bicycle with the training wheels on.

It's time to take the training wheels off and use that same insight you already possess and look at other businesses. Now, you're moving into Level Three.

There are three primary business cycles that you will be exposed to for business and other forms of investing: (1) Start-up. In this case the founder or founders need capital to get going. You'll be looking at prospectus financial statements that can range from well thought out extrapolations of known data to "I sure hope so" back of the envelope scribbles. (2) Change in the business. In this cycle, something is going to change. The business might need to grow and needs capital for that growth, or the business might need to expand or improve its current way of selling or fulfilling services or products and that's why it needs cash. (3) Change in the ownership. At some point, every business owner thinks about an exit strategy. What happens to the business? The owner could close it down (inevitable if he's never built a business beyond just his own ability to work). He could sell it to insiders. Or, he could sell it to outsiders or simply leave it to his heirs. At any given time, there are hundreds of thousands of small businesses for sale. Selling to outsiders is by far the most common exit strategy for business owners.

In each of these three cases, there is a business owner who is looking for money. The owner could be looking to raise that money through equity (i.e., selling off all or part of the ownership) or through leverage (getting loans). A highly skilled Level Three investor understands these three primary cycles of a business that need him and he knows how to quickly interpret the business financial statements to know if the deal is right for him.

Interpreting Financial Statements for a Start-Up Business

In the case of a start-up business, someone has a good idea or has come across a great deal and needs the cash to make it happen. The initial founder/deal maker is putting up his time and talents and is looking for someone else to put up the cash.

In this case, the financial statements are prospective. They show what could be true if income and expenses are in line with the assumptions. Never forget that the prospectus shows *assumptions*. In this case, you have two tasks: (1) Carefully review the assumptions. Is the amount of income and the timing for it reasonable? Are the expenses reasonable? The best prospectuses show a "most likely case" and a "worst case." (2) Assess the ability of the person or group of people who will run the project. Unless you plan to contribute your own time (in which case this is definitely not a Level Three investment), you're banking on their ability to pull the deal off. Can they do it? Have they done it before in the past?

> ## David's Story
>
> I recently worked with three other entrepreneurs to launch a mining company in the Midwest. We raised over $4 million in less than 21 days to launch the business.
>
> In order to do this, we had to show our investors a detailed business plan including pro forma financial projections. Because our investors felt comfortable that our projections were conservative enough and well thought out, and because they felt our management team had the character and competence to safely guide the project, and because the returns we were offering were fair in relationship to the risk they would take on, they invested with us.

When you're at Level Three and passively investing in other peoples' projects or businesses, you've got to be skilled at quickly understanding the story behind the numbers.

Investing Due to Change in Business or Ownership

It's easier to assess the investment potential of an ongoing business. That's because you can now use the ratios you began using at Level Two on your own financial statements. What do these ratios tell you about the existing financial statements?

There are three keys to analyzing an existing business' financial statements:

1. Are the numbers correct? Make sure the financial statement is at a minimum reviewed (preferably audited) by a certified public accountant or chartered accountant. If the business is actually so small that it has never had a professionally prepared financial statement, request to see the tax return for the business.

2. What are the major problems facing this business? You don't want to know everything that can go right at this point. You want to know everything that can go wrong and be sure that you or someone else on the team will know how to fix the problem.

3. How much will your return be on your investment? Don't fall in love with an idea at this point, fall in love with the numbers.

The Four Key Level Three Financial Formulas*

Here are the four key formulas you'll need to learn to use as a Level Three investor investing in other people's businesses or opportunities (note: If you're not ready for these formulas yet, just flag this page to come back to when you are. There is no rush. Give yourself time to learn the Language of Money properly).

1. *Cash-on-Cash Return (COCR):* This is the total net cash received annually divided by your total cash investment. So, if you buy a business with $100,000 down that gives you a cash return of $20,000 per year (after all cash expenses), you will have a COCR of 20 percent ($20,000 divided by $100,000.) Purpose: This is a great back-of-the-envelope calculation to see whether further investigation is even worth your time. Risk: Relying only on the COCR calculation to make a business or investment decision leaves you vulnerable to making major mistakes.

2. *Return on Equity (ROE):* Like the cash-on-cash return, the return on equity is a relatively simple calculation. It is calculated by dividing the annual net income for the company by the average equity for the year. For example, let's say that three shareholders have equal ownership in the company for a total of $900,000 of equity ($300,000 each). The annual net income for the company is $300,000. That means the ROE is $33\frac{1}{2}$ percent ($300,000 divided by $900,000). Purpose: A quick ROE calculation gives you a measurement for management's handle on profitability, asset management, and financial leverage. Risk: As with the COCR, the risk is relying just on this measurement to determine a company's worth. It does not take into account unrealized gains that have not yet been converted into cash or profit.

3. *Present Value (PV):* The present value calculation is based on the premise that money is more valuable today than it is tomorrow. The PV calculation tells you what the value today of a future chunk of money will be. One variation is to calculate the present value of a series of cash flows. This is called a net present value (NPV) or present value of future cash flows. Purpose: The PV and NPV calculations take into account time and the value of compounding. If your Uncle Fred shows up with a great deal—invest $100,000 and

---

*For a list of resources available to help you master these Level Three skills, go to **www.MauiMillionaires.com/book**.

get back $200,000—that is absolutely completely guaranteed, your next question should be, "When do I get the $200,000?" If it's 20 years, it's not a good deal. Risk: The calculation requires some higher math ability or a good financial calculator. The one variable is the rate at which you discount the cash flow. Small changes in that rate could create big differences in the value.

4. *Internal Rate of Return (IRR):* The PV calculation tell you the dollar amount of an investment at a future date. The IRR takes into account both the income and the speed at which you earn it and expresses it in the form of a percentage. This is another calculation for which you'll need a financial calculator. Purpose: With the IRR, you can contrast different investments. Businesses use the IRR to determine the "hurdle mark" of a proposed new project or expansion. It answers the question, "Is this worth the capital investment and risk?" Risk: The calculation process is complicated and so people sometimes shy away from the results. The IRR is highly valuable in determining return and time for investments and is one that Level Three business owners will want to get to know.

Move to Level Three, But Don't Forget Level One and Two

Remember to keep your personal financial statements current. You might have already noticed how much larger your personal net worth statement has become. Your investments in your business and in the businesses of others are reported on this statement. The income streams you receive from them go on your personal P&L. You'll find that these statements act as a powerful control panel—a quick way to see where you are and where you're going. Your personal financial statement lets you keep track of your monthly expenses so you can continually compare your budget-to-actual costs. This puts you in a position to determine your true S-Factor™, which is your true lifestyle cost (we discuss this in great detail in Chapter 15).

The best way to master the three levels in the Language of Money is practice. Because we don't have room in this book to lay out practice financial statements and investment opportunities for you to look at through the Language of Money, we decided to go one better. Diane will walk you through a powerful series of exercises on Level Three Language of Money as part of the Millionaire Fast-Track Program. To get immediate access to this online workshop, including instructions for downloading the worksheet pages, just go to **www.MauiMillionaires .com/book**. (For full details see the Appendix.)

Congratulations! You've made it through your first immersion course on the Language of Money. Remember, it isn't necessary for you to get this all in one sitting, but it is necessary to master it over time. And like any language, the more time you spend speaking the language, the faster and easier it will be for you to learn. We promise you that if you're diligent in your practice and application, there will come a day that you'll be fluent in the Language of Money.

Now it's time to move on to the Business Wealth Line and learn how to speak the Language of Business and the Language of Leadership.

CHAPTER 12

The Business Wealth Line (The Languages of Business and Leadership)

The Language of Business

If the Language of Money is spoken in the vocabulary of accounting, then the Language of Business is spoken in the vocabulary of the law. It's a language where contracts and agreements clarify arrangements and commitments. It's a language that is influenced and interpreted through the legal system in the country in which it is being spoken. In essence, the Language of Business is the legal expression of how deals, joint ventures, partnerships, investments, and business as a whole are conducted.

Buy something from a company? You've entered into a contract of sorts, whether it be written, oral, or implied. Sell a product or a service? Again, you've entered into a contractual relationship. Combine resources with another party to do a business deal? Borrow money from a commercial lender? Hire an employee? Do any of these along with a myriad of other business actions, and you are entering the world of the Language of Business.

This is a world of contractual relationships, rights, and responsibilities. This is a world that is influenced and interpreted by the body of law that's come before, and by the changes in legislation that get enacted at various levels of government.

It's the language that encompasses contracts and asset protection. It can be dry, boring, couched in the almost incomprehensible language of *legalese*, and tempting to overlook. But that can be a financially *deadly* mistake that can lead you to lose everything you've ever worked for.

What's essential is not for you to become a legal scholar or get your law degree. Instead, what is essential is that you become fluent in the basic concepts of contracts and learn to intelligently leverage your legal support team to safely, equitably, and profitably navigate the commercial waters of today's business world.

Let's start off with some important general concepts on exactly what a contract is, then we'll move to some specialized examples such as partnership agreements, which show you why it's so important to become fluent in this language if you want to succeed in building wealth.

The Five Essential Elements
of Every Contract

Contracts are the purest expression of the Language of Business. Every time you buy a product, enter into an agreement with a service provider, sell someone a product or a service, buy, sell, or lease a piece of real estate, you are entering into a contract. You use contracts all the time in just about every aspect of your consumer and business lives.

Every contract must contain certain elements. Without *all* of these elements being present, the contract will not be held valid or binding in the event of a dispute that gets into a courtroom.

1. *Parties.* Everyone involved in the contract must be clearly identified. If you aren't named in a contract, you aren't a part of that deal, and you can't be held liable for nonperformance. Later in this chapter we'll share with you why we think you should never (or at least rarely) sign a business contract in your own name. Rather, we suggest you sign on behalf of a specific company you're legally using as a liability shield.

2. *Mutual agreement.* In order to be valid a contract has to be agreed to by everyone involved. This is usually evidenced by signatures. In the fancy language of lawyers they'll say there needs to be an offer and acceptance of that offer.

3. *Consideration.* Something of value, in fancy terms called "consideration," has to pass between the parties to make a contract valid. Now, what that thing of value is can often be very subjective. This is one of the most highly litigated areas in contract law.

4. *Lawful objective.* You can't contract with someone to perform a criminal or unlawful action and have that contract be binding.

5. *Capacity of parties to perform.* Everyone has to be able to do what they say they are going to do in order to make a contract binding. If you sign an agreement knowing you won't be able to do your part, you won't be able to hold the other side accountable for not doing their part. You may also find yourself being sued for fraudulent breach of contract, that is, for signing the contract knowing you couldn't perform on your side in the first place.

Here are a few other things to understand about contracts:

1. *Minors may not enter into binding contracts.* Did you ever wonder why a 16-year-old can't legally buy a car, although she can drive one? Minor children are not considered to be legally responsible and hence may not enter into a contract.

2. *Ambiguities are resolved in favor of the nondrafter.* If your contract language isn't clear, then the other party may be able to get out of the deal. The courts have consistently held that where contracts are fuzzy, the person who didn't write it gets the benefit of the doubt.

3. *Not all contracts are written.* You can make handshake contracts and oral agreements just as easily as you can make written agreements, but it's not a good idea. They are a lot harder to enforce, particularly if the only two people involved are you and the person you're fighting with, and there is no other witness.

4. *Make independent legal advice a requirement.* If you are dealing with someone who is inexperienced or unsophisticated in the world of business and financial matters, and you want to make sure the deal doesn't go south, you should always add in language requiring that person to either seek independent legal advice before signing the agreement or to sign a waiver confirming he or she has been told to get legal advice and has refused or waived that requirement. This may not always hold up, but it's a great way to protect yourself.

If there is any one point we want to stress above all others it is this: Understand the contract before you sign. If that means you stop the deal and ask for time to get legal advice, so be it. If someone pressures you to sign without talking with your attorney or understanding the agreement, we think this is a signal to rethink the deal and walk away.

Don't sign anything until you clearly understand and agree with what you are signing.

When it comes to contracts, we could write a book . . . not that there aren't thousands of books out there already. The points we've gone through are fairly simple versions of complex ideas. Get help. This is one area where the old saying, "An ounce of prevention outweighs a pound of cure," really holds true. Legal advice proactively used *before* you enter into a contract isn't anywhere near as costly as the legal bill you'll owe *after* the fact when you try to get yourself out of a bad contract.*

Now let's look at the specific area of partnership agreements as one expression of the Language of Business. The best part about the Language of Business is that once you get the feel for it in one area, many, if not most, of the concepts apply to other areas. As long as you use your understanding of the Language of Business to intelligently use attorneys to help you navigate the world of contracts you'll do fine. Beware the temptation to do it yourself. This is one area where the costs are too high and the work is too specialized for you to do this without great peril.

Partnerships

Key Questions to Ask Before You Form Any Partnerships

First, remember that a long-term business partnership is like a marriage; you want to ease your way into it with open eyes and lots of communication on the important issues that will eventually come up.

Here is a list of questions to consider as you think through the viability of any long-term partnership:

- *Values:* Do you share similar values? Will you both fundamentally be moving in the same direction?

- *Conflict:* How does your prospective partner deal with conflict? Is this a match for your style? In times of stress will your partner stay the course or cut and run? How has your prospective partner dealt with conflict in past personal and business relationships? What clues are you able to uncover that reveal the real story?

- *Work ethic:* What type of hours will this person work? How much work will she put into those hours? How effective is he?

---

*Make sure you register right away for your Millionaire Fast-Track Program, which includes a detailed, in-the-trenches, workshop called The Language of Business. For full details see the Appendix or go to **www.MauiMillionaires.com/book**.

- *Integrity:* Do you trust this person? Is that trust based on real data or an emotional connection? How has this person behaved in the past? Does this person consistently meet his commitments, big or small? Will this person do what's right, especially when it isn't convenient or profitable?

Once you've made the decision to enter into a long-term business partnership with someone, make sure you choose the right legal arrangement for that business. One of the reasons we invite two of the top attorneys in the United States with us as guest teachers for Maui is because we know that you need sharp legal advice when putting together partnerships of any kind.

We all know we are supposed to "get it in writing," but here are five things that your partnership agreement *must* cover that many entrepreneurs let slide. We call them the "Five Ds" of partnerships, and too many entrepreneurs let the discomfort of confronting the tough issues up front intimidate them. Alas, nine times out of 10, this comes back to haunt them later.

The Five "Ds" of Partnerships

Death: What happens if one of the principals of the partnership dies? Usually this is handled by a buy-sell clause, and often this arrangement is funded with a life insurance policy.

Disagreement: What happens if you and your partners reach an impasse, an irreconcilable difference on a fundamentally important issue? How will you handle it? The last resort is to have a carefully thought through buy-sell agreement. Will you have the disagreement be handled by an escalating progression of mediation then binding arbitration? Will there be a forced buyout with a set price or formula that is triggered? If you don't spell this out in your partnership agreement you might find yourself forced up the very expensive avenue of a formal lawsuit and jury trial.

Debt: What happens if any of the partners becomes financially insolvent and declares a bankruptcy? Will you have to take on that partner's creditors as your new partners? Usually in the case of bankruptcy the economic interest of the insolvent partner will revert back to the other partners. This protects members of the partnership.

Divorce: Let's say you're a partner with Sally. But she and her husband Jim get a divorce, and in the settlement Jim gets half of Sally's interest in your partnership. Do you really want to be forced to take Jim into your partnership? You need to decide up front how you want to handle this contingency.

Disability: The final "D" is disability. What happens if one of the partners is hurt and is no longer able to contribute time and talent to the partnership? How will this affect his or her ownership interest and the way profits are split?

You'll need to consider all five of the Ds and incorporate your answers in your written partnership agreement.

Ten Bottom Lines to Consider When Forming a Partnership

Here are 10 more key lessons when it comes to partnering.

1. Get your agreement in writing.

2. Make sure you share common values and vision.

3. Integrity is a *must* in any choice of partners. Evaluate your prospective partners' past exits from business and personal relationships to see what that reveals about how they will behave if your business relationship ends.

4. Put the emphasis on making the partnership work out. Make it less favorable to leave or quit the partnership. Beware buy-sale arrangements that economically incentivize the exiting partner.

5. Divide up contributions all partners are making to the business and put an equitable value on each of these contributions. Rewards and control should follow contribution and risk. Remember, not all partnerships are meant to be 50–50.

6. Choose the right legal structure at the *start* of the partnership. The right attorney can help you intelligently choose.

7. Get your written agreement done during the honeymoon stage of the partnership—up front! (If you can't talk about it at the start of the venture how in the world will you handle the tough issues when tensions are running high?)

8. Consider doing a one-off joint venture to see what it's like working together first before you jump into a long-term business partnership. And remember, even a one-off joint venture needs a clear, written agreement between you and the other parties.

9. If you have a buyout triggered, will there be a noncompete agreement required of the selling partner? If so, what are the main terms that the noncompete agreement will require? Who owns the intellectual property that is created out of the partnership? Does

the business? The creating partner? A smart partnership agreement must address this issue, too.

10. Incorporate your answers to how to handle the five Ds in your written partnership agreement up front.

Now let's take a look at the other side of the Language of Business: asset protection.

Asset Protection—The Forgotten Key to Sustain Your Wealth

The real purpose of asset protection is to protect yourself from risks. Those risks can come in all kinds of forms, such as:

- Government agencies (IRS, SEC, EPA)
- Lawsuits (divorce, personal, and business)
- Creditors
- Fraud

We've put government agencies at the top of this list because something the government can often do what no one else can do—seize assets first, and ask questions later. Have you ever received a letter from the IRS demanding that you respond or pay something within a certain amount of days or risk having the IRS levy your bank account?

Lawsuits, on the other hand, can come from all over the place. We've listed divorce because it's a reality in our society. In many states you can literally lose half of what you've built in a divorce. But one of the most common places lawsuits arise for most people is in their cars. There are millions of cars on the road at all times, and thousands of accidents happen daily. In fact, it's probably harder to find someone who's never been in an accident than someone who has.

Two other sources of lawsuits are your home and business. Home-based lawsuits usually arise because someone has been injured on your property and is attacking your homeowner's insurance policy. For example, Diane knows of a case in Miami where a parent, picking up his child from a friend's birthday party, twisted his ankle badly on a sidewalk crack in front of the party house. The father of the party host happened to be a surgeon. Even though the sidewalk is a city responsibility, and not the problem of the homeowner, the injured parent still sued the party host's father. Why? Because as a surgeon, there was an expectation that he was rich, and therefore a good lawsuit target. This is the same reason that many business lawsuits arise, particularly where there is a professional involved. People see successful professionals as having money, and therefore, as tempting targets.

Fraud is another risk—not that you will defraud people but that people will defraud you. If you aren't fluent in the Language of Business, you risk someone taking advantage of you, and trying to take the things you've worked so hard to build.

Let's look at the 10 most important steps you can take to build a financial fortress around your assets.

The 10 Asset Protection Barriers You Must Erect to Protect Your Financial Fortune

1. *Keep a Low Economic Profile*

   We're not suggesting that you hide your wealth the moment you step out of your front door. However, we are suggesting that you don't make your life one of conspicuous consumption. If you are driven everywhere in your Rolls Royce, grocery shop with your fingers covered in jewels, and live in the largest, most opulent house in the neighborhood, like it or not you will present a target. You can mitigate many of the risks by erecting some of the asset protection strategies you're about to learn here, but you may also have to defend yourself more often than if you kept a little lower economic profile.

   But the real place to keep a low economic profile is in the public record. By using business structures to hold your assets, your name can stay under the radar. Are you still traceable? Sure, in most cases there are services and agencies that specialize in peeling back ownership layers to get to the true owner. However, those services cost money, and often that cost is a deterrent to the casual plaintiff (someone who brings a minor or nuisance lawsuit against you in an attempt to evoke an if-I-give-you-this-money-will-you-please-go-away-type of settlement).

2. *Use Entities as a Liability Shield*

   Entities, plain and simple, are business structures. The two most common types are corporations (C Corporations and S Corporations) and limited liability companies (LLCs).

   Doing business through a properly structured and maintained entity means you have a liability shield between you and the world.

As the owner or operator of a business structure you aren't personally liable for the acts and debts of that business unless you do something wrong, like commit criminal acts in the name of the business or steal from the business. You could be a lousy businessperson, making bad decisions and driving your business into the ground, but as long as you follow the entity maintenance procedures, you will be safe from the personal consequences of your bad decisions. (Of course if you've invested everything you own into your business that's another story, but we digress.)

What you spend setting up and maintaining a business structure is nothing compared with what it might cost you if you don't!

If you choose to forego the business structure route and operate a business in your own name as a sole proprietorship or hold real estate in your own name, not only are you painting a huge target on yourself economically, but you're also guaranteeing that in the case of a lawsuit everything you own is at risk. Your business and investments have absolutely zero protection from you, and vice versa. If insurance isn't enough to cover the cost of a claim the balance is coming out of your pocket. If your pocket isn't deep enough to cover that amount, then you will probably be stripped of one or more assets, which will likely be liquidated for pennies on the dollar, until there is enough money to cover the claim. It is absolutely inconceivable to us that anyone would knowingly take on that risk, and yet we see it *all the time*.

Not only that, the excuse for not putting entity protection into place is almost always the same: It costs too much. Someone please tell us what is too much when there are potentially millions of dollars of business, real estate, and personal assets at stake.

From a tax perspective, not all entities are good for all assets. For example, you will pay more in taxes if you offer a service through an LLC than you would through a C or S Corporation. And you will pay more in taxes if you hold real estate in a C or S Corporation than if you hold it through an LLC. We have a fantastic special report called, *Choosing the Right Business Structure: How a Little Knowledge Can Save a Lot of Money*, that goes into detail on the different entity types, how they are structured, and how to maximize the legal and tax attributes each has to offer. You can download this special report for free as part of your Millionaire Fast-Track Program. Just go to **www.MauiMillionaires.com/book**.

No matter which entity you choose, each of them has five common elements that are required to maintain your liability protection.

1. *Your paperwork must be properly drafted.* If you don't form it properly, your business structure may not protect you the way you want—if it protects you at all.

2. *Your business structures must be adequately funded.* While you don't need to stuff your entity full of assets, you do need to make sure your business has enough so that a reasonable person would conclude it was a functioning business.

3. *Don't comingle funds.* This is an entity protection killer! Your business has a bank account. You have a separate bank account. Keep it that way! Nothing will pierce through your corporate protections easier than a record of you using your business' bank account as your own personal piggy bank. If it means writing yourself a business check, depositing that check into your personal account and paying your phone bill from there, *do it*.

4. *Operate as a business.* If you want to be a business, act like one. Use business cards and letterhead for your correspondence and invoices. Don't take checks made out to you personally; only accept checks made out to your business. Make sure you keep separate business records and that you can easily make a distinction between business records and your personal records. Don't lend yourself money from the company without having a promissory note or some record of the loan, and make sure you pay it back! Never sign contracts without using your business title.

5. *Observe corporate formalities.** This means making sure you take the legal steps required to prove you're acting like a business. That means making sure your business is up to date with any state filings, such as those required by the Secretary of State's office or the Department of Taxation. Hold annual meetings, and keep minutes of important business decisions.

3. *Compartmentalize Risk*

The easiest way to compartmentalize risk when it comes to businesses is to have more than one entity. This is something many people don't realize. We've both heard stories from participants about how they are operating over a dozen successful businesses from a single entity, which is a risk no savvy entrepreneur should take.

---

*For a list of courses and resources to teach you how to properly use your entities, go to **www.MauiMillionaires.com/book**.

Why? Because in the event of an accident at one of the businesses, an attorney looking at whether you are a good lawsuit candidate will first find your entity . . . and will then find out that your entity is absolutely *stuffed* with assets (i.e. the other successful businesses). And as anyone who's ever been sued knows, it is amazing how injuries are inflamed when there is a lot of money at stake.

However, on the other extreme, having 50 entities doesn't make sense either. Few people are able to maintain them all properly, even with a maintenance service, and the costs become prohibitive, which often leads to resentment and a lack of will to keep things maintained. Depending on your business type you may want to look at some newer legal protections that have recently become available, such as a Series LLC*, which is one LLC that breaks down into as many sub-LLCs as you need. Each sub-LLC is protected from the others, but there is only a single set of records to be kept at the end of the day.

4. *The Inside/Outside Asset Protection Plan™*

This is another approach to risk protection and involves creating vertical layers, rather than an expanding circle of single-layer entities.

At Level One, people tend to operate personally, through sole proprietorships or holding real estate personally. They have a single layer of ownership—themselves—and no protection. In this case, the inside and outside layers are one and the same.

In Level Two, people begin establishing entities and now have two layers of protection—their business structures and then themselves personally. The outside layer is the business structures they use to operate in the business and investing world. However, the inside layer is still themselves personally.

At Level Three, people operate on a three-layer system. At the very top layer—the outside layer—are the business structures that deal directly with the public and which have the most risk associated with them. However, rather than owning those structures personally, at Level Three, people develop a second set of business structures to act as a second barrier. That's the inside layer. Any type of lawsuit or other risk that is able to penetrate the first layer almost always is stopped at the second layer, meaning that the Level Three business owners remain safe from liability.

---

*You'll find more information about Series LLCs, what they are, how they work, and where you can go to get one set up at our web site, **www.Maui Millionaires.com/book**.

David's Story

A little while ago, I decided to invest in a business project with a group of other people. It was a "private placement" offering, meaning that all of the investors were buying into a single new structure that was not available to the rest of the world. Although I knew and trusted the management team implicitly, rather than buying into the new project directly, I used an investing company I also own to invest through instead. My reason was that just in case anything ever went wrong with the new structure and the corporate protection was pierced, I was still not vulnerable personally, as the liability would then fall on my investing company. It had nothing to do with not trusting the management team. This is just the method I use to manage my risk in this type of situation.

5. *Encumbering Assets*

Encumbering an asset is a term used to describe attaching some kind of debt to the equity you hold in that asset. The more equity you hold in that asset the higher your risk.

For example, let's say you own your own home, free and clear, and it's worth $500,000. If there is ever a lawsuit brought against you personally, for example, you cause a car accident in which the other driver is seriously injured, all of that equity is at risk. Will you lose your home? Probably not if your car insurance covers any damage award granted to the other driver. But what if your insurance doesn't? What if it expired, or you breached your policy and the insurance company refuses to cover the damages? Now you will risk a huge judgment being recorded against your house, and depending on other factors, possibly face losing your home.

There are several ways to encumber assets. For your personal residence there is something called a "homestead exemption,"* which is a piece of equity you are allowed to carve off and hold safe from any and all creditors (except secured creditors or the IRS). In some states, such as Texas and Florida, this is a very effec-

*You can find a list of state homestead exemptions and requirements at our web site, **www.MauiMillionaires.com/book**.

tive strategy, as the homestead exemption amount covers the entire property value. But other states don't have high homestead exemption amounts (California, for example, even with some of the priciest real estate in the country has a homestead exemption of just $75,000), while some states such as New Jersey don't even offer homestead protection. In those states you may want to use one of the other encumbrance methods, such as "friendly" mortgages, lines of credit, refinancing to pull equity, and liability separation. New credit laws have changed the process for the homestead exemption. Make sure you have the most current information when you create your own asset protection plan.

Friendly mortgages are mortgages you take out over a property but don't spend down. For example, if your $500,000 property was held in California, you could file a homestead exemption to protect $75,000 and then get a line of credit from your local bank for $300,000 secured with a first mortgage. While you will have no interest or payments due on that line of credit until you tap into it, the bank will still record a mortgage as a lien against your property. Any potential creditors will see on the public record that you have a first mortgage for $300,000, which reduces the amount of equity they think you have. You can also use advanced versions of the friendly mortgage to "equity strip" your assets through the use of multiple entities. This is a sophisticated technique and one you will need a skilled attorney to help you properly execute.

Another great strategy to protect your assets is to refinance them every several years and pull out some of the equity, and then take that money and invest it into additional projects that return a higher rate than you will be paying on your new mortgage.

Finally, if you have a business with a number of expensive assets in it, consider applying the inside/outside method again. In this case you create an LLC that holds title to the assets and then leases those assets back to the active business operation. A medical or dental practice is a great example: Put all of that expensive medical equipment into a protected structure that doesn't deal with the public but instead leases the equipment to the medical practice at reasonable rates. Now, if a patient sues your practice, there may be some assets at risk but not the equipment.

6. *Proper Insurance*

The best way to use insurance is to cover those losses that you can't afford to handle all by yourself or those risks where the cost of the insurance is a small price to pay compared with the cost of dealing with life if you didn't have the policy.

At its best, insurance is one part of your asset protection plan, but it isn't the entire plan all by itself. There are just too many ways your insurance company defines and limits the extent of its coverage. In fact, one of the biggest mistakes we see people make when buying insurance is looking at the wrong place in the policy. People look to see what's covered, but actually that's the worst place to look. You want to be looking at what items are *excluded* from the policy and what the limits are.

It's like this. Your insurance agent is looking to sell you a policy that will cost the insurance company the absolute minimum if they have to pay out upon it. Much as a casino does, insurance companies try to stack the odds of paying out in their favor not yours. The insurance policy may say, "We cover all of this," but it also will say, "except for that, that, and that," which could mean you don't realize you don't have the coverage you think you do—until it's too late.

So, when you're looking for insurance ask the question, "What's not covered?" If you're looking for a business or a large policy, get someone who understands and knows what to look for to review what's being offered. In fact, consider using an insurance broker rather than an agent. An agent is ultimately working for the insurance company, whereas an insurance broker works for you and is looking to find the best insurance deal for you. And make sure you paper your tail, we mean trail.

Write the insurance company a letter saying, "This is what I understand the policy to mean. If I am wrong, let me know in writing within the next 30 days. If I don't hear back from you in writing within this time, I will rely on this to mean my understanding is correct." What normally happens is you'll get a letter back that disagrees with your position, but it will further clarify what is and isn't covered.

And remember to review your insurance from time to time. If you insured your house years ago, when it was worth considerably less, you may have less coverage than you think in the event of a disaster.

The second most common mistake we see with insurance is people believing that insurance alone is enough. Will the insurance company actually cover your claim or exclude their way out of payment? How is the insurance company doing in terms of ability to pay? Insurance companies in the southern states hit by hurricanes have paid out billions in damages. They may have considerably fewer resources to pay your claim than they did a few years ago. Without the one-two punch of insurance combined with asset protection, you are leaving yourself at more risk than you need to.

7. *Umbrella Policy*

An umbrella insurance policy is a catchall policy that covers you for many of the liability risks that your other insurance doesn't. It also protects you if your other coverages aren't high enough. No matter what level you are, an umbrella policy is something you should at least consider. If you're at Level Two, $1 million may be enough, whereas those of you at Level Three may need somewhere between $5 million and $10 million.

Remember that an umbrella liability policy covers you *personally*, not your business, although you can get an umbrella policy for your business.

8. *Be Unappealing or Intimidating to Sue*

The more hurdles you require a potential claimant or creditor to go over, the less likely it is that you'll be sued. If there are multiple entity layers involved, all with minimal assets, the legal costs to sue go up, and the promise of a reward goes down. The harder it is to get money from you, the less chance someone will take all those steps to try and get it.

When you're well-protected, a claimant has three major barriers to cross to get at your equity. First, the claimant has to know about your equity. Second, that claimant has to pay to bring a lawsuit against you and win. Third, the claimant then has to spend even more money trying to collect on a judgment. Each barrier is progressively higher, more expensive, and harder to cross.

Say you operate a business through an LLC, with one or more partners. If you are sued personally, most state laws prevent a creditor from taking over your ownership in that LLC. A creditor may be able to siphon off your share of the profits from that LLC, but it can't stand in your shoes and make business decisions or elect to sell and liquidate your ownership. If there are no profits, that creditor gets nothing. Or better yet, if there are declared profits (i.e. on paper) but the business chooses not to pay out the cash, then the creditor will get hit with a big tax bill and no income to pay for that tax! This can be a powerful incentive for creditors to settle for a fraction of the judgment amount.

9. *Qualified Pension Plans*

Most 401(k)s and IRAs are protected from creditors. If you go bankrupt, your pension funds stay safe, at least as long as the money remains in the plan. Once you start to pull the money out, it does become attachable, but think about the leverage you have here. Imagine negotiating with a creditor who faces a very real possibility of waiting for years to collect on a judgment in bits and pieces as you pull money out from a pension fund. What do you think that creditor would rather do: take a smaller sum up front to collect *something*, or wait for 5, 10, maybe 20 years to collect in pieces?

10. *Business and Employee-Related Liabilities*

Have you ever sent a blistering e-mail that you immediately wished you hadn't? Chances are, if you have employees, so has one of your employees. It is becoming increasingly important for businesses to train everyone in things that should and shouldn't ever be said. Basically, if it could come back to haunt you some day, leave that thought unwritten or unspoken.

Casual e-mail can be problematic, too. Inappropriate jokes forwarded around an office could land you and your business in the middle of a sexual harassment or discrimination case. It doesn't matter if it's casual. E-mail has the same strength as any other written letter or formal communication.

Train everyone to keep notes of telephone conversations. This is something common in a law firm environment. Attorneys, paralegals, and legal secretaries are trained to keep notes on every discussion they have with people outside the office regarding each case. That way, in the event of a dispute, there are notes to refer back to. Back up conversations with confirmation e-mails or letters. For example, send an e-mail that says, "After our discussion today I understand X, Y, and Z about this matter. If I am mistaken, please let me know within 30 days. If I don't hear back from you in writing within that time, I will rely upon that to mean you are in full agreement with the above understanding." Now you have documented evidence to strengthen your claim if things go south later on.

Once upon a time, when we first entered the business world we thought that we could always count on people to live up to their word. Later we learned that sometimes people didn't honor their word. And after many years in the business world, we now know that sometimes people just have a different way of interpreting what was, in fact, said. All of which has lead us to conclude that not only is it essential to become fluent in the Language of Business, but it's also imperative to remember to use our language skills to clarify our agreements, in writing, *every* time.

Now, in the final part of this chapter we'll move on to discuss the Language of Leadership.

The Language of Leadership: Creating a Business that People Want to Belong To

The second language in the Business Wealth Line is the Language of Leadership. In Level One, you are realizing there is more to life than working for someone else and are breaking free, often by starting a new business. At Level One you may not have a clue where you're going, but one thing you do know is that it's time to make some changes. At this level, your relationship with leadership in the business world is likely following a leader—who may or may not be your boss.

At Level Two, the Language of Leadership evolves into the harried business owner who is looking to build a staff that leverages her time as the main producer for her Level Two business. The language isn't about teamwork so much as it's about getting employees to do their jobs efficiently. The business owner quite likely realizes the need for leadership in her business but laments the fact that she could start being a leader if she could just find some good employees, or if she just had more time.

Leadership really comes into play at Level Three. It's in Level Three (or in advanced stage Level Two) that you are finally secure enough to hire on team members who are more talented than you. When you hire out of strength versus hiring out of weakness, that's when you really can find the team to massively grow your business.

The bottom line is that a business is only as good as its leader. Yet, there is a lot of confusion about what really makes a good leader. Or rather, you know one when you see one, but how do you define that special something that makes an effective leader?

The 14 Characteristics that Define a Leader

Have you ever heard the expression, "He is a natural born leader"? But is that true? Are some people *born* with natural leadership skills and ability? Or is it more likely that some people have received more training in leadership skills, from their parents, family upbringing, positive relationships with teachers, and other early leaders in their lives?

We all teach, guide, and inspire others at some point. In a sense, each of us has the raw materials with which to fashion ourselves into a powerful and effective leader. The first step is to recognize that you are capable of being a great leader. Next, you must learn what it means to be a leader, and what skills and qualities you must cultivate for this transformation to happen. Finally, you must invest the time and energy to grow your leadership qualities and skills. This is not a passive process. It takes discipline, commitment, and focus. But the rewards are an explosion of results and success in your business that you never could have imagined. You see, leadership is the mechanism with which you tap into the extraordinary power lying dormant in other people.

Below you will find the 14 key characteristics we believe all leaders must possess in order to successfully lead others.

We've broken these characteristics down into three lists. The first list defines the three different types of leadership.

The Three Types of Leadership

1. *Meta Leadership*. Meta leadership is the highest level of leadership. It is your way of *inspiring* individuals through your powerful *vision*. At the meta level, you get enthusiastic followers, energetic and ready to be part of the team. At this point, though, there is primarily just enthusiasm, passion, and a general "let's do it" attitude. Meta leadership is where you inspire your team to connect emotionally with your vision and passion for your business. It's the raw energy source that you must direct using the two other types of leadership.

2. *Macro Leadership*. Macro leadership *decisively evaluates* risks and rewards, *strategically plans* out the business path, *defines the values* for the organization, and *persuades others* to commit to these goals. The role of macro leadership is to map out your company's path to a successful future and then to engage and employ your team to reach these goals.

3. *Micro Leadership*. Micro leadership is about the daily process of leadership. It's the level of leadership where you focus on coaching, directing, growing, stretching, pushing, supporting, challenging, and celebrating your team.

The next seven leadership characteristics relate to those things you need to bring to your Level Three business in order for it to excel.

The Seven Core Competencies of Great Leadership

1. *Inspirational.* A true Level Three business has people who are there for more than just the paycheck. To be an effective leader, you need to inspire your team members to show their passion in all they do. In this case your team is more than just your direct employees and contractors. It also includes your customers, vendors, investors, and joint venture partners—in other words, everyone your business touches. The best way to inspire is to help the people you lead find deeper meaning in their interactions with your company.

2. *Visionary.* If you don't know where you're going, you will lead your team into the wilderness with no way back. A good leader creates a vision—a shining promise of the future of the business. Don't be afraid of using emotions in your vision and planning. The best leaders engage their followers' emotions not just their brains.

3. *Decisive.* Leaders lead. They make decisions and take action. The best leaders all move boldly and with clear purpose once they have made their decision. Their force and purpose instills confidence and initiative in their teams. The best leaders are willing and able to make the tough calls.

   "In any moment of decision, the best thing you can do is the right thing, the next best thing is the wrong thing, and the worst thing you can do is nothing."

   —Theodore Roosevelt

4. *Strategic Thinking.* Strategic thinking is critical to keeping your business on track and fulfilling its mission. It's developing the strategies and plans you need to achieve your business goals. How will this project get done? How can we capture that new market? How can you launch a new web site to increase revenues and grow your client base?

5. *Values.* Values determine how we work. Your company's values are the bedrock of your business' culture. A good leader is direct and truthful about his or her values, setting forth the expectations and holding people accountable for their actions and how those relate to the values of the organization. Live up to your values. You are the champion for integrity within your organization. (See Figure 12.1.)

FIGURE 12.1   Financial Character—Values

6. *Persuasive.* Good leaders persuades others with logic, reason, and emotion. They motivate others through persuasion not intimidation. They speak from the heart to the hearts of others. When you lead, do you demand results, or do you ask for results? Or best of all, do you *inspire* results?

7. *Focused.* Once you illuminate the path your business is taking, stay committed! Yes, there will likely be hundreds of new opportunities and ideas that show up every day. But if you constantly change gears to grab hold of the next great new thing, your overall business purpose becomes diffused and unclear. Your team will become confused and unmotivated, particularly where team members have invested time and energy on a project that is summarily dropped in favor of something new. Don't ignore those new opportunities, but don't divert all your business resources, either.

The final four leadership characteristics are the mastery skills and are the advanced skills that take people to the very top of the leadership ladder. If you were to sit down with our recognized business titans—the Jack Welches, Michael Dells, Bill Gateses, and Warren Buffets of the world—and talk with them at length, these four skills would become evident during your discussions.

Four Mastery Skills of a Level Three Leader

1. *Mastery of Self.* Discipline, self-awareness, and emotional fluency are all skills that you must cultivate. Because so much of leadership is expressed indirectly through example, self-mastery is essential to ensure that you consistently and congruently lead by your best example.

2. *Mastery of Communication.* A leader must be able to clearly lay out her vision and get people to buy into that view of the future. He must be able to articulate goals, strategy, roles, and expectations, whether with vendors, clients, independent contractors, or employees. How you communicate will be emulated throughout your company. Make sure your communication skills are deserving of being copied.

3. *Mastery of Rapport Building.* While mastery of self means understanding yourself, mastery of rapport building means understanding others. It's the ability to pick up on the small, unspoken cues about other people and how they are feeling. It's the talent that helps you choose the right people to add to your team. Your ability to empathize and connect emotionally with other people is what allows you to deepen relationships and ultimately grow your influence and impact.

4. *Mastery of Systems.* Systems are critical for the Level Three business to grow and thrive. A mastery of systems means that you can create a system of systems that includes the principles of chunking (breaking a big project down into little steps or aggregating many smaller steps into fewer larger steps for simplicity), thoroughness, relevance, reliability, and scalability. A mastery of systems means that you have also learned to see the deep connections within your business that help you understand root causes and how the whole system interacts.

If you've spent most of your life at Level One, then the ideas of leadership may seem intimidating. But don't let that stop you. Over time you *can* master these skills. Have faith in yourself. Will it mean stretching yourself? Yes! You will be stretched in ways you never knew possible. And yet, years from now you may find yourself looking back to right now, and wondering how it was that you ever doubted yourself.

In the final chapter of this section of the book you'll learn about the two languages of the Personal Wealth Line: The Language of Cash Flow and the Language of Wealth.

CHAPTER 13

The Personal Wealth Line (The Languages of Cash Flow and Wealth)

One of the biggest mistakes we watch entrepreneurs make is never learning the wealth skills they need to build wealth independent of the success or failure of their primary business. Your goal is to not just build a successful business but to successfully build a fortune. And this requires that you master the personal wealth skills you need to become financially fluent so that you make smart moves and solid decisions.

Just as the Business Wealth Line can apply to you personally, the Personal Wealth Line can apply to your business. You really need all five languages (Language of Money, Language of Business, Language of Leadership, Language of Cash Flow and Language of Wealth) to truly become financially fluent.

In the Personal Wealth Line, the focus isn't necessarily on contracts, asset protection and legalities (Language of Business); nor is it on how to successfully lead a business to greatness (Language of Leadership). Instead, the focus is on two things: building the cash flow you need to be financially free (Language of Cash Flow), and internalizing the key wealth distinctions and habits required to be wealthy (Language of Wealth).

The Language of Cash Flow

It's time to focus on the Language of Cash Flow. What does that mean? Well, cash flow is money you receive. The trick is to receive money without having to slap on a tie or roll up the panty hose and climb into the commuter lane with your carpool everyday to earn a paycheck. When you are able to create enough cash flow for yourself to live off of your passive income and passive, residual investments, you will have mastered the Language of Cash Flow. The challenge for many people, especially those at Level One or Level Two, is wrapping their heads around the idea that not only *can* you create cash flow without actively working for it, but you *must* create this cash flow if you want to be truly financially free.

There are two sides to the Language of Cash Flow—offense and defense. The offensive side is how you are able to create passive income and passive, residual income. You do this by finding and investing in the right wealth vehicles to generate wealth for yourself. Most entrepreneurs never learn how to be savvy investors. Instead they pour all of their attention into their businesses and in the end, they are trapped. Even if they sell their business for a large lump sum of money, they lack the investing skills to consistently turn that lump sum of money into passive, residual streams of income. And if they fail in their business, they have no real wealth independent of that business, and they are caught in an even worse place.

Instead, we urge you to learn the investing skills you will need when you exit your business. And rather than learn them later, we advise you to learn to invest along the way, incrementally. Not only will this put you in a much stronger position to wisely invest your profits if and when you sell your business, but it will also likely mean you will make a lot of money along the way.

We'll have a lot more to say about choosing and harnessing the right investment vehicle for yourself in the next several chapters, what's important for you to understand now is that it's not enough to know how to build a business to generate active income. You must learn how to passively invest so that you can create passive, residual streams of income.

Let's talk about the defensive game of cash flow—controlling and minimizing your expenses. Did you ever stop to think what the single greatest expense that you'll ever have is? By far, the single greatest expense most people will ever have is taxes. For example, in the United States the average person pays a blended rate of over 40 percent of their income in state, federal, and employment taxes. Forty percent! Well we know that with a little bit of planning and knowledge you can legally slash that tax burden by thousands of dollars. And every dollar you save is another dollar of cash flow you have left to use the way you want to use it. This area is so important to your cash flow that we want to spend more time on this topic.

Cash Flow from Tax Savings

When it comes to creating cash flow, tax savings is one of the best strategies. That's because just about any other kind of cash flow that you can create at Level One and Level Two will be subject to tax, whereas tax savings is actual, real money in your pocket. For example, if you pay a total tax rate of 50 percent (which is quite common for a high earner in the United States), and you make an extra $100,000, you'll put $50,000 in your pocket. But, if you can save $100,000 on the amount of taxes you pay, you'll put $100,000 in your pocket.

First, we have to examine some of the beliefs that you might already have about taxes. For example, do you believe some or all of the following tax myths?

- Tax loopholes are illegal.
- If I pay less in taxes, I'm more likely to be audited.
- Tax breaks are only for the rich.

Do you remember the saying about how if a lie is repeated often enough it eventually becomes regarded as truth? Well, no matter how many times you see or hear the above three statements repeated, it still won't make them true. Let's take a closer look at these three damaging myths.

Myth #1: Tax Loopholes Are Illegal

False! Tax loopholes are the government's incentive to promote public policy. Most tax loopholes are found in the areas of business and investing, because the government thinks it is an extremely good idea that we, as taxpaying citizens, invest and start businesses. In other words, if you do what the government wants you to do you'll be rewarded—in this instance, with tax loopholes. The trick is that it's up to you to find them. The government does not draw you a map to each and every available loophole.

Myth #2: If I Pay Less in Taxes, I'm More Likely to be Audited

False! As long as you take advantage of legal tax loopholes to *avoid* paying tax (as opposed to tax scams to *evade* paying tax—there's a big difference—and you have the business records to back up your deductions, there is no reason you will have an increased audit risk.

However, if you file your tax return with any of the big red flag mistakes present, such as math errors, reporting errors (your business is misclassified so your deductions don't match what the IRS is expecting), or underreporting income (you miss a W-2, 1099, or K-1), you *are* more likely to be audited. You're also more likely to be audited if you run your business as a sole proprietorship: Even the IRS concedes it selects this business structure for auditing about *10 times more* than any other structure. Why? Because historically sole proprietorships are good targets that tend to lack good financial statements and records.

Myth #3: Tax Breaks Are Only for the Rich

False! Tax breaks are for everyone. According to the IRS, the top 10 percent of income earners (defined as those with $100,000 or more in taxable income) currently pay 68 percent of federal taxes. Now contrast that with another IRS statistic: The bottom 50 percent of income earners (defined as those with $30,000 or less in taxable income) pay only three percent of federal taxes, and the argument that tax breaks favor the rich falls apart.

The reality is people who start businesses or who invest in real estate and other assets—in other words, Level Two and Level Three business owners and investors—receive additional tax breaks because they are taking advantage of the government incentives specifically designed to promote those activities.

We believe that the only true part about this entire argument is that people at Level One—those people who aren't financially fluent and who depend entirely on their W-2 income—do pay more taxes than people who are financially fluent and who don't depend entirely on W-2 income. Here's why.

Level One Tax Planning

There is a tax formula that determines how all tax is calculated, and it's amazingly simple.

(Income – Deductions = Taxable Income) × Tax Rate = Tax Due

So, if you want to pay fewer taxes, there are three ways to do that:

1. Decrease your taxable income.
2. Increase your deductions.
3. Decrease your tax rate.

Let's look at these in greater detail.

Decrease Your Taxable Income

To effectively decrease your taxable income you first have to under-stand that not all income is the same. There are three major categories of income:

Taxable   Tax Now

Tax-deferred   Tax Later

Tax Free   Tax Never

Taxable income is further broken down into three more types:

Earned: You work for your money.

Portfolio: Your money works for you.

Passive: Your investments work for you.

At Level One, you work for your money as a W-2 employee or a 1099 contractor. Your income is primarily all active, or earned, income, which pays the highest tax of all. The top federal tax rate on earned income is 35 percent, plus you have Social Security and Medicare deductions (or self-employment tax if you're a sole proprietor), and state income tax. It's not uncommon for an average wage earner to pay 50 percent in taxes.

Portfolio income comes from your money working for you. The pri-mary sources of portfolio income are interest, dividends, and capital gains. Interest income is taxed at your regular ordinary tax rate, which again, can be as high as 35 percent. Dividend income and capital gains income that comes from the sale of an asset you've held for one year or more are both taxed at a maximum rate of 15 percent.

Don't gloss over that last paragraph too fast. Did you see what hap-pened to your tax rate with the various income types? If you work really hard, you'll pay the highest amount of tax. But, if you instead make your money work for you, you could pay somewhere between 20 and 35 per-cent *less* in taxes.

Passive income comes from your investments working for you. The best example here is rental property. The rent you receive is passive income to you, because you aren't doing anything to earn it. The tax rate on passive income varies. But if you set it up right, you can actually generate passive income while paying *zero* in taxes.

The best Level One tax strategy to reduce your taxes begins with reducing your taxable income (remember this doesn't mean you earn *less* money, instead you earn better *types* of income). Start changing the character of your income by investing to create portfolio and passive income.

Increase Deductions

The second strategy to reduce your taxes is to increase your deductions. The best way to do this is through starting a business. The worst way to do this is by spending money on something just for the tax advantages. Yet this is something we see people in the traditional wealth model do all the time—buying a bigger house with the idea that the larger the house, the larger the tax break. But the reality is that there are limits on both income and the cost of a house, so this strategy can easily backfire. If you hit either the income or mortgage interest limits you begin losing the deduction.

Not a good idea! The way we see it, the best deductions come when you have a business, and for most people, that starts at Level Two.

Level Two Tax Strategy

At Level Two, you're starting to invest from the money you have left over. Now is the time to consider starting a business. Businesses give the best tax breaks at this point. Let's look at the two major categories for tax benefits for Level Two:

1. *Hidden business deductions.* Hidden business deductions are those expenses you could attribute to your business, but you aren't. Things like a cell phone, Internet bill, and automobile expenses are just a few that immediately come to mind. We get into this in more detail in Chapter 20, Preemptive Tax Strategy. You'll also find a powerful assessment tool on our web site, where you can review your present expenses against a list of over 300 potential business deductions to see where you may be missing out on legitimate business deductions. It's a great exercise to do with your mastermind team, and then have reviewed by your CPA! Just go to **www.MauiMillionaires.com/book**.

2. *Business structures.* Using a business structure can save you thousands, or cost you thousands, if you don't use the right one for the job. Not all business structures are taxed the same, and you need to match the business structure to the income it earns in order to get the best and most tax-efficient one possible. If this area is unfamiliar to you, then your best bet is to get some assistance from your CPA or attorney.

If your business is investing in real estate, you can also get some fantastic tax relief here at Level Two, if you get things set up right.

Besides maximizing your hidden business deductions and using the right business structure for your real estate business, real estate investors also have a phantom expense called *depreciation.* And, best of all, this phantom expense is a deduction for which you don't have to pay out any cash in order to get it!

Even though we know that real estate goes up in value over time, the IRS tells us that it in fact goes down; and furthermore, they will give us a deduction for that decrease in value—in other words, we get a depreciation deduction for the amount that our real estate buildings have devalued (there is no depreciation deduction for the land underneath). The deduction differs depending on the property type: You'll get $27\frac{1}{2}$ years to depreciate residential real estate and 39 years to depreciate commercial real estate. This deduction can actually create a loss on paper, meaning that while your investments are putting money into your pocket each month, at the end of the year the tax return will show a loss. That's how you can get to a point where you pay zero taxes on your passive income.

But wait, there's more! (We've always wanted to say that in a book.) You can actually break out the value of personal property items from the real estate buildings and depreciate those items over a quicker timetable. That means more depreciation, sooner, and a bigger deduction in the early years.*

Level Three Tax Planning

Up until now the tax planning ideas we've set out have primarily focused on how to invest after-tax income into businesses and real estate in the best

---

*To find out more about the books and resources that we have created for you to legally save thousands on your taxes just visit our web site **www.MauiMillionaires .com/book**. Plus, while you're there, you can download four free e-books on tax strategy as part of your Millionaire Fast-Track Program. See the Appendix for details.

tax-advantaged ways. That's why in Chapter 20, we talk about two tax percentages that are specifically designed to work with your taxable income:

1. Blended Tax Rate
2. Tax Efficiency Rate™

But when you reach Level Three, your tax planning needs to change again. Now you are starting to experience investing just like the wealthiest people in the country do. You're investing now from your assets instead of from your income that's leftover after you've paid all your bills.

Two key strategies for Level Three are:

1. Asset Appreciation
2. Pension Plan Investing

Asset Appreciation

One of the quickest and easiest ways to build wealth is to make your business worth more by creating additional cash flow from it. Earlier, we discussed strategies to increase your cash flow. Each and every one of those will make your company worth more.

As an example, let's say you take advantage of the strategy that helps you pinpoint expertise in your company that is being given away for free. And, in the first year, you increase your income by $250,000, just like Diane did in her first year of developing and selling a new way of doing tax strategies. In Diane's case, there was no extra cost associated with the income, so that $250,000 is both the gross income and the net income.

Now comes the fun part. How much did that add to the value? Well, if you have a Level Three business that typically sells for five times net income, you have just increased your net worth by $1,250,000! If you have a Level Two business that sells based on gross income at one times gross, you'll have a still respectable increase of $250,000. How much tax do you have to pay on your $250,000 to $1.25 million of increased net worth? Zero! You've created unrealized gains that incur no tax. This is another reason why the second million comes so much faster than the first. You're using your wealth to create more wealth as opposed to investing your leftover income to build your wealth.

Pension Plan Investing

There are lots of ways you can use your existing pension funds as a Level Three investing strategy. Diane's book, *The Insider's Guide to Tax-Free*

A Preemptive Tax Strategy Success Story

A client knew that he had a good thing going when he saw it and invested $1,800 using his Roth IRA in a new dot-com company.

Luckily, it was one of the dot-coms that didn't go bust in the early 2000s. Instead, it was bought out by another company. After a few stock splits, it was bought out again. The pattern kept repeating until the stock was worth over $6,000,000!

Now, here is the amazing part. How much tax did he pay on that amazing investment? Zero! That's because of the careful investment planning he did ahead of time. By using his Roth IRA to make the initial investment, he made sure that all of the money this investment made stayed in his Roth IRA, where it will come out *tax-free* at the time he begins to take withdrawals.

Real Estate: Retire Rich Using Your IRA, goes through over 20 different ways to do just that.

Rather than restate what Diane has already written, let's just talk briefly about what's possible.

Because you're using either tax-deferred vehicles—regular IRA, SEP, rollover 401(k)—or tax-free vehicles—Roth, Solo Roth 401(k)—you'll be able to defer or avoid taxes on all of the income. What can that mean for you?

At Level Three, it's time to begin measuring your tax cost in a different way. That's the third ratio we go through in Chapter 20: Your Tax Power Percentage™. Instead of comparing the total amount of tax you pay to your taxable income, the comparison is instead the ratio between the total tax you pay and your net worth. The other calculations aren't as important any more, because at Level Three, the best Preemptive Tax Strategies involve very little taxable income. You've moved so far away from earned and taxable income that those percentages simply don't make sense to use anymore.

So there you have the basics of the Language of Cash Flow. It's time to turn our attention to the habits and thinking patterns of the wealthy as we focus on the Language of Wealth.

The Language of Wealth

When we talk about the language of wealth, what does that mean to you? Do you imagine we'll be coaching you to move gracefully about in high society? Will we tell you about different forms of etiquette and just exactly what all those different forks at a high-class restaurant are really for? Or will we talk about investments, and explain what high-yield bonds are, or how to understand the commodities market?

Actually, the answer is none of the above. The Language of Wealth is more than just words. It's really a comprehensive set of habits and beliefs about money, wealth, and financial matters that the wealthy have cultivated over their lifetime.

At the core of the Language of Wealth are 21 key distinctions that the wealthy have mastered that clearly and definitively set them apart from Level One or Two people. You may notice patterns emerging. For example, common words found in Level One are *can't* and *won't*. In other words, "these ideas are not even in my realm of possibility." At Level Two, can't and won't begin to be replaced with *should* and *shouldn't*, which usually means at some level, "I am relying on someone else's advice and opinions when making decisions." But in Level Three, the language changes to one of *will* and *won't* and *choose* and *decide*. In other words, "I choose, based on my conscious decision, rather than through fear or by blindly accepting other people's opinions."

As you look through each distinction, make a mental note of which language level resonates with you. You may find that with respect to some distinctions you're Level One, while with others you may be Level Two or Three. That's okay! The thing to take away here is what level resonates with you the *most*. That, more than anything else, will help you to understand your current wealth level, and show you how you need to step up your habitual wealth thinking and language in order to get to the next level.

We've created a printable version of these 21 key distinctions for you to download and keep with you to study. Just go to **www.Maui Millionaires.com/book**.

1. *Your Wealth Frame™ (How far forward do you look financially?)*

   Level One: This day, this week, until my next paycheck, or to the end of the month. I focus on *survival*.

   Level Two: How do I get by financially for the next three to six months, or at the very most, the next year? I focus on *security*.

   Level Three: How do I look at my wealth for not only my entire lifetime, but the lifetimes of my children and grandchildren? I focus on *freedom* and *contribution*.

2. *Business Focus (How do I think about businesses?)*

   Level One: How do I get and keep a job? It is absolutely critical to my survival!

Level Two: How do I create my own job? I don't want to work for someone else anymore.

Level Three: How do I create a business that is self-sustaining and doesn't need me to work in it every day to be profitable, successful, and continue to grow? I want to be wealthy.

3. *Investment Focus* (*How do I think about investing?*)

Level One: How do I invest to get out of debt? (i.e., pay off my credit card debt before charging it up again).

Level Two: How do I save and invest slowly, over the long term, with my leftover money?

Level Three: How can I build wealth faster, without being dependent on my income to fund my investing? I don't want to be limited by what I earn! What value can I bring to a deal to make it better, not just for me, but for everyone else involved? What are the niches I have an advantage in that I can concentrate on and maximize my returns?

4. *Wealth Focus* (*What aspect of wealth do I focus on?*)

Level One: I can't afford it! My focus is on *not* having enough money. Everything is viewed through a poverty filter.

Level Two: I might lose my money! I'm not sure how I got it, and so I'm afraid I'll lose it. I'm not going to do anything that might risk my savings, because I don't know how I could ever recreate that wealth if I lost it.

Level Three: Money is really just a way of keeping score. If I lost it all tomorrow, I could make it back faster a second or third time around. Besides, I tend to view my wealth more broadly to include time, relationships, health, growth, faith, and peace of mind.

5. *Debt* (*What does debt mean to me?*)

Level One: Debt is something created by using my credit cards. I'm always going to be in debt, so why not treat myself by buying things on credit that I couldn't otherwise afford? Besides, it doesn't feel real when I pay with plastic.

Level Two: Debt is equated with fear or viewed as negative. Credit cards are bad; they teach us bad habits that are hard to break. Cash is king! A mortgage is something to be paid down as soon as possible and shouldn't be too big or it will be with me forever. I pay my credit cards off each month and rarely use debt for investment purposes. (That would just be too risky.)

Level Three: Debt is a powerful wealth tool. Debt is something I can intelligently use to build my wealth. Debt is something that I skillfully manage because its misuse is expensive. It helps me grow and expand my business and enhance my investment returns.

6. *Language Focus* (*What are my key words when I think about money?*)

Level One: I can't/won't do that. It's not possible, or if it is possible, it's just not possible for me. I'm not wealthy, and I never will be.

Level Two: I should/shouldn't do that. As long as I listen and do what I'm told, I should get by safely. They must be telling me the correct things; they're the experts, right?

Level Three: The choice is mine. I will do something or I won't, but I am empowered and will make my own choices based on my experience, knowledge, and confidence in myself to make the right decision. I may look to others for advice and instruction, but I will view their suggestions through my own filter and make an independent decision. I can do this. I will do this. I have done it before, and I will do it again.

7. *Making Financial Decisions* (*How do I make my financial decisions?*)

Level One: I don't really make decisions. I go with the path of least resistance. I'm not looking to make changes.

Level Two: My experts make my decisions, thanks. That way I don't need to. I might miss out on some good deals, but I stay safe!

Level Three: When it comes to financial decisions, I am the leader. I know what direction I want to go, so when I'm looking to my experts for advice, my question is, "I want to do this; what is the best legal/tax-advantaged way for me to make it happen?"

8. *Investment Vehicles* (*What do I invest in?*)

Level One: I invest in a savings account, a checking account, social security, or my children and family.

Level Two: My investment vehicles are conventional: 401(k)s, company pension funds, public stocks, mutual funds, bonds, and so on.

Level Three: My investment vehicles are assets I can either control or invest in with advantages so that I consistently outperform the market in these niches. I look at my business as an investment, because I can grow my business to make it more valuable. I invest in businesses, commercial real estate, private placements, and other alternative investments.

9. *Things that I consider risky are . . .*

Level One: Any investment is risky! Savings and checking accounts are okay, CDs are okay, and my company pension is okay. But investing in anything else is very scary.

Level Two: Anything that isn't talked about in the public media must be risky. Investing in businesses, real estate, private placements—these alternative investments feel very risky to me.

Level Three: Anything I don't have direct control over or which isn't transparent or in which I have no real advantages. Essentially, all those things that Level Two people believe make good investments.

10. *Scorecards* (*With what scorecard do I track my financial success?*)

Level One: How much do I make per hour, or per month? How much money do I owe on my credit cards?

Level Two: I take a look at my annual income, my bank balances, and the size of my nest egg. But I only really look once a year, and I don't spend any time analyzing how I'm doing, or if I could do things faster.

Level Three: I take stock of my financial picture at least quarterly. I look at a balanced picture of my financial results including my lifestyle costs, the return I receive on my investments, my total return on my net worth, and how tax strategies impact my wealth plan.

11. *What do banks and financial institutions mean to me?*

Level One: A bank is a magic place where money comes from. My fantasy is walking up to a bank machine and having money fly out at me that I don't have to repay. Banks are really kind of intimidating, actually.

Level Two: Banks are a place where I get my personal or business needs met. I know my local branch well, and do most of my financial dealings there. But our relationship isn't equal. I ask my bank for loans, and I apply for various services, hoping I meet its criteria.

Level Three: Banks are a consumer service, just like everything else. When I approach a bank, I am asking, "Why should I do business with you, and not the bank down the street?" I have multiple relationships with multiple banks, and I foster relationships, both for competition and as a backup. I'm not afraid to change banks when my business outgrows my current bank and often use commercial banks. I *refuse* to be at a bank's mercy. They provide me with a service that I pay for and must earn my business, not the other way around.

12a. *Team (What does "team" mean to me?)*

Level One: Team? You must mean sports team. Go team go! Barbeque at my house this Saturday—bring your own steaks and beer!

Level Two: I have a team, but I don't like them very much. They make a lot of mistakes, and I don't know that I'm getting value for money. I should probably upgrade, but I like being in control. Plus, they're too expensive to use very often.

Level Three: I'm doing long-range planning, and part of that planning and decision-making process is input from my team members. I am not the smartest person on my team! If I find that I am, then I look to upgrade, because I have outgrown the services my team is providing and I will get stuck without someone else who can help me stretch.

12b. *How often do I consult with my CPA?*

Level One: I don't have a CPA. I do my own taxes using software or I go to a major tax-filing service. I want my tax return done as soon as possible because I want my refund.

Level Two: I guess you could say I consult once a year, at tax time when my CPA does my return. I want it done on time, because that's what the rules say.

Level Three: Tax time is no different than any other time. I'm in touch with my CPA constantly, because she is an integral part of my team. My tax return is complex, and I am not qualified or interested in trying to do it myself. In fact, I file as late as possible because my return is so complex I often don't have the information I need until then.

12c. *How often do I consult with my attorney?*

Level One: Only if I have to . . . like when I'm sued or when they give me my one phone call.

Level Two: I call when I need a service, tell them what I need, and that's about it. It might be years between calls to my attorney.

Level Three: At least once or twice a year. My attorney drafts documents and helps me to structure my business and investing to stay legal, protected, and proactive. My attorney is another integral part of my team, and I value her input and knowledge.

13.   *What does insurance mean to me?*

Level One: State and federal programs. I'm depending on the government to catch me if I fall.

Level Two: I buy insurance, but I'm fairly unsophisticated when I buy. I often under- or overinsure, because I rarely look at my insurance needs strategically or comprehensively. I like buying things with a low deductible, because I can't afford to pay a whole bunch out of pocket if I have an accident or have to make a claim. I think about insurance in terms of health, car, and casualty.

Level Three: I often self-insure for smaller, manageable losses. It's more economic to buy a policy with a low premium and a high deductible than the other way around. I'm not going to have an accident every month, but I am going to make an insurance payment, so I want to maximize the return on my insurance investment. I also think about all kinds of insurance, not only the standard life, health, and auto insurance, but also liability insurance and business insurance. I look at how insurance can be an investment, or how it can help me to protect my business interests. I want insurance for liquidity, so that if I pass away my heirs have a quick and easy source of income while my estate is sorted out.

14a. *Retirement* (*How am I planning for retirement?*)

Level One: I'll probably keep working until I die. I'm trying to put money away, but it's hard to save and I don't think I'll have a pension or a lot of savings when I get older. I will be relying heavily on Social Security to survive when I get older.

Level Two: I'm going to live a frugal lifestyle and put everything I can into my nest egg. Hopefully it will be big enough. My retirement goal is to make sure I don't run out of money before I die.

Level Three: I'm creating a portfolio of investments that will provide me with passive residual income that lasts well beyond my lifetime. My goal is to create a legacy that lasts beyond me and does massive good in the world.

14b. *What key questions do I have around retirement?*

Level One: "How will I afford health care?"

Level Two: "Will I outlive my nest egg?"

Level Three: "Is my passport up to date?"

15. *Financial Statements* (*How often do I review my financial statements?*)

Level One: I never do, mostly because I don't have any. I don't want to know anyway.

Level Two: I take a look, probably once a year around tax time. My focus is on my adjusted gross income and how much tax I'll owe.

Level Three: I keep an eye on them all the time. I take a look monthly, quarterly, and annually. I often review my financial statements with my team, to make sure I'm interpreting them correctly, and to see where there are areas I can improve.

16a.   *Asset Protection (My ideas about asset protection are. . . ?)*

Level One: I really don't have much to lose, so I don't give it much thought. I lock my doors at night and look both ways before crossing the street, though.

Level Two: I'm beginning to invest, so I may start some basic asset protection, if someone tells me to, such as forming a corporation. I'm not sure what that means, though. I'm also trying to get my house paid off, so it's free and clear.

Level Three: I've got a multiphase plan that I established in line with my advisors' suggestions. I keep a low economic profile and look for ways to make myself less appealing in the event of a lawsuit. I use asset protection strategies, liability compartmentalization, and work to integrate everything into a comprehensive plan. I have my team review my plan and fine-tune it annually.

16b.   *The entity I select to run my businesses through is a . . .*

Level One: If I have a business at all, it's in my own name. Sole proprietorships are cheap, and I don't need anyone's help.

Level Two: I might use a single-member LLC or an S Corporation, depending on what I hear or read.

Level Three: I've got multiple business structures, because I know that to maximize my asset protection and tax benefits I need to use the best structure for my different assets and income streams.

17.   *Estate Planning (My thoughts on estate planning are . . .)*

Level One: I really don't have a plan. I hope I get an inheritance from someone else. I don't have anything anyway, so why plan?

Level Two: I've got the basics done. I've got a formal will or revocable living trust, so my heirs can avoid probate. But I still need to get my assets into my revocable living trust. I'll get there as soon as I have time. When I've got some extra cash I might even have it reviewed at some point.

Level Three: I've had a plan done, but because my circumstances change I keep my estate plan reviewed and up to date. That probably means I meet with my attorney once or twice a year, just to make sure I don't need to adjust or tweak something.

My estate plan is designed for ease, tax efficiency, proper distribution of my assets, and comprehensiveness.

18. *Record Keeping (My financial groundwork consists of . . .)*

    Level One: I throw my financial records into a shoebox. When that gets full I either empty it into the garbage or get a new shoebox.

    Level Two: I do it all myself. I keep all of my receipts together in file folders, and sort things through and update my records when I get time.

    Level Three: I've got bookkeepers and experts to take care of this aspect of my life. I review the reports they prepare for me regularly.

19. *Tax Planning (My tax planning begins . . .)*

    Level One: I'm just waiting for my refund.

    Level Two: When I get around to it. That can sometimes be early December, or, if I'm really busy, I start it in January of the next year and see what I can still do. Remember, IRAs don't have to be funded until the middle of April!

    Level Three: I start my tax planning at the beginning of the year, but usually for the *following* year, or the year after that. I look several years down the road and prepare today to execute my Preemptive Tax Strategy several years from now.

20. *Living (With respect to giving money . . .)*

    Level One: I hold my hand out hoping to get some.

    Level Two: I'm going to give, but only because I should. It scares me because I don't have enough.

    Level Three: I love giving! I've got more than enough and it feels good.

21a. *Learning Focus (My learning focus on wealth and financial fluency is . . .)*

    Level One: Welcome to Lifestyles of the Rich and Famous! People magazine keeps me up to date on what the rich are up to.

    Level Two: I mostly get my information passively from the mainstream media and financial press.

    Level Three: I spend a lot of time educating myself through listening to my advisors, as well as through books and magazines. I make sure I take advice carefully. If someone has been successful in their field I am more apt to take their advice than that of someone who sits on TV and tells me what I should and shouldn't do.

I want my advisors to have proven track records in the areas they are advising in, so I ask my network for referrals frequently. I use the mass media and financial press to see what the average person is doing and often use contrarian strategies.

21b. *I learn about rich people by . . .*

Level One: What I see on TV and in the mass media.

Level Two: Mostly through the mass media. They sure are a different breed.

Level Three: I have friends and peer groups who are wealthy. I attend wealth-building events to connect with people and watch them, to see and learn about them and what they do. I do keep an eye on the media, but I also recognize that most mass-media publications tend to present caricatures of the rich rather than accurately inform me.

Congratulations on making it through this key section of the book. It will take time and dedication to master all five languages of financial fluency, but the rewards are more than worth it.

In the next section of the book you'll learn how to master your wealth vehicle so that you can convert your net worth into passive, residual income.

SECRET #4: Create Your Wealth Map and Build Your Passive Residual Income

CHAPTER 14

Creating Your
Personal Wealth Map

id you know that *everyone* has a
wealth plan that he or she is following? And your wealth plan will either
lead you to financial riches or financial ruin? Now here's the most shock-
ing part of all: For over 96 percent of the western world that wealth plan
is designed for financial mediocrity at best and for financial failure at
worst.

We've already talked about that traditional wealth plan of get a good
education so that you can land a good job (as determined by its security
and salary). Then work for 40 to 50 years saving as you go. Invest your
leftover money in conventional investments such as mutual funds and
company's 401(k) so that you can retire at age 65 or 70. Then *hope* that
your money doesn't run out while you're still alive. Not a very inspiring
plan is it? Especially considering that this plan flat out fails 9 out of 10
people who end up finding their golden years full of economic uncertainty and anxiety.

Why then would anyone choose to follow a plan that at best leads to financial sufficiency but not real freedom and also has such an astronomi-
cally high failure rate? Sadly, because the average person doesn't know
any better. He simply accepts the barrage of financial programming he
takes in passively from the world around him. She unconsciously gives
up her dreams in order to be "*realistic*" about her expectations in life.

But we know you are different. Otherwise you never would have bought a book called, *The Maui Millionaires for Business*. You may or may not have had a winning financial plan up to this point in your life, but either way, in the next seven chapters you will learn a comprehensive, step-by-step game plan for financial success. We call it your Wealth Map™.

Your Wealth Map is a seven-step plan that you can follow to turn your hard work and business successes into financial freedom and security. When you follow each of these seven simple steps you will be assured of building your wealth the right way and being in total control of your financial destiny.

In the first part of this book you learned over 100 ideas, strategies, and techniques to build a massively successful Level Three business. Now it's time to focus on the in-the-trenches work required to build your wealth *independent* of your business.

Remember, it's not enough for you to be a wildly successful entrepreneur, you must also master the wealth skills you need to build your wealth independent of your business. When you do this you enjoy a level of control over your financial life that allows you the freedom to do what you want, when you want, where you want, with whom you want. It gives you the financial certainty that your family will be provided for no matter what comes. It gives you the financial strength to share your wealth, your time, your knowledge, your skills, and your contacts with the world to leave a lasting legacy.

Let's start out with the big picture.

A Quick Overview of the Wealth Map

Step One: The Strategic Financial Assessment—Determining exactly where you are on your financial journey.

Step Two: The Wealth Curve™—Level-by-level insights to accelerate your wealth building by sharpening your focus and leveraging your investing efforts.

Step Three: The Great Risk Hoax™—The single greatest myth ever perpetrated on the investing public (and how you can escape it).

Step Four: Choosing Your Wealth Vehicles—How to know which investment vehicle(s) is the right fit for you so that you can consistently grow your wealth, eventually converting your net worth into passive residual income.

Step Five: Tapping Into Your Cash Flow Maximizer™—How you can leverage your greatest cash flow advantages to increase your investment returns and accelerate your wealth building.

Step Six: Preemptive Tax Strategy—A revolutionary approach to strategically lower your tax burden and supercharge your wealth building.

Step Seven: Getting Into Action—A step-by-step guided question sequence to help you identify the key action steps you need to take to implement your Wealth Map quickly and easily, plus a system for ongoing financial review that's guaranteed to help you stay on track.

Conquering Fear Before You Begin

You may find that no matter what level you are at, the first step—determining your precise financial picture—might be scary for you. That's okay. Fear is a normal, often healthy reaction to the unknown. It's how you act in the presence of your fear that will determine what your ultimate economic rewards will be.

Have you ever seen a frightened toddler? You go to put him to bed and he clings to you because he is scared of the monsters under his bed. Toddlers deal with their fear by covering their eyes and hiding under the covers. Why? Because they believe that if they can't see those monsters then those monsters won't be able to see them.

Well, what's adorable in a toddler isn't so cute in our adult lives. We know that just because we close our eyes doesn't mean the "monsters"in our financial lives disappear. Yet, there are still people out there who deal with their finances the same way: by covering their eyes and burying their heads under the covers. These are the people who toss their bills, unopened, onto a corner of their desks. They don't balance their checkbooks, let alone have the accurate accounting necessary to generate accurate financial statements for themselves. At the extreme, they work on the assumption that as long as the ATM still spits out cash all is well. Maybe you know people like this. They just aren't willing to face the reality of their financial situations, and because of this, they can't do anything to improve it.

This same behavior manifests in another costly way—in the act of hiding—hiding from partners, hiding from spouses, hiding from themselves. In essence all this fear-based hiding is really just a way of shrinking their world and guaranteeing financial failure. It's a defense that may give temporary relief but ultimately leads to financial ruin.

So what's the way out? Open your eyes; look under your financial bed; have the courage to see if there really are monsters under there. You'll do this in Step One of the Wealth Map—your Strategic Financial Assessment. We urge you to use real numbers from your personal financial situation. In case you don't want to put your personal financial life down in the pages of this book we've made all the worksheets from this section of the book available for you to download for free at **www.MauiMillionaires.com/book**.

But don't continue to hide by saying you'll do these exercises later. If you want to be wealthy then *this* is your chance to step up and play full out. Right now. And the only way to do that is to use real numbers. We encourage you to keep your results private but discuss them with your significant other and your wealth advisors. Remember, if you use pretend numbers, you're still hiding. And nothing grows in the dark, especially not you. So use real numbers and get used to that uncomfortable feeling. It's a sign that you are stretching and growing, and it is the best way to guarantee that you will be growing your wealth.

Are you ready to get started? Good, then go to the next chapter and let's get started with Step One: Your Strategic Financial Assessment.

CHAPTER 15

Your Strategic Wealth Assessment (Step One)

The first step of creating your Wealth Map is to determine exactly where you are financially right now, and what the trend is in your wealth building. You'll do this in three small steps.

First, you'll fill in the financial numbers in Part A of the assessment. This will include things like your net worth, your sources of income, your lifestyle cost (S-Factor), your tax payments, and your return on net worth (R-Score™). We'll walk you through this part in just a moment taking our time so that you really understand this powerful financial snapshot.

Then, in Part B, you'll determine where you stand on seven key scales that will help you better understand your financial values and character.

Finally, in Part C, you'll create some clear financial goals for your net worth and passive, residual income that give purpose and direction to your wealth building.

Let's begin with Part A. (See Figure 15.1.)

Your Net Worth

Your net worth is the sum total of all your financial assets less any outstanding debts you owe. Your net worth is one of the most essential keys

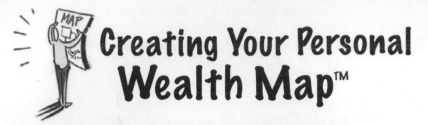

Creating Your Personal Wealth Map™

Step One: The Strategic Financial Assessment

1. _____

2. _____

3. _____

Part A: Your Financial Wealth

		Last Period	This Period	Trend	Insights
Assets					
	Your Net Worth (1)				
Income	Active (2)				
	Passive (3)				
	Passive, Residual (4)				
= 2+3+4	Total (5)				
Expenses	"Total" Expenses (S-Factor) (6)				
	Taxes (7)				
R-Score™					
= 4/1	Strict (8)				
= 3+4/1	Loose (9)				
Giving	Total Giving (10)				
= 10/5	Giving Percentage (11)				

FIGURE 15.1   Part A: Your Financial Assessment

You can download free copies of these powerful financial worksheets simply by going to **www.MauiMillionaires.com/book**. See the Appendix for full details.

to providing future security and freedom for your family. The best part is that your net worth isn't a fixed number. In fact, later in this chapter, you'll learn how you can effectively *double* your net worth overnight.

But first we need you to calculate your net worth. Just follow the worksheet we've provided in Figure 15.2 on the next page.

To really make the most of your Strategic Financial Assessment you'll be comparing your results from last year with your financial results this year. This way not only will you see exactly where you stand financially, but you'll see the *trend*. This way you'll see which way your finances are moving, and how fast. Just like a pilot, you can use this information to navigate with precision through the skies of building wealth.

For your first time through this Wealth Map we suggest you compare your last year's financial results with this year's results. In the future though, we suggest you look at your financial results quarterly, comparing your last financial quarter with your present financial quarter. This will give you more regular feedback that will prove invaluable as you fine-tune your Wealth Map.

That means you'll need to determine your net worth last year and your current net worth this year. Go ahead and take the time to do this now before you move on to the next section of this chapter.

Determining Your Financial Trend

To determine your financial trend you need two sets of numbers to make a comparison. Subtract your net worth figures in the second column (this year) from the first column (last year), and then divide the result by the figures in the first column. This simple formula gives you the percentage increase or decrease, which is the trend you are looking for.

$$\text{Trend} = \frac{\text{(This Period} - \text{Last Period)}}{\text{Last Period}}$$

What do you see? Did your net worth rise, stay the same, or fall? We call this the trend. How is your financial wealth trending?

You'll see another column to the right of the trend column, headed "Insights." As you go through this exercise now, and every time you revisit your Wealth Map, write down your insights—those "a-ha" moments where you see something in a way you've never seen before. Capture those moments as they happen by writing down your thoughts, free form and in as much detail as you need to be able to recall what they were months or years down the road.

MAUI
Net Worth Worksheet

ASSETS		LIABILITIES	
Cash on hand and in bank	$ _____	Accounts Payable	$ _____
Savings Accounts	$ _____	Notes Payable to Banks & Others	$ _____
IRA or Other Retirement Accounts	$ _____	Installment Debt Total Due	$ _____
Life Insurance (cash surrender value only)	$ _____	Loan on Life Insurance	$ _____
Businesses (conservative equity if business is sold)	$ _____	Mortgages on Real Estate	$ _____
		Unpaid Taxes	$ _____
Stocks & Bonds	$ _____	Other Liabilities	$ _____
Real Estate	$ _____		
Collectibles	$ _____	Total Liabilities	$ _____
Other Assets	$ _____		
Total Assets	$ _____	Total Assets	$ _____
		Less: Total Liabilities	$ _____
		NET WORTH	$ _____

FIGURE 15.2   The Maui Millionaire Net Worth Worksheet

One question we often get when we teach this Wealth Map process in our advanced workshops is what to do with unrealized gains. Unrealized gains are increases in the value of your assets that you have not yet realized by converting them to cash. For example, your business was worth $3 million last year, but this year, you and your team increased its fair market value to $5 million. That $2 million of increased value is called unrealized gains, because it's equity in your business that you haven't yet turned into cash.

First, we have to say that you just discovered one of the best kept secrets to building wealth—unrealized gains. Not only can you leverage your unrealized gains by borrowing or using other powerful tax and investing strategies, but you have no tax owed on your unrealized gains! Imagine, in our above example you just created $2 million of value for your business and yet you owe *zero* in taxes until the day you turn those unrealized gains into realized gains by selling. In effect, unrealized gains allow you to compound your asset's growth while paying no taxes— sometimes for years, sometimes *forever*!

But going back to our original question, should you include those unrealized gains in your net worth calculations? Our answer is yes, but we urge you to be very conservative in your estimations of fair market value for your assets. You also need to factor in the realistic costs of selling those assets to unlock that equity such as brokerage commissions, taxes owed, and other transaction costs. Make sure you note the assumptions you made in writing so that in subsequent iterations of your Wealth Map's Strategic Financial Assessment you are consistent. In a real way the choices you make about how to deal with unrealized gains don't matter so much as your *consistency* with applying your assumptions. What makes your Strategic Financial Assessment work so well is the *relative* change you see over time.

Now it's time to move on to look at the next area of the assessment: your income.

Your Income*

The next section is income, which is broken down into active, passive and passive residual. Remember we're not using strict tax definitions of

---

*We urge you to get a copy of our last book, *The Maui Millionaires*, and read pages 167–209. In those chapters we go into great detail about The Five Wealth Factors™ that you are working with in this section of *The Maui Millionaires for Business*. We just didn't have the space in this new book to repeat all the powerful insights and information that we had already shared in the last book.

types of income here. Rather we are using three practical definitions for the three main types of functional income.

Income

Active
+ Passive
+ Passive Residual
_____

= Total Income

The three types of income we use are active income, passive income, and passive residual income.

Active income is money that you work for day after day. This is the typical earned income that 99 percent of the world goes to work to earn each day. Usually active income comes to you in the form of wages or salary that you earn from working a job. It can also flow to you from your active efforts of running a business that you own. Active income is usually reported to you on either a W-2, a 1099, or a K-1 form from an active business partnership. The key distinction that makes a source of income active is the hours you spend earning that income stream. If you work 10 hours or more per month securing that income stream, then that is active income for you.

Where did we come up with that 10-hour-or-less-per-month criteria for when income is passive versus active? We chose it ourselves based on the many years we've spent working with wealthy people and building our own personal fortunes. Every income stream takes some work, no matter how little, to maintain that income stream. But active income sources require many more hours to secure than passive income sources.

Passive income is money you get that you had to work less than an average of 10 hours per month to create. Passive income isn't the same as passive residual income. It's differentiated from passive residual income in that it happens once. For example, it could come from the sale of your business; or the sale of real estate you own; or the sale of stocks, bonds, or mutual funds that you had in your portfolio. Passive income almost always comes to you in the form of a capital gain. A capital gain is the profit you earn when you sell an asset you own for more money than you paid for it.

Passive residual income, on the other hand, is income that flows to you again and again. For example, it can be quarterly distributions you enjoy from a passive business interest you own; interest you earn from money market accounts; dividends from securities you own; royalties you collect from intellectual property you license out; monthly income you earn from commercial real estate you own but have professional managers look after.

The key distinction between passive and passive residual income is that passive income comes in big chunks, but those chunks are one- time payments. Passive residual income flows to you month after month, quarter after quarter, year after year.

Passive income is crucial for you as you aggressively grow your net worth, but to be truly financially free, at some point you must shift your investing focus to transform your net worth into passive residual cash flow. This is what makes you truly financially free—income that regularly flows to you again and again.

It's time now for you to fill in the income section of your Strategic Financial Assessment. Once you're done filling in this information on income for this year and for last year, again calculate your trend and record your insights. Did you increase your active income? How about your passive income? What about your passive residual income? Take the time right now to fill in your real numbers. Remember, saying you'll do it later is nothing more than a way to hide. If you want to be wealthy then you've got to get yourself to do the things ordinary people won't—so fill in your numbers!

Expenses

Being financially free means your passive residual income is more than enough to support your lifestyle. But how much does your current lifestyle cost? What does it cost you to live your life each year? Most people have no clue what their current lifestyle costs them on an annual basis. Is it any wonder that the average person will never become financially free? They don't have a clear understanding of the minimum mark they are trying to reach.

We term the cost of your current lifestyle on an annual basis your S-Factor. As you can imagine, depending on what lifestyle you have chosen for yourself that number may be spartanly low or extravagantly high, or more likely somewhere in between. The simpler your tastes, the lower your S-Factor, which stands for Simplicity Factor.

Are we suggesting that to become a Maui Millionaire you lead an ascetic life and disavow all desires for worldly possessions? Hardly. For now we merely want you be aware of what your current S-Factor is so that you can make some intelligent choices of what is most important to you.

Your S-Factor includes all your personal expenses except for taxes, which are accounted for as a separate line item (7).

Just like you did for your net worth and income, fill in your S-Factor and total taxes paid from last year and this year, then calculate the percentage change so you can see the trend. Fill these in, along with any insights that come to you, in lines 6 and 7 of your Strategic Financial Assessment.

Now it's time to turn our attention to one final area: your ability to convert your net worth into passive and passive residual income.

Your R-Score

The final area of your Strategic Financial Assessment is your R-Score: your *return on net worth*. Your R-Score essentially measures your ability to turn your net worth into passive and passive residual income. The higher your R-Score, the higher your rate of return that you are able to generate on your entire net worth. Most people only measure their cash-on-cash returns on each investment. But this is too narrow a focus to see how you are utilizing your wealth to build more wealth. You need to look at the entire forest, and in the case of your investing prowess, the best number to measure to see this big picture is your R-Score.

Your R-Score

Level Two or "Loose" R-Score
Passive Income
+ Passive residual income
———————————————
÷ Net Worth

Level Three or "Strict" R-Score
Passive residual income
———————————————
÷ Net Worth

There are two ways to calculate your R-Score, and which one you choose depends on where you are. If you're Level Two—aggressively growing your net worth—then your R-Score will be your total passive and passive residual income, divided by your net worth (this is also known as your Loose R-Score). If you're Level Three—transitioning from actively working on creating income to being completely passive and financially free—you'll measure your Strict R-Score, which is calculated as your passive residual income divided by your net worth. When your R-Score is more than your S-Factor, you're financially free.

R-Score > S-Factor = Financial Freedom

Take a moment to fill in lines 8 and 9 in Figure 15.1. As you do, pay attention to what your R-Score figures mean. We believe that your R-Score represents one of your greatest leverage points to create massive wealth *fast*.

It is a mistake to think of your net worth only as a lump sum of money. Instead, Maui Millionaires know that their net worth is really the cash flow factory that produces cash flow. Don't just look at net worth as an asset, but think of it in terms of the passive residual cash flow you are able to generate from it. In fact, Maui Millionaires know that their effective net worth isn't fixed at any one moment. For example, take an ordinary millionaire with a net worth of $1 million. Imagine this millionaire had an R-Score of 5 percent. This means that each year this millionaire generates $50,000 from his $1 million net worth.

But what if you weren't just a millionaire, but instead you were a highly-skilled and financially-savvy Maui Millionaire with an R-Score of 10 percent? Assuming you had a net worth of that same $1 million your R-Score means that your net worth generates $100,000 a year of passive residual income. You have *double* the cash flow from the same net worth. In a very real way when you double your R-Score you effectively double your net worth.

The real lesson here is clear: Your effective net worth is never fixed, it is directly correlated to your ability to invest it to generate a rate of return in the form of passive residual cash flow. In other words, your R-Score multiplies the effective size of your net worth! This is why Maui Millionaires believe so strongly in the leverage of investing in their financial education. They've learned that each dollar wisely invested in their own earning capacity and financial fluency yields a hundredfold return on their effective net worth.

Think about it this way. If you could trade in your car that gets 10 mpg for a car that gets 20 mpg you would be able to go twice as far on the same amount of gas. This is the wealth multiplying power of your R-Score. Now imagine how powerful it would be to be so financially fluent that it would be like having a car that gets 50 mpg!

Part B: Your Financial Values and Character

In this section of your Strategic Financial Assessment you'll clarify where you personally exist at this moment in time on seven key continuums. Your goal here will be to mark where you fall on each of the next seven questions. Remember, there are no right answers, and in fact we'd expect your answers to be all over the place depending on your values, your goals, and your personality. Also, your current financial situation

Part B: Your Financial Values & Character

1. What is the goal of your wealth building?

Spend down wealth   Grow wealth

2. Wealth Frame™?

Your lifetime   Multi-generational

3. Z-Cost™ Tolerance?

Low tolerance for risk   High tolerance for risk

4. Active Participation & Management?

Minimal Time   Full Time

5. Advantages?

Few or no Advantages   Many Advantages

6. Importance of Tax Efficiency?

Low   High

7. Importance of Giving and Legacy?

FIGURE 15.3   Part B: Your Financial Values & Character

will greatly impact your answers. Your Level One answers will probably be very different from your answers at Level Two or Level Three.

Mark your answers to the following seven questions on the appropriate continuums in Figure 15.3. Again, there is no right or wrong answer, just mark what you think is the right place on the continuum for you in that specific area.

1. *What is the goal of your wealth building?* The two extremes here are spending down your wealth, and not tapping into your wealth at all but rather letting it keep growing untouched. If you're in Level One or Level Two, growing your wealth will probably be more important and your mark will likely be closer to the right. But how about those of you in Level Three, who are looking for a way to slow down? You may be looking to spend some of what you've accumulated. Most people will fall somewhere between and will be focusing on growing wealth, while taking at least some time to enjoy what they're working for.

2. *What is your Wealth Frame?* Are you building wealth for your lifetime, or are you looking beyond, to your children, your grandchildren, or to a charitable project you feel passionate about? Depending on your personal Wealth Frame, you could take different approaches to building wealth. If your plan is a multigenerational one, you're going to need more, which means you need to be more aggressive in your investing strategies and much more conscious of your spending patterns.

3. *What is your Z-Cost™ tolerance?* This is what we refer to as your ability to sleep at night. Your Z-Cost tolerance measures your ability to deal with risk. Some of you love risk—you jump out of perfectly good airplanes with a big silk bag on your back. Others of you wouldn't jump out of a golf cart idling in neutral. We're going to talk about risk a lot more in a little bit, but for now, mark where you fall on the spectrum.

4. *What is your active participation and management preference?* Some people love to roll up their sleeves and actively manage their portfolios. Other people like to do a few things and leave the rest to their team. And some folks want to do the absolute minimum and like to stay almost completely hands-off. Your preferences here will feed into your overall strategy. If you want to be completely passive, for example, you'll need a different strategy in terms of which investment vehicles you choose and how you cultivate and utilize your advisor team.

    On that note—there is such a thing as being too passive. If you're too passive, the danger is you aren't paying attention to what's going on, blindly trusting in your advisors and team to keep the car going. But taking your hands off the steering wheel of your wealth vehicle is the same as taking your hands off the steering wheel of your car. No matter how well tuned your car, or how straight the road, sooner or later it's going to start to drift. Not to mention what happens when you come to a sudden curve in the road! You need to check in from time to time, and make sure your vehicle doesn't leave the road. Plus, you need reliable gauges you can consistently look at—monthly, quarterly, and annually—to make sure you're not about to overheat or run out of gas.

5. *What are your Unique Advantages™?* Advantages are the things that help you consistently outperform the market in a specific niche. Are you a great negotiator? Are you a powerful strategist? Are you a promotional or marketing genius? Can you use your analytic prowess plus your experience in a niche or asset class to spot hidden value? Do you have great contacts that you can call on to give you specialized information that gives you a legal edge? The more advantages you have, the more your business and wealth-building strategies will differ from someone who has few advantages. Each advantage you have is a potential leverage point that you can harness to magnify your returns.

6. *How important is tax efficiency to you?* When you make investment decisions, how important to you are tax considerations? We'll be discussing both tax efficiency and Tax Power Percentages later on in the Wealth Map. For now, how important is it to you to minimize the tax consequences of your investment moves when you buy, sell, shift, or move your investment? For example, if you are primarily investing through your self-directed IRA or pension, then in the short run, tax considerations are probably less important to you when you buy or sell a specific asset in your portfolio. On the other hand, if you're looking to compound your investment growth, then you may go to great lengths to minimize the tax consequences of financial moves you make.

7. *How important is giving and legacy to you?* As you build your fortune? How important is it to you to leave behind a lasting legacy that touches the world? We hope that as your wealth grows so will your joy at the thought of using giving to create an inspiring legacy that lives on well past your time here on earth.

This is a great exercise to use to learn about yourself. Part A was fairly cut and dry—you were working with numbers. In Part B, you're beginning to examine your needs and perceptions when it comes to your wealth-building plan. Chances are you'll discover you've got a lot more emotional investment in these questions and where you fall on the continuums than you may have thought.

In the final section—Part C—you'll have the chance to clarify your financial goals.

Part C: Your Financial Goals

It's been said that building wealth without clear goals to engage your passion and energies is like trying to choose the best route to get to a party you don't have the address for. Now is the time for you to reaffirm your financial goals in a simple, yet powerful format that our elite Maui Mastermind clients have used for years.

We encourage you to set your financial goals in threes. The first goal is your close goal, and it's one you should feel very confident that you'll hit. Your second goal is your growth goal, and it should be one you feel confident that you'll hit, even if it may take a bit longer than you put down. Your final goal is your stretch goal, and it should push you to the edge of your self-belief.

We've found that by setting your financial goals in threes you will not overstate your close goals, which means you're much more likely to hit them, plus your stretch goal really works on you to help you expand your ideas about what is possible for you.

Ultimately your financial goals are something you create to engage and energize yourself, not to obsess over.

Take a moment and thoughtfully fill in your three financial goals in Figure 15.4.

Part C: Your Financial Goals

	By when	PRI (annual)	NW
E.g.	By 12-31-12	$200,000	$3 million
Financial Freedom Goal #1:			
Financial Freedom Goal #2:			
Financial Freedom Goal #3:			

FIGURE 15.4   Part C: Your Financial Goals

Congratulations for finishing the first step of the Wealth Map. This step was, in fact, the hardest one of all so you really accomplished something. It's all downhill from here!

By the way, this is probably a good time to mention that you don't have to do your Wealth Map in one sitting. When we use the Wealth Map in Maui we do it bit by bit over several days. Take the time you need to digest and fully work through each step.

When you're ready, go to the next chapter and let's take Step Two together!

CHAPTER 16

The Wealth Curve
(Step Two)

Throughout earlier chapters of this book you've learned about the three-level distinction. You've learned the difference between Level One, Level Two, and Level Three businesses. You've also learned the wealth distinctions between how people at Level One, Level Two, and Level Three view money, wealth, and financial decisions. Now it's time to focus with great clarity and precision on the three levels of wealth building and how where you are in this model will fundamentally inform you on how to best focus your wealth-building efforts. We call this distinction the Wealth Curve because each level has definite strategies and insights that will help you focus your wealth-building activities. By applying the lessons of the Wealth Curve, you'll be able to tap into powerful leverage points to radically accelerate your wealth creation. (See Figure 16.1 for an overview of the three levels.)

Let's get started with Level One.

Level One: Getting Started

Focus: Making the definite decision to be wealthy and quickly creating the knowledge base you need to begin building from in Level Two.

The Wealth Curve

Level 3
Passive, Residual Cashflow!

FOCUS: Converting a large part of your net worth into secure income streams and solid, longterm investments.

LEVERAGE POINT: Invest for Cashflow

Level 2
Aggressive Growth

FOCUS: Building your asset base & financial skills.

LEVERAGE POINT: Invest for "Forced Appreciation"

Level 1
Getting Started!

FOCUS: Building a solid base of financial and investment skills.

LEVERAGE POINT: Invest in self via quality education and outside experts.

FIGURE 16.1   The Wealth Curve

Leverage Points:

- Getting very clear on your driving reasons to be wealthy.
- Reading books, taking online courses, and attending live workshops to help you become financially fluent.
- Creating a mastermind group of other like-minded individuals to help each other become wealthy.
- Tracking your financial life to create accurate personal financial statements.

There are three distinct stages to your wealth building, each with specific, definite goals for you to focus on. For Level One wealth builders the essential focus is to learn enough to get started, with the biggest lesson being to learn to overcome the fear of getting started so that they can get themselves into action. Level One is your departure point. It begins the moment you make the concrete decision to build great wealth. While in Level One, it's essential that you invest most heavily in your own financial education.

The financial education you need is a practical education focused on helping you become financially fluent in all the five key financial languages (Money, Wealth, Cash Flow, Business, and Leadership). *Now* is the time to invest heavily in yourself and your earning capacity by reading the books, taking the online courses, and attending the live workshops. This is also the perfect time to cultivate mentoring relationships with more experienced Level Three business owners who can give you input and guidance along the way.

We also suggest that you create a mastermind group of other like-minded wealth builders who are equally committed to building something special in their lifetimes*. By working together using the mastermind principle, you'll be able to help each other achieve your dreams much faster than any of you could do individually in isolation.

During this stage of your wealth building we recommend that you don't invest large amounts of money in any investment, because you haven't developed the skills or network to give yourself the advantage you need to safely invest for the greatest returns. Instead, use the time

---

*For a step-by-step game plan to create and harness a mastermind group we refer you to *The Maui Millionaires*, pages 125–164. You can also download a free e-book titled *Three Secrets to Mastermind Your Way to Millions*, as part of the Millionaire Fast-Track Program at **www.MauiMillionaires.com/book**. See the Appendix for details.

and money to read the books, take the online courses, and attend the financial and personal development workshops that will help you lay down a solid foundation upon which to build enduring wealth. A little bit of prudence and education will go a long way to helping you make intelligent financial choices in this early stage of your wealth building.

Level Two

In just a moment you'll learn about the three stages of Level Two wealth building. But first, let's take a moment to describe Level Two as a whole. It's important for you to have the big picture first before we break Level Two down into finer detail to help make it easier for you to sharpen your focus to get better results.

As a Level Two wealth builder it's time to begin building in earnest. It is in Level Two where you will have your steepest learning curve as a wealth builder. The focus of Level Two is to invest for aggressive equity growth. As for which wealth vehicle you choose for your investment vehicle, we'll leave this aside for now. (Don't worry, we'll focus an entire chapter on just that question later in the book.) The key to Level Two is to invest not for appreciation but rather to only invest for "*forced appreciation*." The difference is that investing for appreciation is the slow path to eventual wealth, while investing for forced appreciation is the route that all Maui Millionaires eventually find to build their fortune fast—typically in less than 10 years.

Forced appreciation comes when you buy an asset, whether it be a business, a property, or some other asset, and because of how you bought it, or because of the work you add to it after you buy it, that asset becomes massively more valuable. For example, perhaps your company buys a controlling interest in an outside company that is in financial trouble. Because your company is financially stable it's easy for you to get the financing your newly acquired company needs to not only stabilize, but to rapidly expand operations. Perhaps you bought this struggling company for $2.3 million but within 24 months it's valued at $5 million or more. This is an example of forced appreciation. The increased value you enjoy had nothing to do with passive market forces, but rather you forced the asset to become more valuable by the way you bought it and the resources and talent you brought to the company after you closed on the business.

The reason why it is so important for you to invest for forced appreciation in Level Two wealth building is because this is the fastest, surest road to wealth. Plus, since most of your gains will be unrealized gains, it's also extremely tax efficient. For example, you may start a business with a few thousand dollars working out of your home (many Maui Millionaires have started with a whole lot less!). You spend the next five years building and growing your business. At this point it is generating hundreds of thousands of dollars of cash flow for you each year and has a market value hundreds or thousands of times what you started with. This is the beauty of forced appreciation—it allows you to leverage your time, talent, and energy to build wealth fast.

To get this forced appreciation in the early stages of your wealth building you are going to have to put in time and energy to create this value in the world. Later you'll be able to harness other people through teams, systems, and outsourced solutions to unlock this powerful wealth-building potential.

Now let's break Level Two down into three distinct stages, similar to what we did with the three stages of Level Two businesses back in Part One of the book. By doing this you'll be able to hone in on the key leverage points you can use to speed up your wealth building.

Early Stage Level Two

Focus: Getting started building your asset base

Leverage Points:

- Establishing sound financial habits.
- Beginning to build your business and investing networks.
- Investing in your financial education and earning capacity.
- Engaging in "learning deals" and/or launching your own business.

Early stage Level Two is a time where you begin to establish healthy financial habits—getting rid of bad debts, learning how to make smart business deals, and spotting profitable investment opportunities. You'll also continue to invest in yourself and your earning capacity.

At this point it's essential that you begin to build your professional network of contacts that you will later rely on to help you find opportunities and to best maximize the opportunities you select. One of the best ways to grow your network is to create learning deals where you can work with experienced mentors on their deals. Even if you have to volunteer your time, the contacts and experience you will gain will later be worth millions to you. How do you create these contacts? One way to start is through your philanthropic work, but that is something we're going to share with you in Secret Five of this book (no fair reading ahead!).

Usually the best investment you can make as an early-stage Level Two wealth builder is launching your own business. There is no better vehicle to create wealth fast than starting and building your own successful business. But it's also important that you begin in Level Two to build wealth that is independent of your primary business. Why? Because there might be a day when you no longer have that business. For example, when you sell your company for $3 million, will you have the investment skills to intelligently invest that lump sum of money for passive residual income?

Why do we keep reinforcing this point? Because both of us have built multimillion dollar companies that we never expected to sell or let go of, only to find ourselves selling or closing down those companies. It was a painful lesson that we needed to build not only our asset base independent of our businesses, but to also grow the network and skill base we needed to use our wealth to grow more wealth. You can ignore us on this point, thinking that there will never be a day that you won't own your business with its cushy cash flow, but then again we might be right. So prepare for the day you no longer have your business and use early-stage Level Two to start the process of building your wealth in parallel but independent of your business.

Middle Stage Level Two

Focus: Aggressively growing your asset base using forced appreciation

Leverage Points:

- Refining your business and financial skills.
- Strategically using Preemptive Tax Strategies to accelerate your growth of net worth.
- Expanding your network.
- Establishing your financial systems.
- Putting into place at least a basic level of estate planning and asset protection.

In middle stage Level Two you are locked on the aggressive growth of your asset base. Now is the time to take some calculated risks. Here is the place to intelligently use leverage to magnify your returns.

As a middle stage Level Two wealth builder it's critical that you use smart tax strategies to allow as much of your asset growth to happen in a tax advantaged way as possible. For example, you might use 1031 exchanges to delay paying capital gains taxes when you sell a commercial building your business moved from. Or you might use a Roth IRA to invest in someone else's business. Or maybe you won't sell your asset at all, instead you'll tap into your equity by borrowing it out, and invest that money, which is tax free because it's a loan. We'll talk more about Pre-emptive Tax Strategy in Step Six of the Wealth Map, for now just note that it's a powerful leverage point to maximize your net worth as you aggressively grow your asset base in middle stage Level Two.

Do You Know the Difference Between Speculating and Investing?

Speculators buy at market value (or close to it), with the hope that the value will increase in the short-term.

Investors buy below market value, or if buying at market value, make sure the investment will produce cash flow.

In middle stage Level Two it's also the time to begin putting your personal financial systems into place. It's impossible to grow your wealth fast and in a sustainable way without sound financial systems in place. How do you keep your personal books? Who organizes your financial records? How do you coordinate your advisor team? These are all essential elements of building sound financial systems.*

Something else to start thinking about here is your financial fluency, specifically the Language of Money. Many people who are just beginning to look at their own wealth planning may find that their skills in this area are fairly rudimentary. Your system may eventually consist of a book-keeper, personal assistant, CPA, brokers for securities, real estate, mortgages, and insurance, financial planner, and a good attorney. Eventually, your system may be simpler, or it may be more complex. The goal is to get things out of your head and to a place where other people can do many of the things you've been doing (or not doing). Leveraging other people's abilities is a key skill to master—wealth-building is a team sport!

Finally, if you haven't already done so, now is the time to sit down with your advisor team and put into place a clear, comprehensive estate planning and asset protection plan. While few people find this fun, the consequences of not doing it are too painful and costly to bear. That means it's time to bite the bullet and get it taken care of now.

---

*Because this is such an important topic that too many entrepreneurs ignore until it comes painfully crashing down on them later, we have included an online workshop on building sustainable, scalable financial systems for your personal wealth building as part of the Millionaire Fast-Track Program. To get instant access to this free bonus just go to **www.MauiMillionaires.com/book**. See the Appendix for details.

Advanced Stage Level Two

Focus: Transition *part* of your wealth building from equity growth to passive residual income creation

Leverage Points:

- Transitioning cash/assets into cash-flow-producing passive residual income investments.
- Tapping into your network for investment opportunities.
- Refining your financial systems.
- Transitioning your business from a Level Two into a Level Three business.

When you hit advanced stage Level Two, your wealth-building strategies begin to change. Now the focus begins to shift from investing for capital gains to investing for passive residual income. Plus you'll also shift from active involvement in your investing to a less involved role. This means you'll continue to refine your financial and other systems.

You will also focus on turning your business into a true Level Three business. When you do, you'll find yourself in a place where your business functions perfectly well without you, which is great! Now that the business really is working for you—creating a passive residual income stream that will continue with little work on your part—where will you focus your energies? That depends on how in control you're used to being. If you're used to being very hands-on you might find this a challenge at first. Persevere! The rewards are well worth it. Plus, now might be the time that you get time to pursue other dreams.

In this stage you'll also notice your investments are changing. Your focus is increasingly on those investments that generate cash flow, and you're working on your ability to spot good cash flow deals. Your network is going to become even more important. One of the great things that happens here and in Level Three is that you don't need to go looking for the deals anymore, because people in your network are bringing them to you. In fact, the chances are those deals will be coming at you in such abundance that your real challenge will be creating a screening system to filter out the deals you want to turn down! If you think about it, this is a fantastic place to be: You get to sharpen your abilities to analyze deals, be selective and choose only the deals you want, and by leveraging other people's time and skills you don't even have to spend a lot of time working in the deal to make money.

This is one more reason why it's so much easier for people who are Level Three to make so much money. They have built up a massive amount of momentum. As an advanced stage Level Two wealth builder, this is the time that you create that momentum that carries you into Level Three.

Level Three

Initial Focus (first 6–12 months): A graceful transition to true financial freedom

Leverage Points:

- Enjoyment of your accomplishment.
- Keeping your S-Factor under control.
- Giving yourself time for your Wealth Operating System to expand and getting comfortable with your new freedom.

Long-term Focus: Maintaining your wealth and reinventing your life to focus on what you are most passionate about

Leverage Points:

- Solidifying your core passive residual income systems and teams.
- Building from your heart and unique talents.
- Cultivating a Level Three perspective in all your new ventures.
- Initiating advanced level estate planning and asset protection.
- Cultivating the lifestyle of gratitude.
- Looking for ways to share your wealth with the world in healthy ways.

You've Reached Level Three— Congratulations!

There is an emotional context to this stage, and it's important to give yourself the time and space to enjoy it. Explore the world around you. Get more involved with the community needs and causes that you're passionate about, if that works for you. Get comfortable in this new place that may be unlike anything you've experienced before.

Keep your S-Factor under control while you're enjoying your new-found financial freedom. It can be truly intoxicating to begin with, and that can lead to some poor decisions. Without the daily activity and focus of our business or profession, many of us will initially feel empty and start reaching for something else to do, something to fill that emptiness. In our hurry to fill the hole we jump into something that's a poor fit.

Our best advice to you in the first 6–12 months of your transition is to sit tight and don't make any major financial moves. If you've sold a business and come into a huge piece of cash, simply put that money into the highest interest liquid short-term money market account you can find. Give your Wealth Operating System* time to expand around this new abundance. If you rush it, what's a common result? Out of control spending, with its corresponding financial hangover, just like the lottery winners we talked about way back in Chapter 1.

Once you've started to get more comfortable with your new Level Three financial reality, now is the time to start exploring and discovering what you are most passionate about. We think that true Level Three people never retire, they continually find new areas to invest their passions and energies into. But they do it in a Level Three way—on their terms and in a way that fits into their lifestyle.

The two most common things we see Level Three people do is mentor "younger" wealth builders and focus on helping the world. (We had to put the younger wealth builders in quotes because many Level Three Maui Millionaires are still in their 30s or younger!)

It's interesting that one of the most important parts of the Maui Mastermind event is when we go through special processes to help our participants discover what they want the next phase of their lives to be about. You might think that once you've made it financially then you just retire, but it rarely works that way. Maui Millionaires have too much energy, passion, and drive to sit on a beach for more than a few weeks at a time.

It's also critical that you take another comprehensive look at your estate planning and asset protection. Now more than ever it's crucial for you to protect what you've built and plan for your succession.

Level Three is where you have made the transition from active investing and business building to enjoying passive residual income. In Level Three, Maui Millionaires, who are all adept at converting cash and equity into passive residual income, transition a large portion of their net worth into hands-off income-generating investments. Ironically, it is from this place of total financial freedom that many Maui Millionaires take on their next business project that produces more forced apprecia-

---

*For those of you unfamiliar with the concept of your Wealth Operating System (WOS) we urge you to get a copy of *The Maui Millionaires* and read pages 3–78. Your WOS is the single most powerful factor affecting your ability to create, sustain, enjoy, and share great wealth.

tion than all their prior efforts combined. There is something that financial freedom adds to their wealth creations, almost like yeast to the baking of bread, that just makes the size, scope, and success of their projects go through the roof. The key is that they choose to do these projects in a Level Three way—leveraging other people, technology, outsourced solutions, and their past experiences to create huge results with minimal time involvement.

In summary, Level One is about laying the financial fluency foundation and making the definite decision to be wealthy.

Level Two is about fine-tuning your financial fluency skills and aggressively growing your net worth, usually through forced appreciation.

Level Three is all about transitioning your wealth into passive residual income, whether this be by putting a business on autopilot, or by fine-tuning your investment portfolio to churn out consistent, passive residual income—year after year.

Which Level and Stage in Your Wealth Building Are You At?

After reading through this chapter, which stage and level of wealth building are you at? Fill in the answer in the space below:

What does your focus need to be on at this stage in your wealth building? What are the key leverage points for you to tap into to accelerate your financial results?

If you're in Level One, what have you discovered about yourself? Do you need to get busy investing in your financial education? How are your skills? Where will you look to upgrade them? Do you need to work some deals as a volunteer, earning little financially but reaping rewards through education and experience?

If you're in Level Two, what have you learned about the best and highest use of your time? How about your wealth vehicle or vehicles? Are you looking to upgrade some of your skills or learn new skills?

How about those of you who have realized you're somewhere in Level Three? If this is a new place for you to be consciously, take your time! If your insight was that it's time to focus on cash flow and passive residual income, what do you need to know to make that happen? Do you need to take it slowly, perhaps doing some smaller deals so you've got room to make mistakes?

No matter what level you're in, what insights have you had regarding your wealth-building skills and focus in general?

Finally, what three areas do you want to learn about over the next 12 months to help you reach the next stage of your wealth building? What things do you think will have the most powerful, positive impact on your wealth-building strategies and plans?

In the next chapter we'll talk about risk. You'll learn about the single greatest half-truth ever perpetrated on the public with respect to risk, which we call The Great Risk Hoax. You may find that by the end of this next chapter that everything you thought you knew about risk and investing was based on a misleading myth and that you have some serious action steps to take to remediate the damage done to your fortune.

CHAPTER 17

The Great Risk Hoax
(Step Three)

e want to start with a very bold statement that we know to be true but which flies in the face of conventional thinking about investing—the way you were taught to view risk is fundamentally flawed. In fact, it's worse than that. The way you were taught to understand risk in your investing is *deadly* to your wealth.

Before we show you exactly how you have been misled, let's first get clear on what the conventional view on risk is. First, we're talking here about *investment risk*. Conventional thinking says that there is an absolute continuum of risk that starts with ultra-low risk on one end and goes off at the other end to ultra-high risk. Furthermore, the conventional model of risk says that any investment can be objectively placed with a high degree of accuracy on the risk continuum, and that generally speaking, the higher the risk, the greater the potential rewards.

For example, bonds are less risky than income-producing stocks, which in turn are less risky than growth stocks. And that is why bonds pay the lowest return, with income stocks giving a greater return than the bonds, but less than the growth stocks, which as the highest risk investment also have the highest return.

As you hear us lay it out this way you're probably saying well heck, anyone knows that's true. And that, our friend, is where the real danger lies. It's not with what's true, but rather it's that what so many believe to be true is in fact flawed, inaccurate, and downright misleading.

The first place you are taught to look to evaluate risk is the investment itself. What vehicle are you choosing (e.g. stocks, real estate, bonds, business start-ups, etc.)? And which specific choice are you making in that general asset category? These, we are told, are the main determiners of risk. Next of course, you also have the general market risks, which affect broad cross sections of the economy.

But what's missing here? What fundamental risk factor is almost never accounted for, yet is by far the biggest unknown with respect to risk? Do you see it yet? Let us give you a hint . . . where are *you* in the conventional model?

Imagine you are evaluating whether to invest in a piece of commercial real estate. Is that a risky investment? In isolation that question is impossible to answer. Why? Because *you* are still missing! Are you experienced at investing in commercial real estate? Have you developed your advantages of skills, contacts, experience, and information in this niche? If you have, then you will be able to mitigate many of the "risks" other people face when investing in real estate. If you have never developed any advantages in this vehicle, then no matter what the merits of any specific real estate deal, investing in commercial real estate is a risky thing for you to do. The bottom line is that it is impossible to separate discussions of risk from the investor.

Yet that is The Great Risk Hoax that the conventional thinkers have been perpetrating on a naïve public for decades. They pretend that the investor doesn't matter because, after all, any investor can turn to a wise advisor and use their expert guidance to make seasoned investing choices. Bunk! The only way to consistently lower risk is to focus on niches and wealth vehicles that you have paid your dues to master so that you have advantages over the market. How do you know if you have developed advantages in a niche or particular wealth vehicle? Simple, if you can consistently outperform the market in that niche with that wealth vehicle over time then you have advantages. If you can't, then you don't have advantages, and you need to work harder to cultivate those advantages.

The biggest mistake you can make is to ignore yourself in the risk equation. The truth is that *you are the biggest risk variable of all*. And to ignore this fact is the most expensive, the most dangerous, the most damaging wealth mistake you could ever make.

The more advantages you have in connection with an investment, the lower the risk. And, that's where The Great Risk Hoax comes into play. Most financial planners, bankers, stockbrokers, and the like will tell you that the risk is inherent in the *investment*. They'll tell you that all real estate is risky (if that's what they believe) or that all private offerings for investing in a business venture are risky. You might even find someone who tells you that investing in government bonds is risky.

That is completely wrong! Something that's risky for one person may not be risky for another. For example, there are people who make a lot of money with real estate. Just like there are a lot of people who *lose* a lot of money with real estate. The difference is the individual's advantages: their skills, contacts, and strengths. This one risk variable can change everything. Warren Buffett is a great example of someone who is fantastic at assessing risks in businesses and then buying controlling interest in those businesses. It's not risky because he understands businesses and knows what works and what doesn't work. That is his advantage. And he has billions that prove his skill and advantage in using this wealth vehicle.

David's Story

Several years back I stopped investing in mutual funds. Why? Because mutual funds are poor investment choices? Of course not. For many people they are great choices, just not for me. I've spent over a decade learning to master the art of investing in real estate. I can consistently make money in up markets, flat markets, or declining markets. This isn't to say I never lose money on deals that don't work out, but rather to say that I am able to consistently generate wealth-producing rates of return for fairly low risk levels. In fact, my advantages in commercial real estate help me consistently outperform the market by a factor of 200–300 percent. That's why I use commercial real estate as one of my primary wealth vehicles.

Diane is an expert in real estate, but she is also an expert in investing in businesses. That's why she uses both vehicles as ways to build her wealth. The bottom line is that the best way for you to lower your risk isn't to choose "*safe*" investments. Rather, the best way to lower your investment risk is to invest in niches and with wealth vehicles in which you have cultivated advantages.

Okay, now that we've done our best to throw some cold water on you to wake you up from the mass myth of the conventional way of evaluating risk, we want to dive deeper into what really are the factors that influence risk and how you can best manage that risk to create a greater return without taking on a higher degree of risk. (Yes, that is in fact quite possible, and sophisticated investors do it all the time.)

The 10 Risk Factors

Risk Factor One: Your Advantages

As we've already gone to great lengths to convince you, your expertise, experience, and contacts in a specific niche or with a specific wealth vehicle are perhaps the most potent risk factor of all.

What are your advantages? If you're investing in something that is your niche, you've got a built-in advantage, especially if you've been able to achieve higher than average returns on similar investments in the past. The great thing about niche investing is that you often get so familiar with competitors and the market around you that you can see and hear things the average person can't. This allows you to spot imperfections in the marketplace that mean huge profits with fairly low risk. You can only spot these opportunities if you are an expert in that niche or with that specific wealth vehicle.

Of course, if you try this strategy with publicly traded securities that can be bad news. In fact, in some circumstances they have a name for it—they call it "insider trading," and you can go to jail. Not good! But with nonpublic marketplaces this is encouraged and called smart investing. That's one of reasons we don't rely on investing in publicly traded securities as our wealth vehicles—because it's very hard to legally learn information that hasn't already been priced into the marketplace. But with other niches and wealth vehicles, not only is this possible, it's actually fairly straightforward.

Don't fall victim to The Great Risk Hoax. All investments and risks are not created equal. You make the difference. Know yourself and know your true risk with any investment. Now, what are your advantages?

Risk Factor Two: Control

The more control you have, the lower your risk. What do you do when you buy a publicly-traded security? You wait, and hope the stock goes up. If the company is having a bad day, can you call up the president and offer some suggestions on how to turn things around? Of course not. You have no control over the investment (unless you have so many shares that you are a major player, which is unlikely for the average noninstitutional investor).

When you are looking at an investment, consider how the decisions are being made and how the financial controls are set up. If you're in charge, is this investment something you're familiar and comfortable with? If not, do you have some support to help you make sound decisions? And if you're not in charge at all, are you comfortable with the folks who are running the place, controlling the money, and signing the checks?

Risk Factor Three: Transparency

Transparency is another way of saying disclosure. Many of the major stock collapses in recent years happened because of a lack of transparency; those at the top hid things from the rest of the company, from its investors, and from the public in general. This is probably one of the biggest reasons we don't do a lot of our investing in public companies. The lack of transparency can mean a greater risk, and, quite frankly, unless you picked up the stock of a company that has performed incredibly well over the years (like Microsoft or Wal-Mart), you can get bigger returns elsewhere for less risk. When evaluating an investment, ask how you will be able to check performance, and what is going on behind the scenes.

Risk Factor Four: The E-Ratio

E-Ratio™ stands for Effort/Energy/Emotion. The lower your Es, the lower the risk. How much work will you personally have to put in to make the deal happen? How much will this investment weigh on you? Will you lose sleep? (That's a warning sign, by the way.)

Risk Factor Five: Liquidity

There's two parts to liquidity: the liquidity of the investment and your own liquidity. A liquid investment is fairly straightforward—it's easy for you to quickly convert to cash without any harsh consequence. The harder it is to convert that investment, the greater the risk becomes. You see this in a lot of private placements, where private stock is issued that you can't immediately sell or you may invest in a restricted-ownership business like an LLC or LP, where you have a lot of restrictions on how and who you can sell your ownership interests to.

Your liquidity also affects your risk. The more liquid you are, the lower your risk. If you've got cash reserves, you can weather a storm. If you don't, you probably won't. We're seeing this with a lot of real estate speculators, who bought multiple properties with creative financing on the assumption that they could turn around and unload those properties without ever having to make a mortgage payment. Paper rich, and bank poor, if these properties are operating on a negative cash flow the drain may become too much at some point, leading to an unexpected and unwelcome liquidation of one or more properties. This is something Diane talks about at length in her Five Buckets Approach to Your Finances*—making sure you have the cash reserves to ride out a downturn, and how to determine how much cash reserve is right for you.

Risk Factor Six: Principal at Risk

How at risk is your principal? When you make an investment, how do you secure your cash in the event the investment fails? Do you have any tangible assets that secure your investment? Do you have a lien securing your interest or are you an equity investor? The more secure you've made your principal the lower your investing risk.

One of David's strategies when he invests in commercial properties is to not just invest for equity, but to invest as a secured creditor who has a lien against the real property securing his investment. Sometimes he accomplishes this by dividing up his investment with one entity of his loaning the deal money while with another entity he holds an equity stake. Other times he might consider using convertible debt to accomplish this. You see private equity companies do this all the time. It's a powerful strategy to lower your risk while still allowing you an enhanced return.

Risk Factor Seven: Cash Flow

This is a big one. The first thing to look at here is: Are you making a cash-flow-type investment or a capital-gain-type of investment? A cash flow investment puts money in your pocket now—a capital gain investment will pay off down the road. The further down the road you have to wait to get paid, the greater your risk. If you get involved in a cash flow investment and the cash stops rolling in after three months, you've got far

---

*You can download Diane's entire Five Buckets Approach to Your Finances from our web site, **www.MauiMillionaires.com/book**. This is a free bonus we've created as part of the Millionaire Fast-Track Program.

more options than finding out the industrial park you invested in two years ago now is the subject of a native land claim and could be tied up in court for the next 5–10 years.

Risk Factor Eight: Liability

When you make an investment, are you giving anyone or anything the right to sue you if things go wrong? For example, if you're investing in your own business, are you signing a personal guarantee in order to secure a loan? Can you mitigate the risk by negotiating a deal where you're on the hook for a shorter period of time, say 12 or 18 months? Does the liability extend beyond that asset itself? Does your personal guarantee cover just the property itself, or could the creditor reach into your other assets?

The more you are personally liable, obviously the higher the risk. This can extend to other things, too. For example, have you ever been asked to sit on the board of directors of a company? Directors aren't always found liable for the bad or illegal acts of a company—but they can be. Is the company that approached you about a directorship also offering directors' insurance? Are you going to hold your investment interest in your own name or via some liability-protecting entity like an LLC?

Risk Factor Nine: Market Risk

These are outside risks that are specific to the industry for that investment. Take hotels, for example. If the market suffers a collapse—a natural disaster, war, disease, or some such event, hotels in the area affected will suffer. When the dot-com bubble burst in Silicon Valley a few years ago, there was a period of time where high-tech start-ups couldn't find financing, no matter how solid their business plan was. When looking at an investment, consider what impact changes on the customer base or outside market could have on your investment.

Risk Factor 10: Specific Investment Choice Risk

This risk is specific to your investment itself. Let's say you invested in a franchise restaurant and opened the doors, only to have the street in front of your restaurant torn up for the next 10 months while a rapid transit line was being constructed. What's going to happen to your walk-in traffic? What if your restaurant is in a downtown area with limited parking? Or, what happens if the franchise you invested in turns out to have flawed business systems for you to run the franchise with? The bottom line is that you will need to do your deep due diligence to make sure the investment choice you are making is a sound one. The better your due diligence (which you can hire experts to help you perform) the better you are able to manage this crucial risk factor.

Creating Your Own Risk Spectrum

Now that you have a better understanding of the risk factors it's time for you to create your own personal Risk Spectrum™. Which types of investment choices are low risk for you? Which are medium risk? Which are high risk for you? Fill in your answers in the blank Risk Spectrum you see in Figure 17.1. You'll notice in Figure 17.2 David has shared his personal Risk Spectrum with you.

It's important to understand that everyone's risk spectrum is an individual reflection on themselves—their expertise and advantages, their Z-Factor tolerance, their personal financial situation. Remember that to ever look at risk in isolation from you, the investor, is to fall prey to The Great Risk Hoax.

Once you've filled in what your personal Risk Spectrum looks like, let's turn our attention to one of the most powerful ways for you to manage risk.

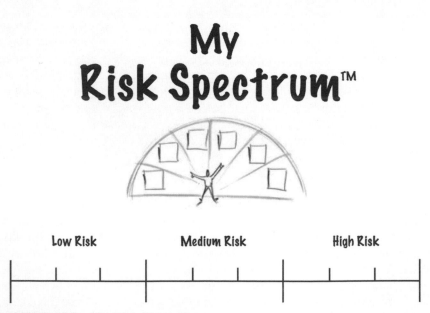

FIGURE 17.1   My Risk Spectrum

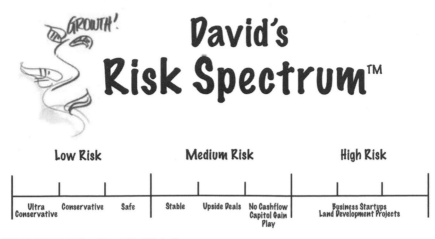

FIGURE 17.2   David's Risk Spectrum

Strategic Asset Allocation

Most people when presented with the opportunity to invest in two investments compare the returns of those two investments. But this can be misleading. It's impossible to accurately compare returns across risk categories because you are not comparing apples to apples.

A much smarter way to sort through investment opportunities is to first strategically decide how you want to apportion your entire net worth across your Risk Spectrum. For example, when David created his plan to strategically apportion his net worth across his personal risk spectrum, he decided as follows: 25 percent of his wealth in conservative low-risk investments, 50 percent in stable cash-flow-producing investments (the upper end of low risk and the lower end of medium risk on his Risk Spectrum), and 25 percent in forced appreciation, growth investments (the middle and upper end of medium risk on his Risk Spectrum.) Remember, your Risk Spectrum and asset allocation plan will probably be different, and that is exactly how it should be. Each person's Wealth Map is tailored to their own starting point and end goals.

What do you want your asset allocation to look like? You must factor in your current wealth stage and level, your age, your financial goals, your current asset base, and your financial values and character that you identified in Step One of your Wealth Map.

The next time you are presented with several investment opportunities the first question you should ask is how do they fit into your personal strategic asset allocation plans? Then and only then should you evaluate

Create Your Own
Ideal Asset Allocation

1. What are your financial goals? _____

_____

_____

_____

2. Where is your financial Starting Point? _____

_____

_____

_____

3. What are YOUR Advantages? _____

_____

_____

_____

FIGURE 17.3   Asset Allocation Plan

the deals that fit your investment needs to assess the risks and potential rewards of these deals.

Congratulations, you've just learned a key part of building wealth that most people never truly understand. In fact, with what you just learned you will now be armed with one of the most effective tools to mitigate risk in all your investing.

Of course, before you can earn those big returns you will need to choose just which investment vehicles you want to harness. This is the subject of the next chapter.

CHAPTER 18

Choosing Your Wealth Vehicle (Step Four)

hat assets are you going to invest in as your primary wealth vehicles? How can you know which investment vehicles are the right fit for you?

Remember, building your wealth isn't done in one move, but rather three distinct phases. In Level One your focus is on creating the right financial habits (e.g. tracking your financials and creating a surplus of money each month) and laying your foundation of financial fluency through sound financial education and training. In Level Two your focus shifts to aggressively building your net worth, primarily through forced appreciation deals. Finally, in Level Three, you need to shift your investing focus to wealth vehicles that convert your net worth into passive residual income.

What this means is that the best wealth vehicles for you in Level Two probably won't be the same wealth vehicles you use in Level Three, or at least you won't approach your investment deals quite the same way.

Let's look at the four main classes of investment vehicles and see which are the best fits when you are at what levels.

The Four Classes of Investment Vehicles

Class One: Businesses

The first class of wealth vehicles you can invest in are businesses. If you're at Level One or Two then the best investment you can make is to actively build a business. As you've already learned in Secret One of this book, when you build a Level Three business you are harnessing forced appreciation to create a multimillion dollar asset.

Of course actively running your own business is not for everyone (although we're guessing that a majority of our readers are up for the challenge). Still you can *passively* invest in businesses.

You can invest in businesses that you hope will later be sold to a larger company or go public. This would be investing for a later capital gain. This has worked for hundreds of thousands of other investors who've made *billions* just this way.

You can also invest in businesses for the cash flow they are able to generate. For example, Diane and her husband invested in a real estate brokerage company that creates a seven percent *monthly* return on their investment! That's close to a 100 percent cash-on-cash return on their investment on an annual basis.

Here are eight quick tips on investing in *other* people's businesses.

1. Focus on industries and business models you have experience with. This will let you leverage all your past experience to make smarter investment choices, lower your effective risk, and potentially let you earn a larger ownership stake by adding your consulting to the equation. Plus, you might very well be able to leverage your existing business network to find deals and add value to new deals you are involved with (e.g. help bring the business new clients, refer them to vendors who are less expensive, etc.).

2. Consider leveraging your skill set to take a larger ownership share than just your money would allow by doing some very limited work or advising for the business. For example, both of us have taken advisory positions in businesses in which we have invested in exchange for a larger equity stake. The company got the benefit of our skills, knowledge, and contacts, and we got the benefit of earning a larger piece of the pie that we helped make even bigger. Everybody won!

3. Do your homework thoroughly. Check out your prospective partners for both character and competence. Pay for a background check on them. Check references. Have your advisor team thor-

oughly vet the deal. Scrutinize both their business plan and their current business operations.

4. Make sure the partnership agreements are equitably drawn up. Have your attorney review the agreements. Make sure you look closely at what happens if one of the 5 Ds occurs: If you reach a disagreement you can't resolve; if one of the partners dies; if one of the partners gets divorced; if one of the partners goes deep into debt and declares a bankruptcy; if one of the active partners is disabled and can no longer perform the work he or she was supposed to do. Pay very close attention to how decisions are to be made, what events would trigger a buy/sell, and what the price or formula for each partner's interest in that buy/sell arrangement is.*

5. Make sure proper financial controls have been established. This includes regular audits of the books, separation of the financial roles to make theft or misappropriation of funds much less likely, and putting reasonable limitations on what the business officers and leaders can or cannot do with respect to borrowing money, spending money, and paying themselves.

6. Make sure you get a clear written disclosure that the deal founders sign that lays out any conflicts of interest. Don't accept this orally, make sure it's in writing. If you are investing in a formal private placement or private offering then their attorney probably has already prepared this document.

7. Carefully choose how much you want to invest. It should be enough so that the payoff justifies your investment in time and energy to do your due diligence up front, but it shouldn't be everything you have. Passively investing as an equity partner in a business tends to be higher on the risk scale than most other wealth vehicles so not putting all your eggs in one basket is smart. But putting your eggs into too many baskets is dumb. Our experience says that you would never want to invest more than 5–10 percent of your net worth in any one passive business venture. (Of course, there is nothing wrong with having much more of your net worth tied into one of your *active* businesses, provided that as you move closer to Level Three you start to run some of your money from the table.)

---

*We have included a free e-book on effectively partnering on an investment as part of the Millionaire Fast-Track Program. You can download it immediately by going to **www.MauiMillionaires.com/book**.

8. Make sure you limit your liability by investing via an entity you own and not in your own name. That way should the active managers do something that inadvertently lets a creditor pierce the liability shield of the primary entity, you still have a second entity layer to protect yourself. Be very cautious about personally guaranteeing any loans. This could come back to haunt you. If you do agree to guarantee any loans, make sure you get your attorney to review the documents and clearly minimize in writing the guarantee's scope and duration.

Class Two: Real Estate

The next asset class is real estate. For many people this means investing in single-family houses as rental properties, or fixing them up for immediate resale. For other players this means investing in commercial real estate like apartment complexes, office buildings, warehouse space, shopping centers, or development projects.

Real estate is a great investment vehicle both for Level Two investors tapping into the power of forced appreciation and for Level Three investors who are looking to convert their net worth into stable cash flow.

David's Story

A little over 10 years ago I jumped into real estate by investing in single-family houses and condos. Year after year I grew my portfolio of homes. At first I did it on an individual basis; later I built up a Level Three real estate investment company. But after house 100 or so I must say that the shine of investing in a portfolio of single-family houses lost some of its luster.

It was at this time that I made the move into commercial real estate, which I found to be a much better fit for me. I loved the fact that the deals were larger but that I could leverage my efforts by putting together the right team so that I could keep my investing to the role of a passive Level Three investor. For example, I worked with a team that bought a $20 million industrial property for less than $10 million from a highly motivated manufacturing company that just wanted to get the property off its books.

(continued)

David's Story *(continued)*

Another forced appreciation deal I did was on a 322-unit apartment complex. At the time we bought it, the building had a vacancy factor of roughly 50 percent! My team filled the property to 80 percent occupied and then we sold the building 18 months later for a $2 million profit. By this point I was making a strong shift in my investing focus to look for stable, high-quality cash flow properties, so we exchanged our profits into a portfolio of office buildings that we still own and which generate a six-figure passive residual cash flow.

I've watched many Maui Millionaires use commercial real estate as one of their wealth vehicles.* For those people who are willing to do their homework and learn about it, I think it's one of the best passive wealth vehicles available.

*By this point in the book you have probably already spotted our bias toward building businesses and investing in real estate. This is how we've made our fortunes. Because we have so much we want to share with you about investing in real estate, we've included 3 FREE online workshops on investing in real estate, both single-family houses and commercial real estate, as part of your Millionaire Fast-Track Program. For full details see the Appendix. Or go to **www.MauiMillionaires.com/book**.

Class Three: Publicly Traded Securities

Publicly traded securities include stocks, bonds, and mutual funds. For the average investor they are an easy way to invest. But they are not necessarily an easy way to make money. Notice the difference here.

It's easier to buy a stock or mutual fund than it is to invest in a private placement or commercial real estate deal. But because it's easier doesn't necessarily mean that you're going to make a profit investing via these wealth vehicles. The saddest thing we see is well-intentioned Level Two investors who have been blindly following the investing advice from a commissioned salesperson, we mean stockbroker, without doing their homework.

If you are going to use this wealth vehicle, and we think it is a very smart choice for a lot of investors, then you *must* put in the energy to become educated in this wealth vehicle.

Now, technically stocks and bonds are two different asset classes, which we lumped under the heading of "publicly traded securities." Stocks are equity investments, which means when you own a stock you own a proportional share of that company. Bonds on the other hand are debt instruments. When you own a bond what you really own is an IOU from a company or government.

We need to be very clear where our expertise is and where it is not. Both of us have made a lot of money building and investing in businesses and investing in real estate. Neither of us has chosen publicly traded securities as our main wealth vehicles. Why? Because we don't have any real advantages here, and because we like the tax advantages of investing in real estate. And we like the better control and transparency we get from investing in businesses and real estate.

So if this is your wealth vehicle then we have the ultimate reading list for you—the 5 must-read books on investing in publicly traded securities. To download this comprehensive reading list just go to **www.Maui Millionaires.com/book**. If you are committed to using publicly traded securities as your wealth vehicle then you must study the books on this powerful list.

Class Four: Alternative Investments

Alternative investments are a catchall for other primary wealth vehicles not already covered. They include investing in fine art, hedge funds, precious metals, annuities, whole life insurance, collectibles, or real estate investment trusts.

Again, the most important advice we can give you about this or any asset class is for you to develop an expertise in a niche before you invest any significant portion of your net worth there. Read the books; take the courses; hire the advisors; interview the experts. The time and effort you invest on the front end will pay for itself handsomely on the back end in the form of higher returns and more consistent profits.

Which Wealth Vehicle
Is Right for You?

So which of the wealth vehicles do you think are the best fit for you and your current level? What do you need to learn about them in order to become an expert in riding them to consistent investment returns? Begin now to pay the price to learn to master your chosen wealth vehicles.

In the next chapter you'll learn about your greatest cash flow maximizer, and how to leverage it so that you increase your investment returns and accelerate your wealth creation.

CHAPTER 19

The Cash Flow Multiplier (Step Five)

How would you like to discover your single greatest cash flow edge? The one asset that you own, free and clear, that is the most powerful cash flow magnifier that you have at your disposal.

We won't keep you in suspense. You are your greatest cash flow magnifier—your earning capacity, your creativity, your contacts, and your unique talents. There is no better way for you to bump your cash flow than to strategically invest your portfolio of time for maximum gain. Level Three people know this and accept this as one of their guiding principles. They understand that you don't get paid for your time, but rather you get paid for the value you create in the marketplace.

Yet what do Level One and Two people focus on? On trading hours for dollars working for someone else.

It's a mistake for a Level One or Two person to get so excited about creating passive residual income that they let go of their focus on running their active income business to focus exclusively on their passive investments. If they did this they would very quickly run into a cash flow crisis that would be financially devastating for them. On the other hand, it would be just as devastating for them to focus only on their active income business and block out all thoughts of creating passive and passive residual investments. There is an important balance point between working to create current income and future wealth, and you must find the right fit for you.

Think about it this way: When you're at Level One, the majority of your time needs to be focused on creating current income, that is, income you'll get within 30 days. In fact, at Level One you'll probably spend 80–90 percent of your time focused on creating current income. Of course, we urge you to intelligently use the remaining 10–20 percent of your working time to move up to Level Two as fast as possible.

At Level Two you'll still focus most of your time on current income. For example, you may spend 70–80 percent of your time running your active income business. The more you are able to invest yourself to create future wealth, the faster you will reach Level Three. At Level Two one of the best things you can invest your time in is in creating a Level Three business. This is by far the best way for you to get the greatest jump to your net worth in the shortest possible time. In essence, building your Level Three business is a way of investing yourself (your time and passion) to build a future asset (your Level Three business). Again, you've got to be careful not to live in tomorrow and take care of your business needs today.

David's Story

One of the companies I started and grew to a market value of several million dollars was a coaching and training business. The business model worked exceptionally well, and like most of my businesses, it was a sales driven organization. The company averaged 100 percent annual growth over the first seven years.

As you can imagine that kind of growth curve got me very excited as the business owner. It was here that I learned a very valuable and expensive lesson. In anticipation of future growth my company invested hundreds of thousands of dollars in revamping our operational and fulfillment systems to handle our projected growth. We also staffed up from a payroll of $100,000 per month to over $250,000 per month. Although these increases in expenses were meant to put us in a better position to take advantage of our future growth, I soon learned we had overinvested in our capacity and infrastructure, dramatically reducing our operating margins and cash flow.

(continued)

David's Story (continued)

The real lesson I learned is that as a business owner or wealth builder you must balance your current cash flow needs with your future dreams. When the two don't square up, err on the side of being cash conservative!

Now when you reach Level Three a great thing happens. You are able to focus more of your efforts on generating future wealth. No longer are you locked on the short term like a Level One person (focused on generating cash in the next 30 days), nor are you limited by the need to create near-term cash flow like the Level Two person (focused on generating a cash payoff in a 30-to 120-day period). Instead you are able to choose investments that create the best overall returns even if that means that some of your investments may not pay you for several years. In fact, investing for the long term creates those unrealized gains we talked about that dramatically lower the drag of taxes.

When you are at Level Three you have enough passive, residual cash flow to pay for your lifestyle, which frees you up to invest more and more of your time in building your medium- and long-term wealth.

The bottom line is that it is a dynamic dance between taking care of your current cash flow needs, and building your long-term wealth. Because you are your greatest cash flow asset, make sure you invest yourself (i.e. your time) for maximum results. Just like you strategically allocated your net worth over your own personal Risk Spectrum, you would do well to consciously choose how you want to invest your time between creating current cash flow and building long-term wealth.

In the next chapter you'll learn a new way of looking at taxes that will fundamentally change how you look at building wealth. It's called Pre-emptive Tax Strategy.

CHAPTER 20

Preemptive Tax Strategy (Step Six)

Do you consistently think through the tax consequences of each business, investment, or financial decision you make? If you're like most people, tax consequences come to mind only when you are in the process of selling an asset (and faced with a big tax bill) or filing your annual tax return. And yet, as your wealth and net worth grow, tax planning is a powerful leverage point that can accelerate your wealth creation.

Take a look at Figure 20.1. In it you'll see three different tax formulas: your blended tax rate, your Tax Efficiency Rate and your Tax Power Percentage. Each of these formulas is a tool that is helpful to you at a specific level of your wealth building.

Calculation 1: Blended Tax Rate— A Level One Tool

To find your blended tax rate, add up the total amount of federal and state income tax you paid last year, and divide that amount by your total taxable income. This number will probably be more than 10 percent and less than 50 percent. It varies wildly depending on all kinds of factors.

Preemptive Tax Strategy™

Blended Tax Rate (Level I)

Total Income Tax Paid / Taxable Income   My Blended Tax Rate is: _____ %

Tax Efficiency Rate™ (Level II)

Total Income Tax Paid / Business Gross Income   My Efficiency Rate™ is: _____ %
+ Other Income

Tax Power Percentage™ (Level III)

Total Income Tax Paid / Net Worth   My Tax Power Percentage™ is: _____ %

FIGURE 20.1   Preemptive Tax Strategy

Your blended tax rate is the one that CPAs, banks, and financial advisors look at because it quickly gives them a sense of where you're at. But it's just a basic math calculation. It doesn't really tell you much. The sad part is a lot of folks don't go any further, even though this number doesn't indicate how well your assets are working for you or how good your tax planning is.

Part of the reason for this depends on where you are. If you're at Level One, for example, there isn't much more to tell. If most or all of your income is being reported on a W-2, your tax planning options are limited to the industry standards of tax-deferred planning (contributing to an employer's pension fund or your IRA) or after-tax planning (contributing to a Roth IRA if you meet the income test). If it seems like there aren't many tax breaks for employees, you're right. There aren't. Our tax system has been designed so that activities that support public policy, such as starting your own business or investing in real estate, get more favorable tax treatment, as an incentive for people to take on these risks.

The other two calculations in this section are much more insightful. Next up is your Tax Efficiency Rate.

Calculation 2: Tax Efficiency Rate— A Level Two Tool

In this calculation, you start with your total income tax paid (state and federal) and divide it by your Business Gross Income + other income. This is an important rate for Level Two because it begins to show you how efficient you are being with your deductions.

Ideally, your Tax Efficiency Rate should be quite a bit lower than your blended tax rate. If it isn't, the first place to begin looking is your current deductions. Do you have enough deductions? If your income is largely made up of W-2 income, and you don't have a business, you won't have a lot of deductions available to you, and your Tax Efficiency Rate will probably be fairly close to your blended tax rate. It really does take getting to Levels Two and Three to start to see a difference here.

Finding Your Legitimate Business Deductions

In Level Two, you are starting your journey to financial freedom, usually by beginning a business or investing in real estate, or both.

If you are operating a business or investing in real estate and your Tax Efficiency Rate is close to your blended tax rate, chances are you *aren't* maximizing your deductions potential as efficiently as possible.

We've created a powerful online tool for you to download called the "Where Does Your Income Go?" exercise. You can download this two-part test for free at **www.MauiMillionaires.com/book**. It's part of the Millionaire Fast-Track Program we have created for readers like you.

The key to maximizing your deductions is to have good records (i.e., receipts with who, what, when, where and why notes on the back), and to ask, each time you spend money, "Was this expense ordinary and necessary to the production of income?"

A more powerful way to phrase that question may be, "What needs to happen for that expense to become a business deduction?" When you put it this way, you give your imagination a chance to engage. In fact, you'd be amazed at what qualifies as an ordinary and business expense. Here are just a couple of examples of legitimate, deducible expenses.

In Hawaii, a junkyard was successfully able to deduct the costs of a watchdog, as providing security was an important business function and the dog helped in that regard.

In Florida, a businessman who wanted to operate a yacht sales company was able to deduct the costs of purchasing and operating a yacht that he used as a sales vehicle for potential customers.

This section is, hands down, one of the most entertaining and lively portions of every seminar we do. We usually begin by asking attendees to shout out what they'd like to write off as a business deduction and then go through some of their answers. And, because we're sure you are curious, here are some of the questions we've gotten.

Can I write off clothing? Yes, if you do certain things. For example, the addition of a business logo can make clothing a write-off (although it may look silly on an evening gown). Certainly uniforms and clothing needed for safety are deductible, as well as clothing you buy specifically for video or television (as long as that's the *only* time you wear those particular outfits). You can even deduct laundry and dry cleaning charges for clothing you use on business trips even after you get home, as long as you have the cleaning done within one to two days of your return.

What can I write off in my home office? Just about anything that goes into your home office can be a write-off, as long as you follow the rules. That means using the space *exclusively* for business and *regularly* using that space in the work that you're doing. So, your first deduction is the initial big one (i.e., if your home office takes up 10 percent of your home's total square footage you can deduct 10 percent of your mortgage, rent, interest, homeowner dues, janitorial costs, utilities, and so on). Then you have a depreciation deduction for that same 10 percent, because it's being used for a commercial purpose, not a residential purpose. All costs to remodel that space into your home office are deductible, as is the artwork on the walls and the furniture in the space. Don't be afraid of taking the depreciation deduction on that percentage, either. In 1997, a new law was enacted that said you no longer have to declare and add the depreciation back into your profit on the sale.

Another great thing to note about your home office, especially for those of you who have offices you commute to as well is that the trip down the hall to your home office in your bunny slippers counts as a commute. That means when you get in your car you can begin tracking mileage immediately, as everything else (with the exception of purely personal trips) is a business write-off.

I have more than two businesses running out of my home office. Which one gets the deduction? Look at the business making the most money and take the deduction where the income is. If all of your businesses are making money split up the deduction between them all in ratios that maximize the deduction.

Business Structures

After deductions, the second area to look at when trying to lower your Tax Efficiency Rate is the type of business structure you're operating through.

This is an area where tax advice and asset protection advice will often differ. Tax advice is designed to help you pay the lowest amount of tax possible. Legal advice is designed to keep your assets as safe as possible and to keep you protected from any lawsuits involving those assets.

One place we see many people make mistakes is in choosing the wrong business structure for the job. You already know that different types of income are taxed differently; but the same thing also applies to business structures. Using the wrong one for the job (e.g. using a business structure that is tax-optimized for an active income business to hold an appreciating passive income asset like real estate) can wind up costing you extra money in taxes. Even among the three pass-through structures (LLCs, limited partnerships and S Corporations) there are differences in how assets will be treated. S Corporations require you to remove assets from a business at fair market value, which makes selling a property your business owns to yourself an expensive proposition. If you had held that piece of real estate through an LLC instead, it could be sold for the much lower basis at which it's on your books.

There are so many things to know here, that trying to do it all yourself will make you crazy, and probably cost you money on things you've missed or misunderstood. It's always a good idea to check with your tax advisor, attorney, or business formation service before launching any new business venture.

Diane's Story

About three years ago I had some clients with a successful retail chain of fabric stores. These clients had started life off in an S Corporation, which was a good choice for that type of business. Then they bought the building the store was housed in and put that building into the S Corporation. Not such a good idea. Then they added another location into the same S Corporation, and another, and another, until these clients had 15 fabric stores and their buildings all held within this same S Corporation.

When the clients came to see me they wanted to know how they could begin splitting off some of the stores amongst their five children. The incredible risk notwithstanding (at this point, having all of their business operations and real estate in a single entity

(continued)

Diane's Story *(continued)*

wasn't much better than owning all of these things personally) they had a tax nightmare on their hands! They needed to divide out the assets, but things were in a mess because the assets were going to have to come out at fair market value.

We finally got them squared away, but as I recall their legal and accounting bill was around $50,000. However, if they'd just gone ahead and paid the tax without restructuring things, it would have been far higher.

How much easier it would have been if they had compartmentalized their real estate and retail operations into separate business structures, and started a new combination each time they opened a new branch!

Even if you start off right, in a great, tax-optimized business structure, you may still need to make some changes down the road. For example, if you operate in an S Corporation you will generally want to look at changing over to a C Corporation once your taxable income hits about $150,000 or more. The same goes for those of you with high medical insurance or expenses: You can often save tax dollars by operating in a C Corporation.

You also need to plan for flexibility as you grow. For example, something a Level Three business owner is beginning to focus on is how to create passive income streams. Often a Level Three business will be full of things like intellectual property (copyrights, trademarks, and patents), real estate and equipment, which can be spun off into separate business structures and then leased back to the original Level Three business, creating passive income streams for the asset-holding business owner (i.e., you).

The third reason your Tax Efficiency Rate may not be as low as you'd like is your current level of income. You may have hit the point where your income is so high that your itemized deductions begin to phase out or disappear altogether.

So what do you then? Make less money so your tax bill goes down?

No way! Our suggestion is to change the way you make income instead. We've already gone through the three ways to make income: earned income (W-2 and 1099 income), portfolio income (capital gains, usually created by selling off appreciated assets), and passive residual income (assets work for you, creating hands-off streams of income, such as rent, interest, dividends, and so on). The sooner you can break away from the Level One trap of depending on your earned income for your wealth, the sooner you will begin to see changes in your Tax Efficiency Rate.

Calculation 3: Tax Power Percentage— A Level Three Tool

Your Tax Power Percentage is the ratio between the total tax you pay and your net worth. It's probably the most powerful of the three ratios we've discussed, especially when you are making the transition from Level Two to Level Three.

Diane's Story

The Tax Power Percentage came out of a conversation I had with David, where he made a passing comment about how taxes relate to wealth. While I was thinking about *why* he said what he said, I had this huge "a-ha." What if he was right? I turned things around and realized there was a whole new level of tax strategies out there I hadn't even thought about before! Instead of looking at tax as it relates to income, look at tax as it relates to wealth. That's what the ultra-rich do—they build net worth without paying tax. Level Two wealth building means using income to create wealth. Level Three wealth building means using assets to create wealth. And that's why the Level Two plan will mean you always pay more in taxes.

The key to the Tax Power Percentage is net worth. In Level Three, you are finding ways to increase your net worth without increasing your net taxable income. The higher your net worth goes, the lower your Tax Power Percentage. This is exactly what you want, because it shows your net worth is increasing without you having to convert income. Think back to typical Level Two investing for a minute—taking after-tax income (leftover money) and investing that to build your wealth. In Level

Three, you're taking your wealth and using that to create more wealth without paying taxes first.

A good example of this is appreciation, forced or passive. Imagine your business owns the building you operate out of. When that property goes up in value, your net worth goes up. Do you pay tax on that increased value? No. You don't pay tax until you sell that building and realize the gain. Is it possible for you to get at the cash without paying tax? Yes! Is that cash something you can use to create passive residual income? Yes! Do you see how you can begin using your existing wealth to create cash flow?

This is a critically important idea. If you're stuck in the "earn more save more" habit, and you aren't at Level One, break it! At Level One, where you have no savings habit and lots of consumer debt, you need to budget and get in control of your finances. But to make the move from Level Two to Level Three, you need to break the need to be frugal. Saving more is a very slow way to wealth—it can take you most of your working life. With the Maui Millionaires plan, you may be able to get to Level Three in anywhere from 5 to 10 years. We've even see people do it in 3 years or less.

Another good way to grow your net worth is using pension funds to invest in business and real estate.* But we do want to add a caveat here. Messing with your pension isn't something to be taken lightly and really isn't something you want to tackle until you are either a Level Three investor or a very experienced Level Two investor. If you aren't fully committed here you risk blowing your lifestyle right back to Level One. Make sure you have the habits that bring in money and have proven your investment skills.

Diane's Story

I remember back in Reno years ago I invested in a start-up beer company. Their beer was everywhere! When I asked how they were getting such great market coverage I was told that the company was offering some really fantastic incentives to the sales team. They were selling beer like crazy, but they were paying some really big bonuses. In fact, the bonuses were so

(continued)

---

*You can learn more about how to invest with your pension by reading Diane's book, *The Insider's Guide to Tax-Free Real Estate: Retire Rich Using Your IRA.*

Diane's Story *(continued)*

good that at the end of the day the company was losing money on each case of beer it sold.

In the short term, the loss wouldn't necessarily be a bad thing. But the beer company hadn't put a time limit on the promotion. In fact, they proudly showed me the contracts they had signed with each member of the sales team, guaranteeing those huge bonuses for the duration of the contracts.

When I pointed out that it actually cost them more to sell the beer than they made from the sale, the answer I got back was— I kid you not—"We'll make it up in volume."

Well, what could I say? I pulled my investment and advised my clients to pull their investments, too. Naturally the company went out of business . . . but not without completely destroying the pension of one of the founder's uncle who had invested almost his entire pension into the company and left his money in.

Take a look at Figure 20.2. As we've said, the middle-class solution is to use income to create wealth. Make money, pay taxes, take the leftover cash and invest it. Those investments are typically industry standards like stocks and mutual funds and are made mostly because the middle class are too busy working to really pay attention to how their investments are doing. To get out of this head space, you've got to change how you make money.

The Level Three solution is to use wealth to create cash flow. Remember, cash flow *isn't* income. Cash flow means creating streams you don't have to pay taxes on. (See Figure 20.3.)

The Preemptive Tax Strategy for the middle class is pension funds, and using that money to invest in "safe" investments. We've put the word "safe" in quotations because many people have trouble moving out of what they understand about investing and taxes, because to them, that feels risky. But the truth is that the middle-class solution is riskier! If you look at Figure 20.2 you can see some of the risks we've listed. Alternative Minimum Tax (AMT) is at the top of that list. It's a parallel system of taxation that catches millions of middle-income Americans each year and forces them into a flat 26 percent tax bracket. AMT will get you if you've got stock options or capital gains. Many real estate

Level Two
Solution

Use Income to Create Wealth

Techniques:

- Save
- Invest with after tax money
- Invest in publicly traded companies & securities

Traditional Goals:

- Save with after tax money
- Invest with after tax money
- Find income tax loopholes

Risks:

- Alternative Minimum Tax
- Non or under-performing investments
- Inflation
- Dollar devaluation
- Tax law changes
- No investment control
- No transparency (particularly with frictional costs)
- No asset protection

FIGURE 20.2   Middle Class Solution

Use Wealth to Create Cash Flow

Techniques:

- Cashflow Maximizer™
- Forced appreciation
- Pension investing
- Home Loopholes
- Always invest with Advantages
- Strategic asset allocation

Goals:

- Create easy-to-manage system for review
- Increase velocity on wealth, without increasing tax rate
- Unrealized gains
- Legally circumvent income tax/AMT system
- Intelligent financial controls
- Strong asset protection

Risks:

- R-Score™ decreases
- Short term focus
- Increase in velocity can mean more time required

FIGURE 20.3   Level Three Solution

professionals get absolutely hammered by AMT, because under the AMT rules they can't offset their real estate losses against other income.

The bottom line of all this focus on Preemptive Tax Strategy is to minimize the frictional drag that taxes can put on your wealth building so that you can create more wealth, faster and easier. This is what Maui Millionaires do, and so can you!

In the final chapter of this section of the book you'll get the chance to organize what you have been learning into a coherent and practical plan of action.

CHAPTER 21

Getting Into Action
(Step Seven)

ou've just completed six of the
seven steps of the Wealth Map. Now it's time to put it all into action in
the real world. In this final chapter of this section of the book, you'll organize and clarify your action steps so that you are able to apply what
you have learned to increase your wealth. Then, at the end of this chapter,
we'll lay out a simple yet extremely effective system for regular financial
review that is guaranteed to accelerate your financial results.

Again, as with the earlier steps, it's critical that you participate in this
section of the book, not merely passively read it. If you want these ideas
to work for you making you money and increasing your net worth then
you'll need to actively answer the following questions.

Congratulations! You've just completed your first pass at creating
your own personal Wealth Map. We've watched the overwhelming majority of our Maui Millionaire clients use exactly these same seven
steps to radically transform their financial life and build Level Three
wealth.

You've got one more wealth secret ahead of you. It's the source of
your ultimate competitive wealth advantage, and it is the key ingredient
to move from success to significance. See you in the next chapter!

Part A:

One: What were your 3 most important insights from your Strategic Financial Assessment (Step One)?

1. _____

2. _____

3. _____

Two: What were your 3 key insights from where you are on the Wealth Curve™ (Step Two)?

1. _____

2. _____

3. _____

Three: What were your 3 key insights from the Asset Allocation (Step Three)?

1. _____

2. _____

3. _____

Four: What were your 3 sweet spots to actively enhance your business and Investing cash flow you uncovered from The Cashflow Maximizer™ (Step Four)?

1. _____

2. _____

3. _____

FIGURE 21.1 Action Time

Part B:

What are your 3 90-day targets/outcomes based on what you have just discovered?

Completed

☐ 1. _____
_____

☐ 2. _____
_____

☐ 3. _____
_____

Part C:

What are your 3 key action steps that you will take in the next 30 days to help you create your 90 day targets/outcomes?

Completed

☐ 1. _____
_____

☐ 2. _____
_____

☐ 3. _____
_____

Part D:

What 3 things will you eliminate or reduce to create the time you need to accomplish your 3-5 key 30-day action steps in a fun and energizing way?

Completed

☐ 1. _____
_____

☐ 2. _____
_____

☐ 3. _____
_____

FIGURE 21.1   *(Continued)*

Regular Strategic Wealth Reviews

Monthly: (2 hours)

- ❏ Leveraged bookkeeping and financial record keeping
- ❏ Review your financials
  - P and L
  - Balance Sheet

Quarterly: (4-6 hours)

- ❏ Complete your Strategic Financial Review worksheet (from step one)
- ❏ Complete your Strategic Asset Allocation worksheet (from step two)
- ❏ Brainstorm leverage points, bottlenecks, and sweet spots that you can utilize to actively enhance your wealth building. Review your actions from the prior quarter. What did you learn? How will you apply these insights?
- ❏ (Optional) Have a Preemptive Tax Strategy session with your tax strategist.

Annually: (1-2 days)

- ❏ Complete your quarterly review
- ❏ Goals check in and refinement
- ❏ Attorney review of wealth plan, asset protection, and estate planning
- ❏ Tax strategy review
- ❏ (Optional) Review your updated Wealth Map™ with your Mastermind Team to get their independent feedback

FIGURE 21.2   Your Regular Strategic Wealth Reviews

PART THREE

INVEST IN
THE GREATER GOOD

SECRET #5: Invest in the Greater Good and Reap Enduring Rewards!

CHAPTER 22

Six Reasons Why Giving Creates a Competitive Advantage for Your Business

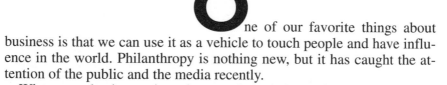

ne of our favorite things about business is that we can use it as a vehicle to touch people and have influence in the world. Philanthropy is nothing new, but it has caught the attention of the public and the media recently.

When your business gives, it expands its sphere of influence and extends the richness of its relationships, both internally and externally. When you build giving deep into the marrow of your business, it energizes your team of employees, vendors, investors, and advisors. When your business gives back in meaningful ways for the right reasons it is a powerful bridge to deeply connect with your clients and the community in which you do business.

The more you reach out, the more people reach back. No one exemplifies this to us better than Beverly Sallee, who began her working life as a music teacher and is now a business owner with foreign affiliates in over 50 countries around the world, and hundreds of thousands of people working with her. For Beverly, giving is a passion, and a part of her business model. "The bed can only be so soft," is one of her favorite sayings, and it's true. So for her, the mission is to find everyone a soft bed. Each time Beverly enters a new market the first thing she tells people is that she and they are going to both make a lot of money—and that her money is staying in that country, to be put to work for the good of all. In many ways Beverly exemplifies what we both aspire to become, as do many of our Maui Millionaires and Maui Mastermind participants.

But besides having a giant heart and philanthropic muscle, Beverly is also a very shrewd businesswoman. She recognizes that making philanthropy and giving a part of her business model also gives her a competitive edge in business, which is fine with her. After all, the more she makes, the more she can give away, and the more lives she can touch, who then touch back, making her business larger, so she has more to give away . . . are you getting the picture?

With that in mind, here are six reasons why building a giving component into the core of your business model will help you grow, no matter what level your business is at, nor how big or small it is.

Reason 1: It will generate positive publicity for you and your business.

Giving provides you with a forum to get publicity for your business and to promote it in the public's eye. The more that people know your business is out there, the more who may enter your deep funnel and become steady clients. Plus, what a great way to be seen by the public—as a business that wants to make a difference.

Do you remember when you first heard the announcement of Warren Buffett's $27 *billion* donation? Or when Bill and Melinda Gates donated over $10 billion to start their foundation? Or when Oprah donated millions to fund a school for girls in Africa? Or, on a smaller scale, can't you think of at least one example of how a local business owner in your community stepped up to make a difference in your hometown? It's powerful actions like these that radically revamp how the world perceives you and your business. And while we hope you have bigger reasons to do your giving than just to generate positive PR, we also think it's perfectly appropriate to generate this positive press for your business' good intentions and philanthropic commitment.

Reason 2: It will help you deepen your client relationships.

The act of philanthropy and giving helps to deepen your relationship with your existing clients and to attract new clients. People will buy from you because they recognize your business also gives back. They see what you do for the community and want to support your business so it can continue that work. It creates a tie between you, your clients, and your community. Just consider the phenomenal success of the Product Red™ campaign rolled out by musician Bono and Debt, AIDS, Trade, Africa (DATA) Chair Bobby Shriver in January 2006. How many people purchased one of their partner products—a cell phone, sneakers, an iPod®, and so on, not because they necessarily needed that product, but because they *knew* a portion of their purchase went to fighting HIV/AIDS in Africa?

We believe that when done for the *right* reasons, when your business steps up for a cause or purpose beyond itself, the world your business operates in will not only expand, but will also see your business in a fundamentally improved way. This one simple idea has radically transformed the way we operate our businesses. For example, in the past 12 months, Maui Millionaires has hosted four charity wealth workshops with over 1,200 people attending and raising over $1 million for 22 different charities. The part we never could have anticipated, nor even intended, was how deeply this model resonated with our clients who are now our biggest source of new business. In fact, of those 1,200 people who attended these charity events over 50 percent of them came because of a direct referral from a client of ours. What would it mean for your business if you had a 50 percent referral rate? Can you imagine how powerful that would be to promote your business.

Reason 3: It allows you to network and connect with the movers and shakers of the world.

What would it mean to your business if you were able to build relationships with the five biggest players in your industry? How would you personally like to be mentored by one of the best business people in your community? But how will you get past the gatekeepers and open the door to initiate those relationships? That's where giving comes into play. Philanthropy just may be the fastest way to cut across social boundaries and connect with the who's who of business.

We've both observed a simple fact: The most influential people in the world all tend to be involved in philanthropy and all have giving projects and causes that are near and dear to their hearts. This means giving just might be the best way to get close to the movers and shakers in the world to whom you would otherwise find the doors barred.

David's Story

As an author of several prominent business books I get a lot of people who want a piece of my time. In fact, I am like a lot of successful business owners I know, who have elaborate office systems to screen out people who want to take up their time. Yet, I'm actually a very easy person to spend time with, if you approach me the right way (as are 90 percent of the business people you want to develop relationships with). So what's the "right way"? Don't ask me for a few minutes of my time; don't try to wheedle your way past my assistant. Instead, just take the time to find out what charities and philanthropic projects I'm passionate about, and find a way to help me help those charities. Along the way we'll start a friendship that just might make the difference your business needs.

For example, about a year ago I went with a group of entrepreneurs on a trip to St. Jude Children's Research Hospital in Memphis. For those of you who don't know, St. Jude Hospital was started by actor Danny Thomas as an institution dedicated to the research and treatment of catastrophic childhood diseases. One of the women on the trip, Sharlet, (who had volunteered to help organize the whole trip), was starting up a new business in an industry that I had just sold my last company in. The night after our tour of the hospital, Sharlet and I spent close to two and a half hours going over her business plans and strategies she could use to make her business incredibly profitable. The real lesson here is that had Sharlet come to me and asked for two and a half hours of free consulting there is no way I would have agreed to it. But in the context of giving, and after watching how much energy she had invested in a cause I felt passionate about, was it any wonder I felt compelled to reciprocate?

I believe that you can open any door if you find the right key. And I have never found any key so universal or powerful as the key of philanthropy.

Reason 4: It lets you add *meaning* to the money.

Businesses certainly exist to make money, and there's nothing wrong with that. But is the money really enough? We can remember the hungry days when we launched our first businesses, but once you get past the momentary Level One struggle of seeing if your business will survive, your business must be about more than just the money. You need it to be about more than just money; your team needs it to be about more than just money; and your clients need it to be about more than just money.

When you add meaning to the money, you step up to a whole new level. And when you involve your team and clients in giving, you help them discover meaning for themselves. You foster an atmosphere that makes people *want* to stay connected to your business and its compelling cause.

Everyone needs something to care about, something that matters to them. By helping your team connect their success with a cause, you create an enormous competitive advantage because there is now more than just a paycheck at stake.

For example, the Maui company's passion is to help connect entrepreneurs to causes. Our passion is to spark and inspire business leaders and investors to step up and discover the joys of giving—their time, their talent, and their money. To this end, we sponsor many different giving trips where we bring business owners out into the world to personally connect with their giving, versus trying to help from a distance. This has been so successful that our clients have stepped up and expanded this, creating giving mastermind groups of their own, each with meaningful ways to get people involved in making a difference. Well, in our office, our operations manager has been on more of these giving trips than *anyone*. In the past year, she's built homes for people in Baja; she's played with orphans in Mexico; she's delivered furniture to families in need in New Orleans; she's traveled to Rwanda to help vulnerable children and micro-lending programs there. All of these trips were organized in the Maui community. Can you imagine the passion that she brings when she comes to work? She isn't just organizing workshop logistics or arranging fulfillment services, she is connected to a company that is making a real difference in the world.

How do your team members feel about your business? Is it a place they come to work, or is it a vehicle that allows them to make a difference? Remember, your people crave meaning, and by using your business as a vehicle to give you are providing them a powerful outlet to make that difference.

Reason 5: It will inspire and strengthen your family.

This may sound like it's kind of far-fetched and starry-eyed, but really it's just hard-edged practicality. The biggest strain we see within the families of entrepreneurs is a distance between the entrepreneur and the rest of the family. Sometimes that's caused by the entrepreneur working long hours and pouring all his energy into his business and his family grows to resent the business, which they see as having taken their husband or father away from them. Other times it's caused because the entrepreneur feels unsupported, like her family doesn't stand with her as she works to build a better life for the family.

When you add giving into the heart of your business, you create an easy way to meaningfully involve your family in your business. At the very least you have helped your family see that the hours you invest in building your business are about more than just making money; they are also about making a better world.

We've both felt firsthand how by making giving a core part of our business our families were touched. Once upon a time, David's wife Heather used to resent the days David traveled to teach workshops. She wasn't all that interested in the world of business so traveling with David wasn't much fun for her. But now that giving is such an integral part of the business, Heather travels with David on over half his business trips, because she loves connecting with his clients around the ideas of philanthropy and making a difference.

As for Diane, well, the philanthropic work Maui has done has quite literally given her a family.

Diane's Story

I'd like to share a deeply personal story with you. It's how my family changed because of designing giving into the core of the Maui businesses.

You might have heard or read how the Maui Mastermind event started way back in 2003 during a meeting of my own personal Mastermind group. The whole concept of the Maui Mastermind began because one of my buddies kept pushing me with questions to find out what I really wanted. What did I love most about teaching? If I could create the perfect event, what would it look like? Who would I allow to come? Who *wouldn't* I allow to come?

The answers flowed easily. I loved teaching people who actually took action and used the ideas I shared to improve their financial lives. I wanted to make sure that the business had a meaningful giving component because money didn't inspire me anymore, but

(continued)

Diane's Story *(continued)*

making a real difference in the world sure did. And I wanted to choose people who, while diverse, shared my core value of how joyful it was to give.

The end result was the creation of Maui Mastermind—an event with proven "do-ers" who were prepared to make a huge impact on their life and in their community.

We agreed that a large part of the proceeds would go to charities. This was just one of the ways we wanted to make giving a real part of Maui from the start. That first year at Maui we gave over $100,000 to charities around the world. Rob, one of the Maui Masterminds, had suggested an orphanage in Juarez, Mexico. We knew that the money was sorely needed due to some problems with their current building, but we didn't know the extent of it.

There was a property dispute and they were going to have to move out of their current building. Sergio, the director, didn't want to ruin the kids' Christmas and so he let them celebrate the holiday without telling them. His plan was to tell them at the end of December that the orphanage was shutting down. Chances were that most of the 15 kids would then be living on the streets, separated and abandoned again.

The check for $10,000 from Maui Mastermind arrived on December 26th. It was enough for them to get their building started. The children moved in the facility immediately, although there wasn't yet a roof or a kitchen. At least they still had a home.

The impact on the kids was even more significant. They had grown up believing they weren't anything special. Now, they had tangible evidence that sometimes prayers do come true.

I never knew that the actions I took might create the answer to someone else's prayers. My husband Richard and I were so moved that we flew down to Juarez to do a short film on the orphanage and meet Sergio.

When we visited Sergio's orphanage, Casa de la Nueva Vida (House of the New Life), one of the teenage boys living there captured Richard's and my hearts. He was so personable and

(continued)

intelligent. Something happened inside my husband and me when we met this special boy. At the end of the day we knew we had to adopt him. Several months and a whole lot of legal red tape later, we brought our 14-year-old son David home from that Mexican orphanage.

How important has it been in my life to connect my business with giving? It's quite literally given me the family that I've always dreamed of. He is the greatest blessing I have ever received.

But the story doesn't end there. We adopted David over three years ago. Since that time, David has grown a lot. Last fall, he was asked to visit a 4th-year Spanish class at a local high school and talk to them in his native language. David visited once and found that the kids were fascinated with his story of spending his first 13 years in Mexico in six orphanages—two bad, three good, and one very good. And, now he was one of their peers. He was asked back to tell more of his life story, but this time he came prepared. He showed a photo montage with music that pictorially told his story and after it was done, he spoke from his heart, in a darkened room, with music softly playing.

When the lights came up, the teacher saw the students were crying and laughing, all at the same time. He was asked back to speak to other classes, eventually presenting to over 650 people. And at the same time, he spoke about his dream—to create a camp in Juarez, Mexico, where groups who were helping the orphanages and building homes could safely stay and where children from the orphanages could play.

That's when David (age 16), along with high school teacher Shawna Thue, started the nonprofit organization, Thunder Mission. They, along with volunteer high school students, bring presents, food, clothing, and educational supplies for the orphans. And they've raised over $20,000 toward the goal of building the camp in Juarez.

In today's fast-paced world of family challenges and breakdowns in communication between parents and teenagers, it's a true gift

(continued)

Diane's Story *(continued)*

to have something we can agree on and work toward together. The joy of giving brought our family together, and it strengthens us as we learn how to be a family.

Would you like to see the actual video that Diane shot down in Juarez that very first visit? Then go to **www.MauiMillionaires .com/book** right now!

Reason 6: It's great for your heart.

We spend so much time in business thinking with our head, that it's a welcome relief to feel with our hearts instead. When you focus on giving you expand your emotional capacity. This helps you become a better person and leader. This also magnifies your capacity to feel joy and your emotional resilience. It's what helps you to make one more call, work a bit longer, and go a bit further.

Take the example of Blake, a past participant of Maui Mastermind who has gone on to become one of the Maui Faculty. When Blake first came to Maui he was already an incredible financial and business success. He had built up a thriving Level Three construction management company and owned a good bit of real estate. But these successes felt empty.

Over the three years of attending Maui, we watched Blake emotionally blossom. His heart was captured by a cause called, Estrellas Para Ninos (Stars for Children), an organization started by Maui grads that supports several orphanages in Mexico. Blake has led multiple trips down to Mexico to work on the orphanages and play with the kids. He's also helped Estrellas raise hundreds of thousands of dollars to improve the lives of these children. Watching Blake over the past several years we've seen him grow his capacity to care for and connect with people heart to heart. His philanthropy was one of the prime sparks to help him grow.

We both believe that when you make giving part of your business that you and your team will grow, and your emotional fluency will mature. And as a result your life will be blessed in ways you can't imagine at this moment. If you trust us about any one thing, trust us about this.

Spread the Word About Maui Giving

The Maui message of freedom through Level Three business and investing and giving from abundance is spreading. While we were writing this book a letter came in from Marichiel Ewert, a first-year Maui Mastermind attendee who wrote to us just two months after attending Maui. This letter more eloquently expresses the power of combining business with giving than we ever could.

Dearest David & Diane,

I wanted to write and let you know what kind of impact you have had on me. Bear with me, this is a long story!

Kelly Fabros entered my life in 1999. She was partnered up with my husband, Nathan, at the Los Angeles Police Department. At this point, we were all in the same financial boat . . . typical middle class. She told us about this book she had just read about how the game of money really worked and how to win that game. She expressed how this book really made her mad because most of what she had been taught about how to succeed financially had been wrong. I completely blew her off because I thought she was talking craziness.

A few years later, we were having dinner with Rob and Kelly, and they were telling us about flipping houses. We couldn't explain how they could flip homes when my husband and I didn't see how we could. After all, we all made the same amount of money. They must have just been lucky.

We were surprised and confused when Kelly quit her job about four years ago. We weren't sure what she was doing.

Kelly and I worked out regularly. She trained me on the beach and in the water (she's an amazing swimmer) and I trained her on the mat at jiu-jitsu. She dribbled a little "Maui" on me every now and then. I wanted so much to be able to quit my job so I could stay home with the kids more. I can remember my language back then. "I can't . . ." "I don't . . ." Kelly patiently stepped back.

Rob and Kelly moved far away in 2004. We didn't see them as much, but when we did, they were more and more successful. We're talking multimillion-dollar deals here. One day I called her up and said, "I have $30,000 to invest. Can I just give it to you and you do something with it?" She told me, "No. If you're going to make more just to spend more, what's the point?" I ended up paying off a credit card and putting a down payment on a new car, something dumb like that.

A year later our two-year-old daughter Trinity was diagnosed with an extremely rare bone marrow disorder—aplastic anemia. One way to explain our life back then ... picture a big rock in a clothes dryer, being tumbled around and chipped away with each spin. I was lost, angry, and confused.

Kelly showed up at my door on the day I was supposed to go back to work with a check she had raised from her Maui friends. "Here. You shouldn't have to work. Stay home and be with Trinity." I told her I wanted to go to Maui one day, meet her friends, and someday be able to do for another family what they just did for me. Throughout the year Kelly shared what Maui Mastermind was all about, bit by bit. I liked what I was hearing!

They say people can't hear it from their own friends, they have to hear it from a third party. Totally true. In February of the next year, I was talking to my realtor about her investing out-of-state and what kind of cash flow she got from these inexpensive properties. I wanted in on this. So I called Kelly for advice, the only other investor I knew. She took me through an exercise involving my goals and dreams. I was dreaming again! She told me my first step was to read that book that she had read several years back that had started her out on her path to financial success. So I did and like her, I was angry, and ready to take control of my life. I guess Kelly saw this as the right time to not dribble Maui on me anymore, but to dunk me in it! Like a sponge, I listened about the mastermind groups, the giving, the wealth attitudes, our fears, all of it. We budgeted and documented every single penny spent to see exactly where our money was going. Most of it doodads and "want" items. That changed real quick. With Kelly's guidance and advice, we formed an LLC and purchased two investment properties. I also quit my job as a real estate appraiser and started my own appraisal business.

Trinity passed away later that year in April. Words can't explain the transformation that happened within me. I grew stronger as opposed to weaker. I refused to take life lying down curled up in a ball. I still had Trinity's baby brother to raise, and what kind of messed up life would that be for him if his mommy moped around all day?

Another reason why we sold our house was to be able to afford the hefty price tag for me to go to Maui. As the weeks got closer to the event, I took notice. I looked around. These were going to be the last days of life as I

(continued)

knew it. I left Los Angeles on a plane crying. Goodbye old life. Hello new life.

David told us to play full out in Maui. I told myself I would. I was ready to get uncomfortable and take action in the presence of my fears. After day one ended, Kelly asked what I thought. I told her, "If I went home and that was all Maui was about, I would be completely satisfied and still ever changed." It was all good. I literally felt like I had died and gone to heaven, and my old friends were surrounding me to greet me. I just can't explain it. The love I felt that week was overwhelming. I met people I knew would be in my life forever. I learned how much more rewarding giving was compared to receiving a paycheck. I learned how to supersize my life and my businesses. Although it didn't show on paper, I truly became wealthy at that event.

Since Maui (two months ago) to present:

- I have increased my passive income by a multiple of eight through a network marketing business I joined. I estimate our passive income to exceed $8,000/month by mid-year. At the rate things are going, Nathan will have the option to retire from police work within the next 12 months.
- We have raised over $30,000 for the Aplastic Anemia Foundation in Memory of Trinity Ewert for research. Our Mastermind Group is working on raising another $250,000 this year. This will be break-through-type research we're funding with the help of Maui Master-mind. We're also searching for needy families with children stricken with aplastic anemia to help them financially. Giving is in my everyday vocabulary.
- I am currently involved in four mastermind groups: one for growing my business, a second to help me succeed investing in commercial real estate, a third to focus on raising money for the Aplastic Anemia Foundation, and a fourth as a "Big Dream" leader for attendees at the Mini-Maui charity events.
- I am actively working on my first commercial real estate deal with a group of investors. I have an accountability group to keep me focused and on track.
- I dragged five people with me to Mini Maui in Las Vegas in January. 1) Jocelyn came home from the event and gave her two-week notice at her corporate job. She is in process of purchasing our coach's jiu-jitsu academy! 2) Robbie has taken control of his life, embracing his fears and we are working on that commercial deal together. His plan

is to quit his job by the end of the year. 3) Jan has plans to quit her corporate job once she gets her CPA license, and in six months wants to start her own real estate CPA consulting business.

- I have taken words like "nice" and "good" out of my vocabulary and replaced them with "amazing" and "awesome." Life is too short to live small. I challenge life to throw fears at me. I eat fears for breakfast now.
- I have hired an assistant at my appraisal company and am currently restructuring it into a Level Three business. I have reduced my hours at this "job" to about five hours a week. (Compared to before Maui . . . six to eight hours a day!)
- I have hired a bookkeeper to free up time. I have implemented David's time mastery strategies to eliminate my lower value activities and focus instead on those things that really matter to me and my businesses.
- I am grateful every minute of every day.

Did I get to the thank you part of this letter yet? I can't even express in words how grateful I am that you two have come into my life. Not only do I have what you have taught me, but so do my children and future generations to come. I am creating a legacy, leaving a dent in this universe, and living big. Because of you. Thank you for creating Maui Mastermind. Thank you for your time and hard work, setting an example, changing lives. CHANGING LIVES!! I'm looking forward to next year's Maui and seeing you both throughout the year at the Maui events.

With all my heart,

Marichiel Ewert

This is why we do it. This is why we're here. And this is the power of Maui Giving.

Our Final Question for You

We've essentially reached the end of our time together in this book. We have saved the most important question for last. And now is the time to ask it: When? When will you start dreaming big again? When will you step up and turn your dreams into tangible reality? And most important of all, when will you embrace your power and greatness and do something extraordinary with your life?

The world needs your special gifts. Give them—with an open heart and joyous spirit. The rewards are overwhelming and certain when you do.

Thank you for sharing a part of your life with us and connecting with the Maui message. We arranged a special gift for you that is described fully in the Appendix. We think you'll love it.

We hope the strategies we've shared will help you build an extremely profitable and successful Level Three business and that you use your business to fuel an extraordinary life.

Our best to you,

David and Diane

The Millionaire Fast-Track—Your FREE $2,150 Bonus From the Authors!

Congratulations on finishing the book! As our way of rewarding you for reading it and the hard work you've put in so far, we've created a very special online program for you that will help you to increase your wealth, your cash flow, and your freedom.

It's called the *Millionaire Fast-Track Program* and it's our **FREE** gift to you for stepping up and taking action to build the life of your dreams.

This detailed online wealth program is your fast track to turning the ideas, techniques, and strategies you learned in this book into tangible results.

Because this valuable gift is only available for a very limited time we urge you to register online right now. (Note: We reserve the right to withdraw this offer at any time.)

To register, simply go online to **www.MauiMillionaires.com/book** and use the access code:

Cashflow17

When you've finished registering online, you'll get immediate access to the *entire* program, which includes wealth tools like:

- **Private access to over 5 hours of in-depth, money-making, how-to online workshops** that will make growing your business and your wealth *easier* and *faster*!

- **Eight free e-Books** on wealth, business, real estate investing, and tax strategy!

- **Free downloads** of all the worksheets and wealth forms shown in this book!

- **Free 30-Day trial membership to Maui Mastermind Online**, the online Maui community of entrepreneurs and investors who help each other succeed financially!

- And much, much more!

You'll also get access to proprietary wealth tools like the *Wealth Factor Test*, a personalized assessment of your current Wealth Operating System; a free download of the *Wealth Map*, a revolutionary new approach to creating a detailed road map for your financial life; and the *Wealth Level Worksheet*, a simple, yet extremely powerful worksheet you can fill out and in less than five minutes know *exactly* what wealth-building level you are at and what you can do to accelerate your financial progress.

These tools, and others like them, are designed to help you take the guesswork out of creating enduring wealth and put you on the fast track to financial freedom and the Maui Millionaire lifestyle you desire.

Three More Special Bonuses When You Register Within 30 Days of Buying This Book

Bonus One: Behind-the-Scenes Audio Interviews with 10 Maui Millionaires!

When you register right now, you'll get exclusive access to more than six hours of private interviews conducted with 10 Maui Millionaires. Imagine the power of listening to these one-on-one interviews in which they share directly with you how they really built their wealth, what obstacles stood in their way, and how they would build their wealth differently if they had to do it all over again.

Bonus Two: Five Free e-books!

- The Five Most Important Financial Controls You Must Activate in Your Business (or You Could Lose Everything)
- 10 Paperwork Pitfalls of Real Estate Contracts
- The Core Accounts System for Managing Your Money: The Simplest Way to Get Your Financial Life Under Control Fast
- The Three Secrets to Mastermind Your Way to Millions
- Escaping the Self-Employment Trap: How Doctors, Lawyers, CPAs, Consultants, and Other Experts Can Turn Their Expertise into Residual Streams of Income

Bonus Three: Six Additional Hours of Online Business, Investing, Tax Strategy, and Financial Fluency Training!

Watch and listen to dozens of ideas to help expand your business, increase your wealth, and enjoy a level of financial freedom only dreamed about by the average person. You'll learn how to boost your investment returns, lower your investing risks, and tap into your real passions through your business.

Each of these online workshops can be viewed or listened to from the convenience of your home or office, streamed to you over the Internet!

How to Enroll in the Millionaire Fast-Track Program Right Now—FREE!

Simply go to **www.MauiMillionaires.com/book** and complete the short enrollment form. When you are prompted for the "Book Access Code," enter the following access code:

Cashflow17

It's literally that easy! Just go to the web site, enter in your registration information, and hit enter.

But remember, this offer is only available for a very limited time, so make sure you don't miss out. Go online and register now that you're thinking about it.

In closing, we want to thank you for choosing to work with us as your wealth mentors. We wish you a lifetime of success and happiness.

Enjoy your "graduation gift" of the Millionaire Fast-Track Program!

Our very best to you,

David and Diane

P.S. To get immediate access to your FREE Millionaire Fast-Track Program ($2,150 value), go online right now and register at **www.Maui Millionaires.com/book**.

P.P.S. Register within 30 days of purchasing this book and you'll get all three of those *extra* bonuses you just read about! Register now!

David Finkel

In a cluttered marketplace of "how-to-get-rich" books and infomercials, ex-Olympic-level athlete turned business and real estate multimillionaire David Finkel is one of the nation's most respected wealth masters.

David first retired after selling off one of his successful multimillion-dollar companies at age 35, but he soon grew bored with the quiet life. Taking advantage of his fresh start, David carefully chose what he was most passionate about, and then launched and built successful businesses, Maui Millionaires™ and Maui Mastermind™, which focused on that passion—helping entrepreneurs and investors create, enjoy, and share great wealth.

David's mission is to share the real story on how to build wealth that debunks the prevailing money myths that keep so many good people living below their real potential.

His investing background started with interests in single-family houses across the United States, and since then has grown to focus on apartment complexes, office buildings, shopping centers, industrial parks, and other large commercial real estate projects.

A *Wall Street Journal* and *BusinessWeek* Best Selling author of over 40 business and investing books and courses, including the wildly successful *Real Estate Fast-Track* and co-authoring *The Maui Millionaires*, his how-to financial articles have appeared in over 4,000 periodicals across the United States.

He and his wife Heather first met in San Diego, but now live part of the year in Jackson Hole, Wyoming, and part of the year in Charlottesville, Virginia.

His web site (**www.MauiMillionaires.com**) is home to one of the most popular wealth-building communities on the Web, and has dozens of free tools and downloads for visitors.

Diane Kennedy

Diane Kennedy, the nation's preeminent tax strategist, is owner of Diane Kennedy & Associates, a leading tax strategy and accounting firm, and founder of TaxLoopholes.com, a tax education company. Diane is the author of *The Wall Street Journal* and *BusinessWeek* best sellers *Loopholes of the Rich* and *Real Estate Loopholes*, and co-author of *The Insider's Guide to Real Estate Investing Loopholes*, *The Insider's Guide to Making Money in Real Estate*, and *Tax Loopholes for eBay Sellers*.

Diane's extensive teachings have empowered people throughout the country to minimize their tax liabilities through the use of legal tax loopholes.

Diane has written for numerous financial publications, and has been featured in *Kiplinger's Personal Finance*, *The Wall Street Journal*, and *USA Today*, and on CNN and CNBC.

A highly sought-after international speaker and educator, she has dedicated her career to empowering and educating others about financial investments and the tax advantages that are available. Through Diane's knowledge and execution of tax loopholes in her business and real estate investments, she and her husband Richard are able to contribute to special life-changing projects and charities in the United States and around the world.

For the latest expert advice on tax loopholes and critical tax law updates, as well wealth building resources, visit her web site: **www.taxloopholes.com**.